POLITICAL QUESTIONS

Other books from Automatic Press ♦ $\frac{V}{I}$P

Formal Philosophy
edited by Vincent F. Hendricks & John Symons
November 2005

Thought$_2$Talk: A Crash Course in Expression and Reflection
by Vincent F. Hendricks
June 2006

Masses of Formal Philosophy
edited by Vincent F. Hendricks & John Symons
October 2006

Philosophy of Technology: 5 Questions
edited by Jan-Kyrre Berg Olsen & Evan Selinger
January 2007

Game Theory: 5 Questions
edited by Vincent F. Hendricks & Pelle Guldborg Hansen
March 2007

Philosophy of Mathematics: 5 Questions
edited by Vincent F. Hendricks & Hannes Leitgeb
June 2007

Normative Ethics: 5 Questions
edited by Jesper Ryberg & Thomas S. Petersen
June 2007

Legal Philosophy: 5 Questions
edited by Ian Farrell & Morten Ebbe Juul Nielsen
August 2007

POLITICAL QUESTIONS

5 Questions on Political Philosophy

edited by

Morten Ebbe Juul Nielsen

Automatic Press ♦ $\frac{V}{I}$P

Automatic Press ♦ $\frac{V}{I}$P

© Morten Ebbe Juul Nielsen 2006

This publication is in copyright. Subject to statuary exception and to the provisions of relevant collective licensing agreements, no reproduction of any part may take place without the written permission of the publisher.

First published 2006

Printed in the United States of America
and the United Kingdom

ISBN-10   87-991013-2-7   paperback

The publisher has no responsibilities for
the persistence or accuracy of URLs for external or
third party Internet Web sites referred to in this publication
and does not guarantee that any content on such
Web sites is, or will remain, accurate or appropriate.

Typeset in $\LaTeX 2_\varepsilon$
Jacket design by Vincent F. Hendricks

Contents

Preface	iii
Acknowledgements	vii
1 Kwame Anthony Appiah	1
2 Richard Bellamy	13
3 Allen Buchanan	29
4 William Galston	41
5 Amy Gutmann	53
6 Chandran Kukathas	63
7 Andrew Mason	75
8 Martha Nussbaum	83
9 Philippe Van Parijs	99
10 Philip Pettit	105
11 John E. Roemer	121
12 George Sher	135
13 Larry S. Temkin	147
14 Peter Vallentyne	169
15 Michael Walzer	179
16 Andrew Williams	187
17 Jonathan Wolff	195

18 Bernard Yack	211
About Political Questions	225
About the Editor	227
Index	228

Preface

If you are not wholly skeptical about representations of reality, you will probably find the following well-known metaphor appealing: when we try to depict or describe something – a vase, say – a single snapshot might prove helpful, but it does more justice to the represented object if we take several. Different pictures using different angles and different settings of light will provide a more truthful representation. There are limits and exceptions, to be sure, but everything else being equal, a plurality of depictions of the same object will purvey a more complete, a more truthful picture.

◆

With this volume about political philosophy, I hope to provide a picture taken from one of the less common angles. Philosophers, including political philosophers, are seldom public figures in the straightforward sense. They work in highly specialised and competitive fields, filled to the brink with specialised terms, juggling with an impressive array of esoteric canonical arguments and positions. They must follow strict standards and rules of formulation when they put forward their views, always with an eye to the immensely critical eye of the philosophical community. It seems to be a part of the philosophical spirit of inquiry to go towards extremes. And philosophical positions almost never seem well fitted to be expressed in neat sound bites. Small wonder, then, that philosophers are not normally seen as public figures—by themselves as well as the public.

However, the object of political philosophers, at least, is public *par excellence*: how ought we to arrange our political institutions? What kinds of reasons and arguments are legitimate for the state? What is a fair political distribution of goods and burdens? Which rights ought we to have as citizens? In Mill's words, what is "the nature and limits of the power which can be legitimately exercised by society over the individual?"

The alternative picture, the extra dimension, I hope to convey with this collection of interviews with some of the world's most eminent and influential political philosophers, aims to be both true to the nature of political philosophy as well as public or accessible. Here, the philosophers can state their views in a straightforward manner, unimpeded (and unaided!) by the normal constraints of academic publishing and review.

I believe – and hope – that what motivated me to do this book is shared by many interested in political philosophy and philosophy in general: I was – I still am – curious about what political philosophers themselves believe they are doing; why they are doing it; what they believe about the current (and future) state of the art; and how they see their own work in the larger context of political reality. Obviously, some of the questions are sometimes answered, at least implicitly, in the academic writings of political philosophers. However, it is probably unique to this collection that they answer these questions explicitly and without the usual constraints of academic publication. I believe that the individual contributions will serve as both introductions and appetizers (for newcomers to the field) and explanations and teasers for further work (for more seasoned members of the philosophical community.)

Hopefully, the volume should at least provide a fascinating look into the opinions and ideas of leading contemporary philosophers, complementing the picture for scholars and newcomers alike.

A few words on the selection and format of *Political Questions*. Whereas I have tried to get a reasonably broad selection of distinguished and influential political philosophers to participate, this selection is constrained in two major ways: the philosophers are, with one exception, predominantly or exclusively Anglophone, and work within what some call the analytic (or perhaps "post-analytic") tradition, sufficiently broadly construed. The other major restraint is vis-à-vis political theory understood as the empirical study of actual political institutions. Whereas all of the philosophers here present obviously have something important to say about actual institutions, and often do so on a background of studies of these, they are philosophers rather than empirical scientists.

Regarding the format, I decided from the outset that the interviews/essays should, as far as possible, retain whatever "impromptu" feeling they might have (if any.) Accordingly, the contributors had very free hands in answering the questions. As you will see, the ways in which the contributors have chosen to answer the questions vary to a very large extent, not only in substance (as could be expected) but also in style and form. The lists of literature are provided by the contributors.

Morten Ebbe Juul Nielsen
Copenhagen
December 2006

Acknowledgements

I am indebted to my publisher Automatic Press ♦ $\frac{V}{I}$P, in particular senior publishing editor V.J. Menshy, for support and encouragement throughout and to Elizabeth Pando and Christopher M. Whalin for proof-reading the manuscript. Also, I'm indebted to colleagues at Roskilde and Copenhagen Universities for valuable input, and, naturally, first and foremost to the contributors.

Morten Ebbe Juul Nielsen
Copenhagen
December 2006

1
Kwame Anthony Appiah

Laurance S. Rockefeller University Professor of Philosophy and the University Center for Human Values

Princeton University, USA

Why were you initially drawn to political philosophy?

This might seem to be a particularly good question to ask *me*, since my first published papers and books were in the philosophy of language. At the most general level, I explored questions about the role of conceptions of truth and assertibility in semantic theory; and I was interested, more specifically, in the semantics of conditionals and in ways of understanding their behavior that used subjective probabilities to explain assertibility. The rough idea was that you should assert only what you take to be very probably true. The only obvious preparation for thinking about political philosophy in this work was that I had to think about decision theory, in which subjective probability theory is embedded; and that theory has played a prominent role in recent political philosophy.

My first *job*, however, after I finished my doctoral thesis, was a joint appointment in Philosophy and African & African-American Studies at Yale University; and my contribution to the latter program focused on questions of central relevance to political philosophy. Of these two were most important.

One was how to understand Pan-Africanism as a political ideology. A second was how to make sense philosophically of the concept of race and, relatedly, of the idea of racism. This last question is obviously of ethical interest. But racism is also a political ideology, a political problem, and a topic that general theories of justice ought to say something about. And these two topics are connected, because race was the central organizing concept of the early Pan-Africanist movement, which was, to use suitably old-fashioned language a kind of racial Negro nationalism; and that form of nationalism was itself a response, in large measure, to anti-black racism. So I have worked on questions of relevance to political philosophy since the beginning of my career, even though that wasn't terribly evident in the first work I actually published.

That I was interested in politics is not hard to explain. I grew up in the home of a politician – my father, Joe Appiah – who was a member of Ghana's first post-independence parliament. I lived through turbulent political times in my childhood – my father was a political prisoner on three occasions; and I spent much of my childhood with my English grandmother, Isobel Cripps, who was the widow of a British cabinet minister and knew and corresponded with political figures in every continent and discussed their correspondence with me. But being interested in politics and in philosophy is perfectly consistent with not being interested in political philosophy; indeed, Michael Dummett, whose work was the focus of my own second book in the philosophy of language, is both a very influential philosophy of mathematics, logic and language, and an anti-racist political activist; but he is not a political philosopher.

It was, in the end, the question of Pan-Africanism – the subject of the first course I taught at Yale – that led me into the scholarly study of nationalism, which is, of course, one of the central topics in modern political philosophy. My route into the subject was not, therefore, the standard one for a philosopher working in England or the United States.

There were two sources of my interest. One was the personal, familial one. My father had been a leading Pan-Africanist in the middle years of the twentieth-century and had attended the famous fifth Pan-African Congress in Manchester in October 1945; and he was a delegate at the sixth congress in Tanzania in 1974. My sisters and I grew up in a household where issues about African and her Diaspora were a frequent topic of conversation. Both Richard Wright and C.L.R. James, major figures in the intellectual life of the Africa Diaspora visited our home when I was a child, and W.E.B. Du Bois (whom my father knew) moved to Ghana, where I grew up, when I was seven. Kwame Nkrumah, one of the founders of the Organization of African Unity, was once my father's close friend and later had him imprisoned without trial. Pan-Africanism was inescapable.

The source of my second major interest – in race and racism

– was also personal, in a way, but it came later. I had to work out how to understand the dominant conceptions of race in the United States, when I moved there in the early 1980s as a young adult. As a person of African (though also of European) ancestry, I found it mattered a good deal to others that I was black. But the challenge here was first of all conceptual. I needed to work out how what I knew about human biology—I had started out at Cambridge University as a medical student and knew, as a result, more human biology than most people—could be put together with the folk-conceptions of race I discovered in the United States.

But if that was what drew me to these questions, I confess they soon seemed to me simply intellectually engaging. The project was to try to make sense of a real problem in the world – racism – or a real ideology – Pan-Africanism or black nationalism – using, as I was bound to do, the tools of my philosophical training and, at the same time, learning from the other disciplines of the interdisciplinary fields of African and African-American Studies. (Because literary studies were so central to these fields at the time and work in them was so interesting, I found myself drawn into literary studies as well and a good deal of my work in the 1980s and 1990s addressed questions in literary theory and the literature of Africa and her Diaspora.) The result of this thinking was *In My Father's House: Africa in the Philosophy of Culture*, which aimed to reflect on the current situation of African and African-American intellectuals in the light especially of the Pan-Africanist inheritance. Because questions about race and racism turn out to be central to that situation, I also discussed both quite extensively in that book.

Immersion for a decade or so in these questions about race and nationalism, and the acquisition of the literary, historical and sociological and anthropological knowledge that they seemed to require, led naturally – at least, for a philosopher – to an exploration of some rather more abstract questions that had arisen in the course of my work. And, since questions about race and justice were obviously important, I began to reflect on the relationship between the work I had already done and the current state of political philosophy. I had been interested in political philosophy since my undergraduate days—I read Rawls's *Theory of Justice* and Brian Barry's critique of it in his *Liberal Theory of Justice* in the summer that I switched from being a medical student to being a philosophy student and it was one of the most exciting intellectual experiences of my life. But I entered the field of political philosophy very much from the matrix of African-American Studies and had not felt until then the need to connect my work more directly with "mainstream" political philosophy. Nevertheless, I wrote extended discussions of Rawls and Nozick in an introduction to philosophy that I published in the mid-1980s and published in 1989, and they were equally important to a second, more recent, introduction to philosophy, *Thinking It Through*, which came out in 2003.

That work led me to think further about race and nationality as species of the more general category of social identity and to read more in the new philosophical literature – by people like Charles Taylor and Will Kymlicka – on multi-culturalism. It also led me back to early work in the liberal tradition and, in particular, to John Stuart Mill; who then led me back to Humboldt, whose work, as Mill said, had been a source of inspiration for the book he sometimes called "the *Liberty*." And, in the end, I was led back to Aristotle's *Nicomachean Ethics*, and his account of *eudaimonia* and the making of a life.

What do you consider your own most important contribution(s) to political philosophy, and why?

I hope I have helped us to understand why ethical identity is central to the best understanding of the liberal tradition. Our individuality – the term is Mill's – is both enabled and challenged by social identities. Standard individualistic (or libertarian) versions of the liberal tradition tend to ignore or resist the role of social identity in constructing individuality. But the new more communitarian forms of liberalism seem too often to share the presupposition that individuality is inconsistent with accepting social identities, and so propose that we should seek a compromise between the two. I have proposed a middle way that rejects this presupposition.

The argument begins with an understanding of social identities and on their role in people's lives inside and outside of politics. The right analysis of social identities, I believe, is nominalist; it begins by focusing, like labeling theory in sociology, on the way we give names to kinds of persons. The assigning of a label, L, which we can call *ascription*, is the first of four central features of the way social identities work. The second is that the labels people apply to one another come to play a role in how they think about themselves. We can call this *identification:* when someone comes to think and feel and act *as an L*. It is important, too, third, that people *treat* L's differently from non-L's, at least sometimes. And finally, fourth, there are *norms of identification,* according to which how people ought to behave depends on their being an L. With this vocabulary in hand, one can explore such issues as the working of the dialectic between treatment and identification; or how contests over norms of identification can be central to what we now call "identity politics."

We can also explore how identities, thus conceived, play a role in the ethical life of individuals; meaning by *ethics* reflection on what it is for human lives to go well, for us to have *eudaimonia.* Ethics, in this sense, has important connections with morality. But it is not reducible to it, since what it is for my life to go well requires more than my giving others their due. Our pursuit of *eudaimonia* is constrained by morality, but also by our historical circumstances and physical and mental endowments. (I was born in the wrong place to be an American President and with the wrong body for motherhood; I lack the patience to do good laboratory science.) But each of us has a great variety of decisions to make in shaping our lives. Liberalism, on this analysis, is essentially the view that these choices belong, in the end, to the person whose life it is.

Identities are central to liberalism because we make our lives as men and women; Americans and Germans; Catholics and Jews; philosophers and novelists; fathers and daughters. They are so diverse and extensive because, in the modern world, people need an enormous range of tools in the task of life-making. Each person needs many options. And, because people are various, the range of options that would be sufficient for each of us won't be sufficient for us all. Indeed, people are making up new identities all the time: "Gay" is basically four decades old, "Punk" is younger. As Mill put it, in chapter 3 of *On Liberty:*

> If it were only that people have diversities of taste, that is reason enough for not attempting to shape them all after one model. But different persons also require different conditions for their spiritual development; and can no more exist healthily in the same moral, than all the variety of plants can exist in the same physical, atmosphere and climate. The same things which are helps to one person towards the cultivation of his higher nature, are hindrances to another ... unless there is a corresponding diversity in their modes of life, they neither obtain their fair share of happiness, nor grow

up to the mental, moral, and aesthetic stature of which their nature is capable.[1]

The work on identity is thus at the interface of ethics – conceived as reflection on what it is for human lives to go well – and political philosophy, which has at its center questions about the role of the state. In justifying the state's exercise of its coercive powers, I think we must always ask whether it is helping or hindering citizens in the making of good lives; and, as I have said, I take the fundamental liberal thought to be Mill's claim that making my life is, in the end, up to me. As a result, certain forms of perfectionist politics, that aim to improve the citizen against her own judgment strike me as indefensible. As Mill said "If a person possesses any tolerable amount of common sense and experience, his own mode of laying out his existence is the best, not because it is the best in itself, but because it is his own mode."[2] The background idea here is that the state is an instrument not an end in itself.

These ideas are sketched out first in my essay in *Color Conscious: The Political Morality of Race*, which began as my Tanner Lectures on Human Values at the University of San Diego in 1994; developed further in "Soul Making," which was a series of Tanner lectures at Cambridge in 2001; and most fully formulated in *The Ethics of Identity* (2005). This book explores the legacy of Mill's development of the idea of individuality – which is the topic of the famous third chapter of *On Liberty* – and develops a philosophical account of social identity in ethical life before going on to ask what this means for national and global politics. Just as I have tried to articulate a version of liberalism that avoids both the Scylla of an unsociable libertarianism and the Charybdis of an anti-individualist communitarianism in thinking about politics within the nation; so in the context of global justice, I have tried to avoid both the extreme impartiality endorsed by some cosmopolitans and the excessive national partiality of some philosophical nationalists. In each case, the argument goes by way of a view about the proper role of identities in our ethical lives.

So I hope I have helped advance thinking about the place of identity in ethics and, thus, in politics. I am glad, too, however – since one is allowed to mention contributions, in the plural – that I was in at the start of serious analytical engagement with questions about race and racism; work that is more in ethics than in political

---

[1] John Stuart Mill *On Liberty* (London: J. W. Parker & Son, 1859), p. 122.
[2] *Op. cit.*, p. 121.

philosophy, but that is obviously, for reasons I mentioned earlier, of central importance for politics.

What is the proper role of political philosophy in relation to real, political action? Can there ever be a fruitful relation between political philosophy and political practice?

There is, I believe, no general answer to the first of these questions. Some issues in political philosophy are of central intellectual interest but of little direct importance for policy. (For example – here I assert rather than argue – work on the logic of rights.) And certainly there are works of political philosophy that have had a great impact on political life: Locke's work on toleration, for example, or Marx's on capitalism.

Whether one wants to bring philosophy and policy together is partly a matter of temperament. Some people are interested in trying to influence politics through their intellectual work and some aren't. But I think it also depends on how much one believes the actually available choices among policy options are produced by applying ideas in political theory to the relevant body of facts. If what lie behind policy disagreements are different pictures of the social (and sometimes the natural) world, then political philosophy will be relevant but not determinative. My own sense is that the role of disagreement about values in politics is often overstated; and that disputes about normative theories play even less of a role. So I am pessimistic about the *application* of philosophical theories to political disputes, unless it is subtly done with a great deal of sensitivity to the actual structure of the world.

Thus, for example, two people who disagree strongly on whether abortion should be legal, may nevertheless agree about the importance of respect for individuality, and thus have – in this sense – a shared political philosophy. Their disagreement might derive from differing views about the moral status of the fetus; and their judgments about *that* are likely to depend both on moral and religious views and on biological and psychological claims about fetuses.

But because political philosophy can't be *applied* in this straightforward way, it doesn't follow that it isn't enormously useful to people outside philosophy. The kind of political philosophy I do in fact strikes me as helpful to the wider thinking of my society, not because it answers questions of policy or motivates people to support or carry out particular policies. It's useful because it provides conceptual tools for thinking about policy questions, allowing people to deepen their thinking as they make up their minds. When political philosophy does shape political action in that way, then, to my mind, they have a fruitful relationship.

I am not sure the distinction between political philosophy and political theory is worth trying to make sharply. But one way to make it is to suggest that political theory is more deeply embedded in answering normative questions – "Is democracy the only legitimate form of government?," say – in the light of more than normative considerations. Political theory requires more attention to empirical political psychology and sociology and to history; to do it well requires not only a knowledge of that sort, but also a kind of practical wisdom. (This is, of course, an idea of Aristotle's.) In particular, that sort of wisdom requires a sense for *which* facts of political psychology or sociology are important. And this is something that is not so obviously necessary in political philosophy of a somewhat more abstract kind.

What do you consider the most neglected topics and/or contributions in late 20th century political philosophy, or in related philosophical disciplines (ethics, philosophy of law, metaethics etc.)?

Recent psychology has underscored what every sane person always knew: people are not terribly rational. The new discoveries have to do with the structure of our irrationalities, the fact that they are often predictable. Political philosophy in the traditions I know hasn't really done enough to take this fact on board. (Jon Elster's work is a notable exception.) Part of the reason is that we don't have a clear answer to the first of the important unsolved questions I mention below.

What are the most important unsolved questions in political philosophy and/or related disciplines and what are the prospects for progress?

Here is a central methodological question in normative political thinking, whether we call it theory or philosophy. Which facts about people and institutions as they currently are may we take as given? The answer will turn in part on what psychology or sociology you assume. Some conservatives take it to be evident that no amount of education or propaganda will make people more than moderately altruistic. Many socialists, per contra, once thought that people could easily be molded to behave in more egalitarian ways. Now each of these positions counts people as changeable only where the changes it contemplates can be brought about justly and at reasonable cost. So the notion of what changes in human nature are possible is also, at least in part, a normative question.

In pursuing normative questions about politics, then, what kind and what degree of idealization should we adopt when? John Rawls discussed this question under the rubric of the distinction between political theories assuming various degrees of compliance. His general theory stated principles of justice for a world in which everyone behaved justly. But many questions of justice only arise once people behave unjustly, as he knew. There is also an extensive recent bibliography on the distinction between so-called Ideal and Non-ideal theory; and, finally, there's a longer tradition of critiques of the unrealistic character of utopian thinking. But these questions strike me as harder than the existing literature—at least so far as I am aware of it—supposes.

Take a simple example. Nozick argued in *Anarchy, State and Utopia*, for roughly the following view of entitlement to property. You're entitled to property just in case:

1. you acquired it justly, or

2. it was transferred to you justly, or

3. it was justly given to you in restitution for some earlier injustice.

No one, Nozick thought, was entitled to property except by (repeated) applications of 1, 2 and 3.

It seems to me that most of the actual real property in the world does not currently meet these conditions, because most unjust transfers have not been rectified. Suppose we had a title deed to every portion of land running back to its first human settlement. Principles (1) and (2) would have required us to apply (3) very early on in the proceedings. But (3) wasn't applied in fact. What should we do then? Should we ask where the property would be if restitution had occurred? But once property has passed into the wrong hands, all the history tells us is what was done with it by people who weren't entitled to it. A stole it from B. Perhaps it should have been returned. If it had been, B would have had it. Where would it have gone from there? Who knows? And if we did know that B would have given it to C; what would C have done with it? The further out the counterfactuals get, the less plausible it is that the actual history helps us answer them. Here is one obvious reason: a different history would have meant that different people would have existed. We should end up having to ask: given that a just history would have produced these allocations to these people who don't actually exist, how should we assign property to the people who do actually exist? Principles of "rectification of holdings," as Nozick called them, are going to be very difficult to work out.

You might think that this was only a problem because Nozick's theory is built on what he calls historical principles of justice, which hold, as he put it, "that past circumstances or actions of people can create differential entitlements ..." But similar questions arise pretty quickly for what he called "end-result" principles, which determine justice in allocation by looking at features of synchronic patterns of distribution. Rawls assumes that people in the original position are self-interested but not envious: so we can appeal to the fact of self-interest and its role in motivating the creation of wealth in justifying principles of allocation, but we can't appeal to envy. But it's no more unrealistic to imagine away envy than it would be to imagine away the current degree of self-interest. So why shouldn't we say that justice demands that societies make efforts to make people less selfish? As I say there are literatures relevant to this question—on ideal versus non-ideal theory and on utopianism; so I expect progress here in the coming years.

My second big question, which is less abstract, has to do with the relationship among different traditions of thinking about politics – neo-Confucian, liberal, Marxist, Catholic, Moslem, for example – and how they can speak to one another. This is a question about the management of disputes about politics, a topic on which all traditions have more or less well-developed views. Much political philosophy in every tradition, but especially in the modern Euro-American one I know best, strikes me as insufficiently attentive to the fact that its premises generally seem implausible or at least unintuitive to others. Because so many questions in contemporary politics involve discussions across nations and cultures, it strikes me that we ought to have something more to say on questions of method here than we actually do. At the very least we might want to know which features of actually existing political ideologies we should take as given—as part of the context for engagement with them—and which should be up for challenge. This is, as you will immediately see, a point where my two questions intersect. As for the prospects for progress, I have no idea. Indeed, part of the problem is that it is not clear to me that there is a non-question-begging notion of progress available in this area. But I am constitutionally an optimist.

Books

In My Father's House: Africa in the Philosophy of Culture (New York: Oxford University Press, 1992).

Color Conscious: The Political Morality of Race (Princeton: Princeton University Press, 1996) with Amy Gutmann.

The Ethics of Identity (Princeton: Princeton University Press, 2005).

Cosmopolitanism: Ethics in a World of Strangers (New York: W. W. Norton, 2006.)

Articles

"Race." In *Critical Terms for Literary Study* Frank Lentricchia & Tom McLaughlin (eds.) (Chicago University Press, 1989).

"Racisms." In *Anatomy of Racism*, David Goldberg (ed.) (Minneapolis: Minnesota University Press, 1990).

"But would that still be me? Notes on gender, 'race,' ethnicity as sources of identity." *Journal of Philosophy*, Vol. LXXXVII, No. 10 (October 1990), 493–499.

"Identity, Authenticity, Survival: Multicultural Societies and Social Reproduction." In Charles Taylor *Multiculturalism: Examining "The Politics of Recognition,"* (Princeton, NJ: Princeton University Press, 1994).

"Race, Culture, Identity: Misunderstood Connections." *The Tanner Lectures on Human Values* Vol. 17 (Salt Lake City: University of Utah Press, 1996), 51–136.

"Cosmopolitan Patriots." *Critical Inquiry* 23 (Spring 1997), 617–639.

"The Multiculturalist Misunderstanding" *The New York Review of Books* October 9, 1997 Vol. XLIV No. 15, 30–36.

"Liberty, Individuality and Identity." *Critical Inquiry* 27 (Winter 2000), 305–332.

"Stereotypes and the Shaping of Identity." In Robert C. Post *Prejudicial Appearances: The Logic of American Anti-Discrimination Law* (Durham: Duke University Press, 2001).

"Grounding Human Rights." In Michael Ignatieff *Human Rights As Politics and Idolatry* (Princeton: Princeton University Press, 2001).

"Ethnic Identity as a Political Resource." In *Explorations in African Political Thought: Identity, Community, Ethics* Teodros Kiros (ed.) (New York: Routledge, 2001).

"Individuality and Identity." In *The Tanner Lectures on Human Values* Vol. 23 Grethe Petersen (ed.) (Salt Lake City: University of Utah Press, 2002).

"Comprendre les réparations: une réflexion préliminaire" *Cahiers d'études africaines*, 173–174, 2004.

"The Politics of Identity," *Daedalus*, forthcoming.

"What's wrong with slavery?" in *Buying Freedom* Martin Bunzl and K. Anthony Appiah (eds.), (Princeton: Princeton University Press, forthcoming).

2

Richard Bellamy

Professor of Political Science

University College London, UK

Why were you initially drawn to political philosophy?

The Neapolitan philosopher Giambattista Vico famously dated his philosophical vocation to when he was dropped on his head as a baby. I can recall no such single moment of enlightenment. I came to political philosophy via an interest in contemporary politics informed by the history of ideas. Though I now mainly employ the idiom of Anglo-American analytical political and legal philosophy to tackle current issues, arriving at this point has been rather a long journey and my approach still bears the marks of my historical origins. So, I think it is justified in this context to tell the somewhat lengthy tale of how I was drawn to political philosophy as it is predominantly understood today.

Politics and philosophy were not taught in schools in the UK in the 1970s, and I do not remember my teachers being particularly political or philosophical. But I had some truly outstanding English and History teachers and these subjects enthused me most. That said, I was always interested in more theoretical approaches to them than we ever got in class. So, largely inspired by my eldest brother, who was reading philosophy at the University of York, I began to tentatively explore a somewhat mixed bag of thinkers. As I recall, Nietzsche and Sartre figured strongly – neither of whom I can claim to read much these days – but I also remember delving into Hume and Wittgenstein. What I do not recall reading was any political philosophy, which was – and I suspect still is – very much a poor relation in British philosophy departments. Certainly, for my brother logic and metaphysics formed the core of the discipline. Perhaps for that reason I never really considered doing philosophy myself because I was already fairly politically minded. My family was quite political and intellectually engaged, with my father and other brother doing their bit in local politics. This familial background fed into my school work and stimulated an interest in the role ideas, particularly political ideas, played in literature and history. In different ways, George Steiner and Raymond Williams both had a big influence here and probably led me to go up to Cambridge to read English. Before the end of my first term, though, I had switched to History.

When I arrived in Cambridge I had not heard of the 'history of political thought', let alone the 'Cambridge School'. In fact, I cannot remember any one using the latter term during my undergraduate career. However, one of the great things about Cambridge at that time was that lectures were more open events for lecturers to intrigue and entertain students, than formal parts of the teaching programme. One really went for the show. I soon found myself attending far more lectures in philosophy and history than in English, though I did sufficiently enjoy those by the notoriously obscure poet Jeremy Prynne to go to them two years running – thereby discovering that although identical in every respect, including dramatic pauses, they also elicited identically rapt responses from the audience. Had politics existed at Cambridge, I would no doubt have sampled that too – but 'social and political sciences' was then just a committee rather than a department, offering a mixture of history, psychology, sociology and economics courses that could be combined to form Part 2 of a degree programme but not Part 1. I found the philosophy lectures stimulating, but I was also a bit daunted by them and it was clear that moral and political philosophy had a rather lowly status at Cambridge. The historians of political thought were a different matter. Quentin Skinner – a famously effective lecturer – was then based at Princeton, so sadly I did not hear him, though in my second year I did participate in an amazing pre-exam 'class' he ran for some 200 students in which he coordinated a remarkably intimate and spontaneous seeming – yet in reality extraordinarily well coordinated - discussion of the set texts. But I soon became an assiduous follower of Richard Tuck, Duncan Forbes and Roy Porter—all, in their very different ways, also extremely stimulating lecturers. They showed me how it was possible to philosophise about politics while seeing ideas as firmly grounded in and engaged with a given political and intellectual context. As I'll note in answer to question 3 below on the relation of political philosophy to political action, I regard the way this kind of historical approach takes that relationship seriously by seeing ideas as political acts as one of its great strengths.

Having changed to history, I ended up taking every intellectual history paper then available, with Duncan Forbes and Roy Porter more or less supervising me for all of them. Both dedicated scholars of the Enlightenment, Duncan was a somewhat urbane, rational Scot, whereas Roy seemed like a figure out of Henry Fielding who drank sherry by the tankard and somewhat disconcertingly expected you to do so too. Roy supervised my undergraduate dissertation, which almost a decade later became my first publication in a refereed journal—a study of William Godwin and the Romantic Poets published as 'William Godwin and the Development of the "New Man of Feeling"', *History of Political Thought*, VI, (1985) pp. 41132. As the topic indicates, my route to political philosophy was still very much entrenched in English and History. Most attention on this topic had centred on Godwin's influence on the romantic poets. I switched focus to look at their influence on him – especially in the writings post-*Political Justice*, including his novels – a change I related to difficulties with his earlier utilitarianism. I also took Roy's special subject on the development of Geology as a discipline in the eighteenth century. Originally, I planned to carry forward these interests and do a PhD with him on the links between the scientific and political ideas of Joseph Priestley. Had I done so, I might well have pursed a career as an intellectual historian. However, just after my finals Roy moved to the Welcome Institute in London to embark on his series of studies into the history of medicine. As a result, I turned to my other Cambridge mentor, Duncan Forbes, as a potential doctoral supervisor.

Though best known as a path breaking scholar of the Scottish Enlightenment, a field that his teaching as much as his writings did much to create, for students of my generation his renown rested mainly on his quite remarkable series of lectures on Hegel. True to the spirit of the time, the vast bulk of these were devoted not to the set book, *The Philosophy of Right*, but to a text that was not part of the syllabus – *The Phenomenology of Spirit*. As well as the Hume to Marx history of political thought paper, Duncan also supervised me for a rather odd paper called 'Historians and Historical Thought: From Bossuet to Burkhardt'. This paper had been devised by the seventeenth century scholar, Brian Wormald. A Catholic convert, his thesis – delivered in his rooms in Peterhouse to the six or so students brave or mad enough to have opted for this somewhat unusual course – was that things had pretty much been downhill from Bossuet onwards, though Wormald himself was tormented by spiritual doubts arising from God's will not being as clearly discernable in the way of the world as he might have wished. Fortunately, no such angst bedevilled Forbes's reading of these texts. Rather, the paper kindled an interest in the philosophy of history and of the relationship of political thinking and acting to different understandings of its past. Vico seemed a key figure in this context and I now suggested to Duncan that I might write my PhD on him. He proposed thinking more generally about Vico and the Scottish and Neapolitan Enlightenments, a potential set of influences he had alluded to in an early article of the 1950s, and gave me a few names of famous Italian scholars I might go and visit., Like many of his generation, Duncan had not written a PhD himself and took a somewhat cavalier attitude to supervising one, and after what was our sole meeting to discuss the dissertation shook my hand and with his inimitable chuckle said 'see you in three years with your *magnum opus*'. Six months and an intensive Italian course later, I set off by train to Turin and Naples having written to the academics on Duncan's list.

Though I did eventually write articles on both the Neapolitan and Scottish Enlightenments partly based on my research at this time, and also produced an edition of Cesare Beccaria's *On Crimes and Punishments* for Cambridge University Press, I soon discovered that this material did not really connect with the philosophical question that most engaged me—namely how was our present thought and action shaped by a confrontation with past thought and actions. However, that issue was very much at the heart of the twentieth century Italian philosopher, Benedetto Croce, whose work I became acquainted with as a result of reading his studies of Vico and the Neapolitan Enlightenment. I now decided to change topic and write my dissertation on him. While, Duncan's Hegel lectures and teaching had in many ways inspired the topic, this also seemed a convenient occasion to get a slightly more proactive supervisor. Fortunately, Quentin Skinner had just returned to Cambridge to the Chair of Political Science. I had now read his methodological essays and thought there was some commonality of themes with my thesis topic, and luckily for me he agreed to take me on. Meanwhile, I had decided that it would be helpful to have an Italian base and had successfully applied to the European University Institute in Florence, which then allowed students to be registered for their degree at another university. The upshot of that experience was that I came into contact for the first time with political scientists and so began my academic political education. As part of my work on Croce I also started to read Pareto and Mosca and I now became interested in the historical origins of current understandings of political behaviour—a topic that I was later to develop.

My eventual PhD was somewhat eccentric in many ways, being as much a study of the influence of Croce's politics on his philosophy of history as an exploration of the relationship of political thought to its past. Along the way, though, I had become thoroughly educated in the social and political philosophy as well as the politics of his times—a resource I was to draw on in what is often seen as my major book *Liberalism and Modern Society: An Historical Argument* (Polity and Penn State University Press, 1992). What I still lacked was any systematic grounding in contemporary political philosophy. That only came when I went as a post-doctoral research fellow to Nuffield College, Oxford. 'Social being determines consciousness', and in that context I soon found myself taking a crash course in Hart, Berlin, Rawls, and their heirs, attending the famous set piece discussions between Dworkin, Sen, Parfit and later Cohen, and engaging in conversations with the extraordinarily rich seam of political and legal philosophers in Oxford at that time, which included along with these four not only David Miller, Joseph Raz, John Finnis, John Gray, Steven Lukes, Michael Freeden, Alan Ryan, Mark Philip, and Nicola Lacey but also, then as doctoral students, Leslie Green, Chandran Kukathas, Adam Swift, Andrew Williams and Keith Dowding—the last two having the room next to mine in Nuffield. I guess I inaugurated my career as a contemporary political theorist with the very first paper to the now renowned Nuffield Political Theory seminar that I started in my rooms in 1984. It was 'Sex, Sin and Liberalism', exploring the issue of pornography and freedom of speech and rehashing the Hart-Devlin debate. However, I was at that stage still more a historian of political thought than a political theorist, and in fact at the end of my Nuffield fellowship returned to Cambridge as a colleague of Richard Tuck's at Jesus College, where I became a college lecturer in modern European history. The shift in focus really only came when I replaced Jeremy Waldron in the Edinburgh politics department in 1987, and became responsible for teaching the contemporary political philosophy paper and participated in the highly stimulating jurisprudence reading group organised by Neil MacCormick in Law.

A final transformation, turning me towards being a theorist of politics, in the sense of addressing the normative qualities and role of political activity and its organisation rather than more general issues of justice, was brought about when I took up the Chair in Politics at the University of East Anglia in 1992. There I had the wonderful experience of teaching the Philosophy, Politics and Economics programme alongside Martin Hollis and Bob Sugden. Martin was very much the team leader of this enterprise and had conceived the course as a dialogue between the three disciplines in which we were all supposed to defend our own turf. As a result, I was forced to think about what, if anything, was so special about political decision-making *per se*. That preoccupation led me to explore the resources of republicanism, particularly the neo-Roman version favoured by Quentin Skinner and Philip Pettit, and to criticise the liberal retreat from politics in my *Liberalism and Pluralism: Towards a Politics of Compromise* (Routledge, 1999). This concern has deepened since. Though I benefited tremendously from co-teaching with two eminent political philosophers and co-contributors to this volume, Andrew Mason and Andrew Williams, when I went to Reading in 1996, the centre of my attention turned increasingly to looking empirically as well as normatively at the virtues of actually existing democratic systems. A move to Britain's pre-eminent political science department at the University of Essex as Professor of Government further stimulated that investigation, culminating in my *Political Constitutionalism* (Cambridge University Press, 2007). Often in collaboration with others, notably Dario Castiglione, I have also pursued this topic in numerous studies of democracy, constitutionalism and citizenship within the EU, the likely subject of my next book.

What do you consider your own most important contribution(s) to political philosophy, and why?

My most important contributions have probably been my three main books to date. Despite their apparently different topics and approaches, they are linked by the common theme of exploring the underpinnings and character of liberal democracy. My first two books, *Modern Italian Social Theory: Ideology and Politics from Pareto to the Present*, (Polity and Stanford University Press, 1987) and *Liberalism and Modern Society* were attempts to mix history and political theory. As I remarked in the preface to the first, my aim was to reach 'Oxford destinations by the Cambridge road', and the second had as its subtitle 'an historical argument'.

In other words, in each case I was using history to make a philosophical point. However, though widely reviewed in philosophy as well as politics and history journals, they have been looked on mainly as interesting works of scholarship rather than as contributions to political philosophy in their own right.

The underlying theoretical issue in *Modern Italian Social Theory* was the origins and character of the modern liberal democratic state. With the partial exception of Croce, all the Italian theorists I looked at – both the positivists and the idealists – regarded politics as epiphenomenal. It reflected either certain universal psychological dispositions of human beings, as Pareto believed, or a given social and economic stage of development, as in different ways Mosca and Gramsci thought, or was the product of a given cultural consciousness, as Gentile and, in part, Croce, argued. As a result, none of these thinkers saw any independent virtue in liberal democracy. Thus, for Pareto it was simply a method for manipulating human passions, for Gramsci a historical stage to be superseded and so on. Though they were right to stress the socio-economic and cultural preconditions of liberal democracy, they had little or no appreciation of its possessing any normative value. Indeed, they were all somewhat dismissive of politics, regarding it as a transitional phenomenon occasioned by certain psychological failings, an absence of cultural unity, the conflicts attending a disorganised system of social and economic production, or some mixture of these.

The book attempted to show how many prevailing notions about how liberal democratic states work – not least dominant views of their failings – might have somewhat uncomfortable historical origins, resting on largely unarticulated assumptions inherited from the past that would hardly stand up to scrutiny today. For example, current views about the nature and shortcomings of mass democracy rest to a remarkable degree on arguments first articulated by Pareto and Mosca that reflect the failings of the system in turn of the century Italy, on the one hand, and the bogus social psychology of the time, on the other. In the concluding chapter, I also attempted to develop an argument for democracy as justified by the shortcomings of any social theory to fully ground its claims in ways that pre-empted all disagreement. In many ways, that sketched my agenda for much of my later work.

Similar themes run through *Liberalism and Modern Society*. The debate between liberals and communitarians was raging during the period it was written (roughly from 1987–92). A prominent version of this *quarelle* turned on whether liberal principles could be seen as 'neutral' or were rather components of a given account of community in which they served to foster a particular kind of human agency. My 'historical argument' was that an 'ethical liberal' tradition had existed that viewed liberalism largely in such communitarian terms. This conception of liberalism had formed the dominant strand in both Britain and France in the mid-nineteenth to the early twentieth centuries, where favourable social circumstances had made liberalism appear as the underlying ethos of well-functioning, modern industrial economies. The discussion of the 'social question' at the turn of the century, and the attempt to give a liberal reading to socialist demands, was particularly revealing in this respect. By contrast, Italy and Germany offered far less propitious contexts for the development of liberal institutions and ideas. Here, as my earlier book on the Italians had shown, the social and cultural underpinnings of liberalism came to the fore as liberal thinkers grappled with the issue of how they might be brought into being. I defended Croce and particularly Max Weber as the most self-conscious and sophisticated proponents of what, slightly infelicitously, I called the 'economic liberal' tradition.

I now think a better term would have been 'realist' liberalism. Weber's (and, to a degree, Croce's) liberalism are realist in two distinct ways. First, they were concerned with liberal reality rather than simply the liberal ideal. As a result, they appreciated liberal practices had many, largely contingent, historical origins that were hard to replicate. Weber also saw that there were features of contemporary societies that were either inimical or challenges to ethical liberalism, even where it had become strongly established—not least their complexity and growing differentiation, on the one side, and the growth of corporate and bureaucratic power, on the other. Second, these thinkers had a realist, almost Machiavellian, view of democratic politics. Not only did it possess its own distinctive logic, and so needed to be separated from ethics and seen as more than a means to certain ethical ends, but also this feature meant it could play a role in mediating between competing ethics and rationalities. I have always rather regretted not writing a historical chapter on the development of liberalism in the United States which would have grounded the main analytical liberal theories in certain preoccupations of the American tradition and politics. Instead, I moved straight to a discussion of contemporary 'neutralist' liberalism, arguing that it was but a more abstract version of ethical liberalism. However, *pace* contemporary communitarians, I argued the ethical liberal world had always been an idealisation and had definitely passed. Far more appropriate for today's conditions was a Weberian 'disenchanted' and realist democratic liberalism.

Critics tended to praise the history and be bemused by, pass over, or be openly hostile to the final argument—not seeing that the one was the basis for the other. As a result, I decided to take a more direct approach and argued straightforwardly for a democratic liberalism in my next book *Liberalism and Pluralism: Towards a Politics of Compromise*. In developing this case, I drew inspiration not just from Weber but also the neo-Roman republican theory of non-domination discovered by Quentin Skinner and developed by Philip Pettit. Its focus on power, with arbitrary rule the cause of domination, served my purpose well. I found a Weberian echo in Pettit's insistence that modern societies contains multiple sources of potentially dominating sources of power that extended far beyond the organs of the state. However, I added a concern, also drawn from Weber, with pluralism and the difficulty of reconciling competing values and conceptions of good, inevitable in a diverse and differentiated society. In seeing democratic politics as a means for confronting both issues, I argued for the liberal qualities of political compromise as echoing the republican injunction 'to hear the other side'.

The book had three parts—first, a critique of contemporary liberalism's flight from politics as it sought to go 'beyond', somehow circumscribe, or simply skirt around conflict and disagreement; second, a defence of a republican inspired democratic liberalism, and the role of compromise within it; and third, an attempt to apply these insights to the analysis of certain concrete policies that revealed the weaknesses of the various liberal strategies and the strengths of my proposed alternative. I suspect few readers felt moved to engage with all three, with the last part being largely ignored because of its applied and mainly British focus. I regard that as unfortunate because part of the case against liberalism was that it rested on unfounded empirical assumptions that the case studies served to illuminate. Meanwhile, though the argument for compromise has attracted both negative and positive attention, it has usually been detached from its normative basis in a republican account of non-domination. My latest book, *Political Constitutionalism*, which is forthcoming from Cambridge University Press at the time of writing, attempts to address both these issues by offering a republican defence of the constitutionality of actually existing democracy that criticises explicitly the normative and empirical shortcomings of legal constitutionalism of a liberal hue - this time using examples from the USA as much as the UK.

I have also applied this argument in a number of detailed studies of the EU, criticising in the process the arguments of David Held concerning Global Democracy and Habermas's views of the potential for a European constitutional patriotism. Instead, I have argued that we should see the EU as a variation on the republican model of 'mixed government'. Its key attribute lies in sharing power between different *demoi* rather than seeking to create a common *demos* or unite around common principles of social justice. Rather, the real achievement of the EU lies in its forcing a degree of mutual accommodation and 'hearing the other side' between the Member States.

What is the proper role of political philosophy in relation to real, political action? Can there ever be a fruitful relation between political philosophy and political practice?

My own work has been increasingly concerned with informing and evaluating contemporary political systems and public policies—particularly in relation to the EU. However, I suspect my view of the relations between political theory and political practice is rather different to many contemporary political philosophers. As the recent concern with relating ideal theory to the real world suggests, the commonest approach among analytical philosophers has been with devising principles that reflect certain ideal criteria. Of course, these idealisations often begin validly enough as abstractions that reflect criteria implicitly employed to justify many current practices yet that are incompletely thought through. The aim is to draw out their consequences and judge social reality by the values people claim should animate it. However, the passage from abstraction to idealisation is easy to make and involves certain fatal distortions. Particular attachments that have force in the real world get sidelined or simply assumed away, the constraints on autonomous agency afflicting most people get passed over, the limitations on practical reasoning when predicting the effects of most policies are ignored, as are the difficulties of getting agreement on what should be done and how, themselves products of imperfections in our powers of moral and political reasoning.

As a result, political philosophy can sometimes seem not so much abstract as abstracted, an irrelevance that makes unwarranted empirical assumptions as to how things are or could be.

How then does my own approach differ? I think there are three respects. First, in not taking the process of abstraction so far that it turns into idealisation. As I noted above, I think one of the key lessons of the so-called Cambridge School's historical approach lay in its seeing how political discourse operates as political action. On this account, ideas serve not simply to legitimate actions undertaken for other, self-interested reasons, but to define what interests are and the range of possibilities open for their pursuit. Much of what goes on in political philosophy is the manipulation and reworking of dominant discourses. Yet it is rarely portrayed or fully conceived in these terms. Instead, philosophers have a tendency to argue as if they were dealing in universal truths rather than battling within and against the limitations of present political thinking. Ironically, though, the search for truth *sub specie aeternitatis* can be more a condemnation to an eternal present than an escape from the restrictions of current thinking. The relationship of political philosophy to its past is instructive in this respect. A prime target of the Cambridge school was the way many philosophers saw the history of ideas as a grand dialogue about certain basic questions of the human condition, in which error was slowly weeded out and progressively better insights achieved. Of course, as Croce famously put it, 'all history is contemporary history'. Today it is almost impossible not to read Plato through Rawls, say, and much other later political thought besides. In doing so, though, we are no longer reading Plato as Plato, to the degree that is possible at all. However, to attempt to do so is not, as is sometimes charged, mere antiquarianism. It forces a reflection on the present and so extends the range of current political thinking by leading us to see how different past ways of thinking and acting have been. Sometimes, as I noted above, it is to be made aware of how ideas we take for granted actually rest on theories we find strange and possibly untenable or abhorrent. In the process, we too can come to think and act differently by being brought to challenge dominant discourses. In essence, that is what Skinner achieved in bringing to light the republican view of non-domination, unearthing a whole new way of thinking about liberty and its consequences for political organisation.

Second, political philosophers rightly seek to formulate principles of justice that can guide policies in given areas—from affirmative action and surrogate motherhood, to global justice and child poverty. Yet in so doing, they must guard against the temptation to suggest that politics must be designed purely to deliver their favoured principles and policies. This instrumental approach to democracy is all too common. It produces an unwarranted faith in counter-majoritarian mechanisms, notably constitutional judicial review – naturally by the 'right' sort of judge, guided by the 'right' sort of bill of rights and the 'correct' interpretation of them – and a naive faith in the probity and talents of experts of all kinds. For a start, such attempts to act as philosopher kings, however well motivated, are dominating. They fail to treat fellow citizens as equals in unjustified ways. Philosophers have no epistemological warrant for their rival ontological claims, nor can they or others fully predict the consequences of their proposals. Democratic processes are required to provide collective decisions with legitimacy and to ensure accountability. It allows citizens to choose on an equal basis between policy proposals and to contest them when they fail. Turning democracy simply into a means to achieve favoured ends, to be rejected or curtailed where it fails to deliver, is to misunderstand the normative role it plays in preventing arbitrary rule, overcoming disagreement and reconciling citizens to common projects.

More generally, how decisions are made is as important an issue as who gets what, where and when. Political philosophers have given too much attention to identifying what seem to them desirable frameworks or outcomes, too little to the procedures whereby decisions are made and the dispositions of those making them. If the best outcome proves disputable or hard to identify, all that can be hoped for is that those who take decisions do so as responsibly as possible – aware of their limitations – and can be encouraged to rectify their mistakes when they appear. The appropriate processes and attitudes are likely to vary according to the public role an individual plays – citizens act differently to politicians, scientists to bureaucrats or generals, and so on. And such public virtues may diverge tremendously from those suitable in the private sphere, so that private virtue can become public vice.

Third, political philosophy needs to be much more informed by social science. To a degree many are aware of the more theoretical branches of economics, but political philosophers tend to take little or no interest in political science. If many political scientists tend to be blissfully unaware of the normative and theoretical assumptions that pervade their work, then political philosophers can be charged for ignoring the often contentious empirical assumptions that underlie theirs. However, if empirical studies of politics that eschew normative theories are blind and lack a sense of where they ought to be headed, political philosophies that are formulated in ignorance of the way political and legal institutions and policies actually work prove empirically empty and so unable to make their ideals engage with reality.

So to sum up, I think we can relate political philosophy to political action only if political philosophers are sensitive to the languages of politics and self-conscious about the ways their arguments abstract from yet engage with past and present discourses, seeking at the same time to avoid empty idealisations; approach their own proposals with due humility and see politics as having intrinsic merits of its own rather than as a mere means to implement those ends they find desirable; and engage with empirical work in the social sciences so that their theories are informed by knowledge about how social, economic and political processes work.

What do you consider the most neglected topics and/or contributions in late 20th century political philosophy, or in related philosophical disciplines (ethics, philosophy of law, metaethics etc.)?

Though there are signs of change, I think political philosophers have tended to ignore theorists and theories of politics, law and society relative to theorists and theories of justice. So the basic courses have tended to ignore Machiavelli and the political writings of Hume, say, rarely teach Durkheim and Weber, and certainly not their political writings, include Dworkin but not Hart and so on. Likewise, philosophers tend to teach courses on professional and public ethics for non-philosophers—business studies and public management students on the whole, rather than seeing these topics as part of a political philosophy programme. The result, as I said above, is a curious disengagement with actual political processes, while offering ever more grandiose schemes for improving the world that bear little or no relation to what is ever likely to happen.

What are the most important unsolved questions in political philosophy and/or related disciplines and what are the prospects for progress?

I find this question almost unintelligible. I do not think there are unsolved political questions in the sense, say, that there are unsolved mathematical ones. The history of the discipline is the asking of different questions and the proffering of different answers, with this questioning and answering shaping and being shaped by the evolution of politics and society—much of which is entirely open and unpredictable. So, it's clear that philosophers will continue to offer variations on the questions and answers that are preoccupy us at present, while moving into new areas we cannot as yet imagine. I certainly have indicated what I hope they will do—re-engage with their past, with social science, and with politics in all its dimensions. How far events force such moves is another matter. However, I suspect the growing turmoil in the Middle East is liable to do so. Here we have issues that cannot be simply seen as matters of 'social justice' and where the need to engage a different tradition of political thinking should make us more reflective about our own. How far that happens may turn out to be of more than academic or disciplinary interest.

Selected bibliography

Monographs

Modern Italian Social Theory – Ideology and Politics from Pareto to the Present, (Polity Press, 1987, Stanford University Press, Ca, 1987, translated into Indonesian).

Liberalism and Modern Society: An Historical Argument, (Polity Press and Penn State University Press, 1992, translated into Portuguese and Chinese) (with Darrow Schecter) *Gramsci and the Italian State*, (Manchester University Press and St Martin's Press, 1993, translated into Japanese).

Liberalism and Pluralism: Towards a Politics of Compromise, (Routledge, 1999).

Rethinking Liberalism: Selected Essays 1987–1997, (Continuum, 2000, reissued 2005, translated into Chinese).

Political Constitutionalism: A Republican Defence of the Constitutionality of Democracy, (Cambridge University Press, 2007).

Selected Edited Books

(editor), *Liberalism and Recent Legal and Social Philosophy*, (Franz Steiner, 1989) (Also appeared as a special issue of the *Archiv fur Rechts-und Sozialphilosophie*, Beiheft nr. 36, 1989).

(co-editor with Dario Castiglione), *Constitutionalism in Transformation: European and Theoretical Perspectives*, (Oxford: Blackwell, 1996) (Also appeared as a special issue of *Political Studies* Vol. 44, n. 3 (1996).

(co-editor with Alex Warleigh), *Citizenship and Governance in the European Union*, (London: Continuum, 2001, reissued 2005).

(co-editor with T. Ball), *The Cambridge History of Twentieth Century Political Thought*, (Cambridge University Press, 2003, translated into Arabic and Chinese).

(co-editor with Dario Castiglione and Emilio Santoro), *Lineages of European Citizenship: Rights, Belonging and Participation in Eleven Nation States*, (Palgrave, 2004).

(editor), *The Rule of Law and the Separation of Powers*, International Library of Essays in Law and Legal Theory - Second Series, (Ashgate / Dartmouth, 2005).

(editor), *Constitutionalism and Democracy*, International Library of Essays in Law and Legal Theory - Second Series, (Ashgate / Dartmouth, 2006).

(co-editor with Dario Castiglione and Jo Shaw), *Making European Citizens: Civic Inclusion in a Transnational Context*, (Palgrave, 2006).

Selected Edited Books (I have excluded those reprinted in *Rethinking Liberalism: Selected Essays 1987–1997*, (Continuum, 2000)).

(with Alex Warleigh), 'From an Ethics of Integration to an Ethics of Participation: Citizenship and the Future of the European Union', *Millennium: A Journal of International Studies*, 27, (1998), pp. 447–70.

(with Martin Hollis) 'Compromise, Consensus and Neutrality' in R. Bellamy and M. Hollis (eds) *Pluralism and Liberal Neutrality*, Special Issue of *Critical Review of International Social and Political Philosophy*, 1, (1998), pp. 54–78.

'Dealing with Difference: Four Models of Pluralist Politics', *Parliamentary Affairs*, 53 (2000), pp. 198–217 (also published in M.

O'Neill and D. Austin (eds), *Democracy and Cultural Diversity*, (Oxford University Press, 2000), pp. 198-217 and translated into Italian as 'Quattro modelli di pluralismo politico', *Ragion Pratica* (2006) pp. 81–100.

(with Dario Castiglione), 'Legitimising the Euro-polity and its Regime: The Normative Turn in EU Studies', *European Journal of Political Theory*, 2:1 (2003) pp. 7–34 (Also published in Italian as 'La legittimazione della forma di stato e della forma di governo europea: la svolta normative negli studi sull'UE', in Etienne Balibar et al, *Europa, Cittadinanza, Confini: Dialogando con Etienne Balibar*, ed. Salvatore Cingari, Lecce: Pensa Multimedia, 2006, pp. 291–335).

(with Justus Schönlau), 'The Normality of Constitutional Politics: An Analysis of the Drafting of the EU Charter of Fundamental Rights', *Constellations: An International Journal of Critical and Democratic Theory*, 11.3 (2004) pp. 412–33 (also translated into French as 'La normalité de la politique constitutionelle. Analyse de la rédaction de la Charte européenne des droits fondamentaux', *Archives de philosophie du droit*, 49 (2006) pp. 85–108.

'Still in Deficit: Rights, Regulation and Democracy in the EU', *European Law Journal*, 12:6 (2006), 725–42.

3

Allen Buchanan

James B. Duke Distinguished Professor of
Philosophy and Public Policy Studies
Duke University, Durham, North Carolina, USA.

Why I was drawn to Political Philosophy

I entered graduate school in 1971, with little or no interest in Political Philosophy, intending to study the highly technical Philosophy of Language. A combination of factors eventually led me to redirect my attention toward Moral and Political Philosophy. I had grown up in the American South during a period in which it was literally an Apartheid society, still characterized by institutionalized racism and violence toward Blacks. As I began to become more critical toward that environment, my appreciation of the importance of social and political institutions began to grow. The cultural and political turmoil of the 1960s stimulated me to begin to be deeply suspicious of the belief structure and system of values into which I had been socialized. I came to the disturbing conclusion that the basic institutions of my society – family, church, school, and government – were deeply implicated in social injustice and helped to perpetuate it by producing prejudiced, unreflective individuals. Some of the grosser injustices of my society began to become visible to me; and I was deeply disturbed that until then they had been invisible to me—and continued to be invisible to most of the people I knew.

I concluded that I had to extricate myself from this noxious environment at the earliest opportunity. I was able to do so, at the age of 18, by entering Columbia University in New York City on an academic scholarship. My undergraduate studies there from 1966 to 1970 exposed me not only to the great social and political thinkers of the Western tradition, but also gave me the opportunity to study non-Western civilizations and literatures by taking courses with professors in Columbia's renowned Oriental Studies

Institute. My most influential undergraduate teacher, the philosopher and art critic Arthur C. Danto, did not work in Political Philosophy, but knowing him and his family, who were true cosmopolitans in the best sense of the word, also helped to widen my political and cultural horizons. Participation in the protest movement against America's war in Vietnam increasingly convinced me that one could not take the rationality or morality of political institutions for granted.

As an undergraduate, however, I did not attempt to integrate my changing political views with the study of Philosophy. Because the center of gravity in Philosophy in the United States at that time was the Philosophy of Language and there was almost no work being done in Political Philosophy, it did not occur to me that contemporary Philosophy had much to contribute to the understanding or resolution of political conflicts or to the moral evaluation of social institutions. All of that changed, in my first year in graduate school, when I began to read Rawls's newly published book, *A Theory of Justice*. I came to believe that it was possible to think rigorously as an analytic philosopher and do so in a way that connected one's academic life with the world of politics.

In graduate school I had the privilege of studying under a brilliant political philosopher, Professor Werner David Falk, a Jewish refugee from Nazi Germany who had been a Professor in Germany and was black-listed by the Nazis after the Reichstag fire. Falk published very little, but he conveyed to his students a deep understanding of the work of major figures in the history of Political Philosophy, especially Hobbes, Rousseau, Hegel, and Marx. Falk helped me to understand how deeply Rawls's work is rooted in the history of Political Philosophy and he encouraged me to write my first book, *Marx and Justice: The Radical Critique of Liberalism*.

I was originally drawn to Philosophy because I admired clear thinking and the refusal to evade the deepest, hardest questions. I began to focus on Political Philosophy because my experiences growing up in a profoundly unjust society convinced me that those who fail to think critically about social and political institutions run a grave moral risk.

Throughout my career, my research and teaching have been equally divided between work in Political Philosophy and work in Bioethics. However, this characterization is misleadingly dualistic, because I have always thought that the best work in Bioethics *is*

Political Philosophy. Accordingly, my work in Bioethics has proceeded on the assumption that one cannot properly understand and respond fruitfully to ethical problems in medicine and the biomedical sciences without seeing that they are at bottom institutional problems and more specifically problems arising from the way in which power is distributed through institutions.

Contributions

I have tried to contribute in the traditional academic way, through teaching and authoring scholarly works, but also by participating in public policy deliberations. To take a few examples of the latter: I have served on a number of national bioethics commissions and similar public bodies in the U.S., including the President's Commission for the Study of Ethical Problems in Medicine and Biomedical and Behavioral Research, the National Bioethics Advisory Commission, the Advisory Committee on Human Radiation Experiments, the Advisory Board for the National Human Genome Research Institute, and the U.S. Secretary of Health and Human Services Committee on Genetic Testing. I have also served as a consultant to the Canadian Government on the possible secession of Quebec from Canada, to the European High Commissioner on National Minorities, and to the Ethiopian Transitional Government on the writing of the Ethiopian constitution in 1993. The basis for my participation in the last three cases was my work on secession and political self-determination.

I believe that my more important scholarly contributions to Political Philosophy have so far been in five related areas. The first is my work on secession or, more accurately, the stimulus it has given to the work of others. I am gratified that *Secession: The Morality of Political Divorce From Fort Sumter to Lithuania and Quebec*, which was to my knowledge the first book-length treatment of the morality of secession, stimulated other political philosophers to explore the moral issues of secession. I had been thinking about secession for some time, but I was fortunate in the matter of timing: it was published in 1991, when the break-ups of Yugoslavia and the Soviet Union were beginning to intrude on the consciousness of even the most reclusive and theoretical of political philosophers. A rich philosophical literature on secession has developed since that time, much of it responding directly to my work.

My early work framed the question of secession almost exclusively as a two-party problem, a conflict between the state and the secessionists. I later came to think of secession as an institutional problem not just at the level of the state but also at the international level. The attempt to develop a view on how the international legal order ought to respond to secession led me to begin to think about international legal institutions more generally and this led to what I believe is a second contribution. I think that my 2004 book *Justice, Legitimacy, and Self-Determination: Moral Foundations for International Law*, has helped to convince some political philosophers that the Philosophy of International Law is a rich and important area for research. Like my book on secession, this work will almost certainly be more valuable for the impetus it gives to better work by others than for the ideas it contains. Through the publication of *Justice, Legitimacy, and Self-Determination* and related papers and through my teaching of graduate students, I think I have done something to stimulate a new generation of political philosophers to become specialists in the Philosophy of International Law.

The third contribution is my effort to engage some of the most interesting and perplexing issues in Bioethics in a way that makes it clear that they are fundamental issues of Political Philosophy. I have in mind here primarily my work on issues of distributive justice in health care, my co-authored work with Dan W. Brock on the concept of decisional capacity and the ethics of deciding for those who lack decisional capacity, and more recently my work on the ethical, social, and political issues surrounding the application of genomic sciences to human beings. My primary authorship of *From Chance to Choice: Genetics and Justice* is an example of my attempt to approach the latter issues from the perspective of Political Philosophy. My current research on the use of biotechnologies to enhance human beings builds on my earlier work, but examines more explicitly the moral significance of the economic effects of the application of biotechnologies to humans.

Fourth, in the last seven years or so I have begun to develop a new topic of research that I call Social Moral Epistemology and I believe that it has considerable potential for changing the way we think about Ethics. Philosophers such as Helene Longino, Alvin Goldman, and Philip Kitcher have done important work in Social Epistemology, which is sometimes defined as the comparative evaluation of alternative social institutions as to their efficacy and efficiency in producing, preserving, and disseminating true or justified beliefs. Much of this work has focused on the epistemic virtues of the institutions through which scientific knowledge is developed. By Social *Moral* Epistemology I mean the comparative evaluation of alternative institutions as to their efficacy and efficiency in producing, preserving, and disseminating true or justified beliefs that play a crucial role in the functioning of our moral powers—our capacity for moral judgment, for moral reasoning, and for moral motivation. The perspective of Social Moral Epistemology transforms the way one thinks about Ethics. Instead of conceiving of Ethics as primarily or exclusively a matter of identifying and critically evaluating ethical principles and arguments, considered in the abstract, we need to develop a systematic understanding of the ways in which institutions shape the beliefs on the basis of which we apply moral principles and the assumptions we make about the interpretation and scope of those principles. For example, I have argued that to understand the most serious moral wrongs of the eugenics movements of the late 19th to mid-20th Centuries it is necessary to appreciate the role of false beliefs about the biological causes of social ills and the way in which these false beliefs were disseminated through the social identification of supposed experts in the science of biological inheritance. ("Ethics, Institutions, and Beliefs: Eugenics as a Case Study," forthcoming in *The Journal of Political Philosophy*).

In his splendid book *Humanity: A Moral History of the Twentieth Century*, the British philosopher Jonathan Glover argues that a central concern of Ethics should be to help us understand the large-scale evils of our own time, with the aim of reducing the risk that they will recur. I agree with Glover on this point, but would add that to achieve this aim we must think more deeply about the role of institutions in forming and sustaining the beliefs that rationalize and motivate morally bad behavior.

A fifth area of contribution, of which my work in Social Moral Epistemology is only one instance, is my increasing emphasis on the importance of what might be called institutional moral theorizing. I have come to have grave doubts about the usefulness of the distinction between "ideal" and "nonideal" theory and have become convinced that Moral and Political Philosophy must take the existence and power of institutions more seriously at every level of theorizing. What is called ideal theory is often either so disconnected with institutional realities that it has no substantive implications for how we ought to proceed in the real world, or it unconsciously assumes that existing institutions are a fixed feature of the moral landscape. In my judgment, political philosophers need to think institutionally "all the way down." It is time to jettison the facile idea that there is a neat division of labor, with true philosophers working out the theory, paying no attention to institutional realities, and mere "applied ethics" people (beings of lesser intellect) assigned the supposedly less creative task of applying the theory.

I believe the application of this idea of institutional moral theorizing in my recent work on Just War Theory illustrates its importance. I have argued that theorizing about the morality of war must take seriously the fact that the validity of norms can depend upon the institutional context in which they are to operate. A particular norm may be valid for a context in which institutional capacity is negligible, but overly-constraining in a context in which appropriate institutions operate. For example, preventive war, understood as the use of large-scale military force to avert a supposed distant harm, carries special moral risk beyond those of war generally, because the inherently speculative character of the notion of prevention invites error and abuse. In recognition of the fact that recourse to "the preventive war justification" is so risky, the dominant view in the Just War Tradition has been that preventive war is never justified and this highly constraining norm is also reflected in international law. It is important to understand, however, that the risks of abuse and error may not be fixed; better institutions for decision-making may be able to reduce the risks to tolerable levels, for example, by being multilateral and including certain accountability mechanisms to help ensure that decision-makers properly utilize accurate information about potential future harms. Thus the question is not "Should we stick with a blanket prohibition on preventive war or abandon the blanket prohibition in favor of a more permissive norm that allows war for prevention?" but rather "Are there feasible institutional safeguards that could make it responsible for state leaders to engage in preventive war?" The choice, in other words, is not only between alternative norms, but also between alternative norm-institution packages. The more general point is that the enterprise of Just War theorizing looks quite different, depending upon whether it proceeds on the assumption that just war norms are to be directed to the conscience of state leaders, under conditions of negligible institutional capacity for guiding their decision-making, or whether we may consider the possibility of a more developed institutional capacity. Almost all contemporary Just War theorizing fails to make this distinction, while unconsciously proceeding either on the assumption that institutional capacity is zero or on the assumption that the only alternatives are unilateral decision-making without any significant institutional safeguards or decision-making in accordance with the current international legal standard, namely, UN Security Council authorization. Institutions are overlooked entirely or, if they are noticed at all, the existing institutions, with all their imperfections, are assumed to be the only alternative. The possibility of developing better institutions for decision-making about war is not considered and the crucial relationship between norms and institutions is unappreciated.

The emphasis on institutions and the refusal to rest content with a dubious distinction between ideal and nonideal theory is closely linked to my interest in Social Moral Epistemology. The character of the institutions within which we live influences our beliefs and through them our conduct in ways that we seldom fully appreciate, but once the epistemic role of institutions becomes clear there is hope that we can deliberately modify our institutions in ways that improve our prospects for acting morally.

I have recently been exploring further the idea that the moral justification of policies relies in part upon institutionalized reasoning and that institutionalized reasoning can play a crucial role in the legitimacy of institutions. Consider, for example, the familiar complaint that some or all of what are called human rights are not really universal, but instead merely reflect the peculiar values of Western culture or liberalism. If this charge is valid, then it undermines the legitimacy of international institutions that are designed to try to implement human rights norms. I believe that whether human rights are universal or are expressions of parochial values cannot be determined by traditional moral-philosophical reasoning but requires an examination of the epistemic functions of the totality of institutions within which human rights norms are articulated, interpreted, subjected to on-going critical scrutiny, and revised over time. In brief, I believe that the ultimate justification of human rights norms is partly institutional and that the legitimacy of institutional efforts to implement human rights norms depends in part upon the epistemic quality of the institutions through which human rights norms are developed and justified. ("Are Human Rights Parochial? Rethinking the Question," unpublished paper).

Theory and practice

For reasons already noted, I reject the hard and fast distinction between ideal and nonideal theorizing in Political Philosophy and this gives me one reason to be skeptical of a sharp boundary between theory and practice. More importantly, my work in Social Moral Epistemology has convinced me that the contrast between belief and action that the theory/practice distinction suggests is also untenable in this sense: institutions inculcate beliefs that shape action and institutions are only able to do this through the actions of those who wield institutional power and the responses of others to their actions. The beliefs that institutions inculcate in us and that in turn lead us to support these institutions are systematically interconnected with one another: they comprise an implicit theory. In that sense, practice is always theory-laden, so it is misleading to ask how we can put theory into practice. When new sets of systematically connected sets of new beliefs come to inform our practices, this is not a matter of the theorist winning over the belief of the masses or of leaders simply by virtue of the intellectually compelling content of the new ideas. Instead, whether particular beliefs come to be widely accepted and to have effects on behavior depends upon institutions in at least three ways. First, institutional processes help us to identify (or misidentify) some and not others as experts, as reliable sources of beliefs, both factual and normative. Second, institutions can either facilitate or block the coordinated action needed for putting ideas into action. Third, and less obviously, institutions can support beliefs that can either help make moral flaws in our social arrangements obvious or hide them from view. For example, liberal social orders, in spite of their flaws, have resources for the correction of false beliefs about social reality that are lacking in other institutional arrangements. Institutions also shape our moral horizons by shaping our beliefs about which parts of our social world are fixed and which are alterable.

The best ideas can be extremely dangerous if they are applied in the context of systematically distorted, institutionally supported beliefs about how the world is and in particular about supposed natural differences among human beings. For example, a Nazi manual for school teachers in the 1930s emphasized that it was important to teach children to act in accordance with the Golden Rule, but with the provision that the Golden Rule only applied to "racial comrades." The distinction between 'racial comrades' and inferior others was inculcated through institutional processes in which some individuals, including physicians and public health officials, were identified as experts in racial science and seen by others as credible sources of true beliefs about supposed biological differences between different groups of people. At the very least, Political Philosophy, if it includes Social Moral Epistemology, can make us more critical of both our institutions and our beliefs, by making clear how they shape and support one another. More ambitiously, a Political Philosophy informed by Social Moral Epistemology can provide guidance for modifying institutions in a way that enables them to help us to get the most out of our limited moral powers.

Neglected issues, unanswered questions

Until recently, Political Philosophy has had little to say about some of the most significant moral and political issues because it has focused almost exclusively on the justification of the state, taken in isolation, and upon the relationship that must exist between the state and its citizens if the state is to be legitimate. The result has been not only a failure to address issues of international justice and more generally the ethics of international relations, but also blindness to the fact that the state itself has changed through processes of globalization and the development of international legal institutions and that these changes ought to be taken into account in our efforts to theorize the state itself. There are already significant efforts to remedy these glaring defects, but it is still an open question whether a coherent and persuasive cosmopolitan Political Philosophy will be developed and will gain adherents beyond the academy.

Fruitful engagement with international issues will only occur if political philosophers are willing to adopt a more interdisciplinary approach. In particular, they must try to understand how international institutions work before they can offer a plausible assessment of their legitimacy and the requirements of international justice.

Just as Political Philosophy has operated largely within the confines of the idea of a single state, considered in isolation, so the Philosophy of Law has generally neglected international law. There are encouraging signs of change here, too. Philosophers are beginning to notice that there is such a thing as international law. Those who agree with me that Political Philosophy must take institutions seriously at all levels of theorizing also are coming to recognize the need for a moral theory of international legal institutions. In my judgment, the Philosophy of International Law is likely to be the most exciting area in Moral and Political Philosophy, at least for the next decade. My hope is that the developing field of Philosophy of International Law will not only contribute to the creation of a larger cosmopolitan moral and political theory, but that it will also make the community of Political Philosophers more cosmopolitan, by forcing them to consider different societal perspectives on international law, on international institutions generally, and on the state itself. Too much of the work of Anglophone political philosophers has proceeded in ignorance of excellent work being done elsewhere, especially in Europe.

If the Philosophy of International Law is to flourish, it must be not only cosmopolitan but also interdisciplinary. Until recently, theorizing about the international legal system, at least in the United States, tended to be the exclusive province of international lawyers who either took a rather narrow "textual" or "doctrinal" approach to the subject or were human rights activists whose moral commitments were considerably deeper than their knowledge of Moral Philosophy. Just in the past few years, a new generation of political scientists has begun to develop empirically-based theories about how the international legal system actually works and to break down the traditional theoretical and institutional barriers between the disciplines of international relations and international law. Philosophers working on international law have much to learn from this new approach to international legal institutions, but lawyers and political scientists focusing on international law can also benefit from the philosopher's expertise in the moral evaluation of political and legal institutions.

Although the morality of war has been a recurring theme in the history of Western Philosophy it has largely been addressed in a rather compartmentalized way, as the phrase 'Just War Theory' suggests, rather than as a crucial element of a larger Political Philosophy that encompasses international relations and international legal institutions. Periods of development in Political Philosophy usually are stimulated by major political events, in particular revolutions and wars. The NATO intervention in Kosovo in 1999, the failure to intervene in Rwanda and Bosnia in the early 1990s, and the recent U.S. invasion of Iraq, which was officially justified in part as a preventive war of self-defense, have together prompted a remarkable out-pouring of work on the morality of war by moral and political philosophers in the analytic tradition. So far this work has been too noninstitutional and too unconnected with the larger task of developing a Political Philosophy that takes international institutions and life beyond the confines of the state seriously. In addition, this new work on the morality of war has, for the most part, not taken up what I take to be one of the main challenges for a cosmopolitan Political Philosophy and for the Philosophy of Law: providing a unified, principled account of the relationship between human rights and the morality of war. Remarkably enough, mainstream liberal Political Philosophy in the United States has largely ignored human rights until very recently and even now some of the most prominent contemporary philosophical work on the morality of war makes no mention of human rights or of the problem of reconciling the practice of war with respect for human rights. In international law, the law of war and human rights law have usually been treated as if they were almost unrelated and that there exists no over-arching jurisprudential theory that encompasses both. I believe that Political Philosophy has a major role to play in remedying this deficiency.

Selected publications

Books

Marx and Justice: The Radical Critique of Liberalism, Rowman and Littlefield, Philosophy and Society Series 1982 (U.S.) and Methuen Publishers (U.K.) 1982.

Ethics, Efficiency, and the Market, Rowman and Allenheld, (U.S.) and Oxford University Press (U.K.), May 1985.

Deciding for Others: The Ethics of Surrogate Decision-Making, co-authored with Dan W. Brock, Cambridge University Press, 1989.

Secession: The Morality of Political Divorce From Fort Sumter to Lithuania and Quebec, Westview Press, 1991.

From Chance to Choice: Genetics and Justice, with Dan W. Brock, Norman Daniels, and Daniel Wikler, Cambridge University Press, 2000.

Justice, Legitimacy, and Self-Determination: Moral Foundations for International Law, Oxford University Press, 2003.

Articles and Book Chapters

"Categorical Imperatives and Moral Principles," *Philosophical Studies*, 1977.

"Revisability and Rational Choice," *Canadian Journal of Philosophy*, 1975.

"Medical Paternalism," *Philosophy & Public Affairs*, 1978.

"Revolutionary Motivation and Rationality," *Philosophy & Public Affairs*, 1979.

"The Right to a 'Decent Minimum' of Health Care," *Philosophy & Public Affairs*, 1983.

"Justice and Charity," *Ethics*, 1987.

"What's So Special About Rights?" *Ethics*, 1987.

"Justice as Reciprocity Versus Subject-Centered Justice," *Philosophy & Public Affairs*, 1990.

"Advanced Directives and Personal Identity," *Philosophy & Public Affairs*, 1988.

"Rationing Without Justice, But Not Unjustly," *Journal of Health, Politics, Law & Policy*, 1998.

"Assessing the Communitarian Critique of Liberalism," *Ethics*, 1989.

"The Morality of Inclusion," *Social Philosophy & Policy*, Vol. 10, No. 2, 1993.

"Choosing Who Will Be Disabled: Genetic Intervention and the Morality of Inclusion," *Social Philosophy & Policy*, 1996.

"The Controversy over Retrospective Moral Judgment," *Kennedy Institute of Ethics*, Vol. 6, No. 3, 1996.

"Theories of Secession," *Philosophy & Public Affairs*, Vol. 26, No. 1, 1997.

"Social Moral Epistemology," *Social Philosophy and Policy*, Vol. 19, No. 2, 2002.

"From Nuremburg to Kosovo: The Morality of Illegal International Legal Reform," *Ethics*, July 2001.

"Political Liberalism and Social Epistemology," *Philosophy & Public Affairs*, 2002.

"The Philosophy of International Law," with David Golove, *Oxford Handbook on the Philosophy of Law* in Jules L. Coleman and Scott Shapiro, eds., Oxford University Press, 2002.

"Political Legitimacy and Democracy," *Ethics*, July 2002.

"Institutionalizing the Just War," *Philosophy & Public Affairs*, January 2006.

"Institutions, Ethics, and Beliefs: Eugenics as a Case Study," *The Journal of Political Philosophy*, (forthcoming).

4

William Galston

Senior Fellow, Governance Studies Program
The Brookings Institution, USA

Why were you initially drawn to political philosophy?

I have always been passionate about politics. I can remember lying in the bedroom at the age of 6 listening to Dwight Eisenhower's "I will go to Korea" speech. Eight years later I accompanied my family on a year-long trip around the world financed (in that vanished age of low inflation and a strong dollar) by a Fulbright grant. As November approached in Canberra, Australia, I plastered my wall with state-by-state statistics and predictions about the 1960 U.S. presidential campaign. The time difference made it easier for me than for the bleary-eyed candidates and their aides to follow every twist and turn of the night when the outcome hung in the balance until near dawn. My parents seemed unsurprised when as a middle-aged academic I participated in a series of presidential campaigns (all losing) and, after finally picking a winner, spent two and one half years in Bill Clinton's White House.

So politics, yes, but political *philosophy*? As I entered Cornell University in the fall of 1963, I was hardly drawn toward philosophy as a major. At that time, students of Wittgenstein dominated Cornell's department. While I was happy enough to take scattered courses on the philosophy of science and Kant's First Critique, I was not at all interested in the questions that defined the Wittgensteinians' agenda, and I was less than impressed by what I learned about relations among them. I remember reading Norman Malcolm's memoir. In one episode Malcolm and Wittgenstein were out in a field at night. Malcolm glanced up, pointed to a small constellation, and said Look, M for Malcolm . . . at which point Wittgenstein rotated 180 degrees, pointed, and said No, W for Wittgenstein. This sounded like the beginning of a joke, or of amiable banter of what it means to follow the same rule from different points of view. But no, it sparked an argument that (if I recall correctly), led to a significant period of estrangement between the two thinkers. This, it seemed to me, was not a model of human excellence. At any rate, I had no desire to emulate it.

But something else was going on. In my freshman year, and for many years after, Allan Bloom was a charismatic presence. His classes filled the largest lecture halls, and with reason: his passionate exposition of the classic texts of political philosophy was irresistible. It was mind-boggling for a boy of 17 to learn that the idea of democracy had a history, that a number of not obviously crazy thinkers had preferred other forms of government, and that even its supporters had found it necessary to warn against its defects. It was equally mind-boggling to discover, not only that philosophers asked how we should live, but also that they thought the answers had a bearing on practical politics. I was amazed at how much light Aristotle's analysis of justice cast on contemporary American institutions and policies. Not to put too fine a point on it, I was hooked, and forty-three years later I still am.

As I slowly learned (and the world more slowly still), Bloom's exegeses were rooted in the febrile European debates of the interwar years. I needed to learn more about Carl Schmitt, Martin Heidegger, Gershom Scholem, and Alexander Kojeve, among others ... and of course about Leo Strauss. And I needed to think through the relation between this tradition and contemporary politics. If you took this European tradition seriously, did you have to become a political conservative? Did you have to become skeptical about the worth of liberal democracy? Did you have to see modern natural science as a problem? (As the son of a biologist, that last question mattered a lot.) As an undergraduate, my preliminary answers, duly qualified, were no, no, and no. (I have not changed my mind since.) It took me much longer to come to terms with Allan Bloom's complex legacy. Readers interested in this journey can consult my review-essay on *The Closing of the American Mind*, which appeared in the obscure (to most) journal *Interpretation*; and also my essay entitled "A Student of Leo Strauss in the Clinton White House." (I am told that this title alone drove some followers of Strauss into splutters of laughter, and others into paroxysms of rage. But I digress.)

What do you consider your own most important contribution(s) to political philosophy, and why?

While I am not blessed with a good memory for events, I confess

I find it easier to trace what drew me toward political philosophy than to specify my contributions to it. Having thought about this for a while, I believe I can now say why.

In the first place, "contribution" is the conceptual tip of an elaborate theory and sociology of knowledge that I don't accept. The underlying intuition goes back to Locke, if not before: while the architect designs the wall of knowledge, the "under-laborers" build it, brick by brick, over time. Once the basic design is locked in, knowledge is discrete, harmonious, and cumulative. Conceivably some areas of human inquiry work this way, but I'm pretty sure political philosophy doesn't.

Second, the concept invites a certain loss of perspective, even vainglory. Plato "contributed" the *Republic* and a few other modest works, which probably will be read as long as the texts and our species survive. By that standard, I have contributed precisely nothing. Have I been one of Oakeshott's voices in the conversation of mankind? Sure, but so has everyone else. Where is the middle ground?

Third, it seems to me that a scholar's contributions, whatever they may be, are better assessed by students, colleagues, and readers than by the author. When I try to specify my contributions to political philosophy, I focus on the extent to which I affected the debate. But that may not be the right metric, and even if it is, I'm not sure I'm in the best position to apply it.

Having elaborately denied that I can address the question, let me try anyway. In my judgment, which may be fatally flawed (see the preceding three paragraphs), I have offered three ideas that to some extent have altered the debate. To begin: from the early 1980s on, I raised questions about the conception of liberal democracy as "neutral" with respect to conceptions of good or worthy lives. That didn't seem right, either as a theoretical matter or in light of observed practice. Nor did I think it sufficient to acknowledge that liberalism embodies a set of all-purpose, instrumental ("primary") goods. The difference between liberal constitutional democracy and other regime-types is not between the absence and presence of non-instrumental theories of the good, but rather in the relative thickness of those theories—in plain terms, the space they leave for individual choice and self-determination. Liberalism insists on certain basic goods as intrinsic to human well-being, but at the same time it recognizes that these goods establish a floor, not a template, for human aspiration. Or so I argued, in a series of exchanges with John Rawls and other leading liberal theorists.

I'm not sure I carried the day, but I did advance an argument that was harder to ignore a decade after I began making it.

Second, guided in part by my enduring regard for Aristotle, I questioned a then-popular distinction between civic republics on the one hand and constitutional democracies on the other. Civic republics depended on virtuous citizens; no one doubted that. But many thinkers, misreading and distorting James Madison, argued that constitutional democracies needed nothing more than institutions artfully arranged to repress the passions and channel the interests. (Kant's famous remark about the problem of republican government being soluble even for a "nation of devils" was much in the air.) I argued to the contrary, that like every regime-type, constitutional democracy had its own civic requisites, which I was bold enough to term "liberal virtues." These civic virtues were understood as instrumentally rather than intrinsically good—as necessary for constitutional democracy but not necessarily part of the human good *simpliciter*. While there was no direct linear correlation, I acknowledged, at some point the attenuation of these virtues would impede the operation, and at the extreme threaten the survival, of constitutional democracy itself.

I wove these two "contributions" into a sustained thesis about modern liberal democracy, published as *Liberal Purposes* in the early 1990s. Shortly thereafter, I entered the Clinton administration, emerging exhausted a few years later. Exhausted, but also changed, in ways that it took me some time to grasp. The most important were these: During my years in government I had repeatedly experienced clashes among sensible arguments and worthy goods that could not be reduced to a common measure of value. The choice between good and bad was easy; the tough choices were between good and good. In thinking this through, I realized that while I had always implicitly been a value pluralist, it was time to integrate this insight into my theorizing. At the same time, as the White House official responsible for a range of religious free exercise issues, I began to appreciate the importance of freedom of conscience as never before. This led me into the thickets of medieval dual-sword theology, to the Reformed Calvinist conception of "sphere sovereignty," and ultimately to the once-fashionable, now scorned British pluralist tradition (J.N. Figgis, G.D.H. Cole, and the early Harold Laski.)

How, if at all, did value pluralism and political pluralism fit together? And could they be used to reformulate liberal democratic theory? These are the questions that I have addressed in my most recent work, *Liberal Pluralism* (2002) and *The Practice of Liberal Pluralism* (2004). Isaiah Berlin was both a value pluralist and a liberal, but he was less than clear about how these two bodies of theory fit together. Along with a handful of others, I tried to bring some precision to these issues. In so doing, I think I helped move the philosophical (as opposed to interest-group/political science) conceptions of pluralism closer to the center of political philosophy.

What is the proper role of political philosophy in relation to real, political action? Can there ever be a fruitful relation between political philosophy and political practice?

Given my somewhat unusual life, which has moved from theory to practice and back again, the relation between political philosophy and political action is for me an existential as well as theoretical question. I remember teaching and implicitly endorsing the message of Plato's *Seventh Letter* as a young assistant professor. My thinking has changed since then. Sure, the relation between philosopher and prince can be a temptation to collaborate with evil, or at least to corrupt the truth, but so can most other human relationships in which scholars find themselves. And given the vagaries of public life, no one thinks that political philosophy can supply recipes for practice. It can, however, help frame discussions and point toward plausible responses to problems. Let me give two examples from my own life.

I mentioned earlier that my theoretical work had led me to the idea of "liberal virtues," which I was able to specify in some detail. No one thinks that these virtues are innate, the product of moral sense; everyone concedes that concrete social processes and institutions are needed to produce them. This simple line of reasoning leads toward a number of areas of public policy: To what extent are well-functioning families needed to lay the foundation for civic virtues, and can public policy help strengthen them? What role should intentional civic education play in our public schools? And to the extent that our public culture shapes the civic consciousness of the young, how if at all should we regulate the broadcast media and other formative cultural institutions? Philosophy cannot answer these questions, but it forces us to ponder them.

A second example: early in my extended encounter with Rawls's thought, I concluded that his rejection of "desert" was among the weakest building-blocks in the entire edifice of *A Theory of Justice*.

(That was a minority view in the early 1980s, but it's much closer to today's mainstream.) But if one brings desert back in, what is the impact (if any) on political practice? In the late 1980s and early 1990s, the answer became clear and highly topical. Guided by the idea of reciprocity and reward in return for civic contribution, a few of us had begun reshaping U.S. social policy around two principles: If you work full-time, you and your family should not live in poverty; and second, welfare should be a temporary bridge to the world of work, not a permanent way of life. We entered into dialogue with a young governor from Arkansas who was thinking along similar lines. By the end of Bill Clinton's first term, programs to support work and make it pay had been vastly expanded, and welfare had been fundamentally changed. These policies were controversial at the time and in some circles remain so today. I offer them to illustrate the point that political philosophy can create a broad context within which specific policies can be developed.

The productive relation between political philosophy and political practice also works the other way around. Political philosophy is one way of thinking about politics. It is not brought to, but rather is drawn from, political life. It should begin by reflecting on the specific features and dynamics of political communities, relations, conflicts, and decisions. When John Rawls published his masterwork, its implicit and very narrow political context—disputes between liberty and equality, conducted through reason and guided by the assumption that constitutional democracy was an uncontested good—seemed plausible to most scholars. Today, developments at home and abroad have renewed the old quarrel between reason and faith as grounds of political authority, and also about the worth of democracy itself. If God is truly the source of law, the people cannot be, and the Western stance toward democracy is recast as a form of idolatry. We may well be moving back toward earlier eras of political philosophy in which the range of debate among regimes and authorizing principles may be much wider than it was thought to be when my generation of political philosophers was coming to maturity.

What do you consider the most neglected topics and/or contributions in post-Rawlsian or late 20th century political philosophy?

Few topics in political philosophy are truly neglected. The most usual situation is that a handful of scholars labor at the margins of the discipline (sometime for decades) until a critical mass of argument accumulates or until circumstances spark increased interest and draw topics from the periphery toward the center of concerns. With no pretence of completeness, let me list seven such topics.

1. Aristotle never forgot that we humans are embodied beings, distinct from other species yet sharing certain attributes with them. For the most part, contemporary political philosophy has focused on the distinctiveness (speech, reason, liberty, creativity) at the expense of commonality. In that light, political philosophers and others are prone to understand fundamental human institutions as social constructions.

I think I know why: appeals to biology and nature generally have often been used to sustain arrangements that are hard to justify before the bar of reason. But as a discipline, we have gone too far in separating ourselves from scientific advances in neurobiology, evolutionary psychology, and others. It is time to reopen lines of communication.

2. During most of my career, political philosophy has been dominated by what I regard as an excessively rationalistic view of human beings. This is in part because of the way that Kant's practical philosophy has been received into contemporary political philosophy, and also in part because of the understandable vogue of "deliberation" as the core of democratic politics. Whatever the cause, the effect is to ignore, or to regard as wholly negative, the role of passions and emotions in political life. As every reader of the *Rhetoric* knows, Aristotle didn't make that mistake, and I don't see why we should continue to. Martha Nussbaum's work during the past decade has shown how we can begin to restore balance to our theoretical enterprise, and I hope that younger scholars will be inclined to follow that trail.

One example will show the practical significance of this move. Suppose a contemporary politician is accused of exacerbating and manipulating people's fears. A political philosophy more attuned to the passions and emotions could provide a template for assessing this charge. Some Aristotelians might argue, for example, that not fearing what is truly fearful is at least as dangerous as fearing what is not truly fearful. If the people are oblivious to a genuine threat, then the use of rhetoric to stir their fears can be an act of legitimate statesmanship. Our inquiry then shifts to the question of what is rightly feared in current circumstances—not a simple question, of course, but a more productive discussion than the exchange of charges over rhetoric.

3. The late Bernard Williams often contrasted two kinds of political philosophy—"political moralism," in which the moral is prior to the political, and "political realism," in which political problems and relations enjoy substantial autonomy from moral philosophy as now understood. This distinction, I believe, raises challenging questions that go to the heart of our enterprise, and I hope we take them up. As I scan the field today, political moralism is the dominant view. Its competitor is dismissed as simple cynicism, or as what Rawls called "mere modus vivendi"—as if the perennial human quest for ways of getting along peaceably with one another were somehow unworthy of serious attention. Perhaps the discussion would go better if more political philosophers had political experience. Lacking that, graduate courses would do well to focus more than they now do on issues such as evil, the Augustinian *libido dominandi*, and the consequences of the breakdown of basic civil order. At any rate, Williams' challenge should not be ignored.

4. Aristotle directed our attention to the distinctive nature of political association and its relation to other forms of human association. I don't think we can accept his answers, but he certainly posed the right question. We need to think harder about the authority political institutions typically claim over families, voluntary associations, and religious institutions, among others. This is one reason why I regard the British pluralists, despite their often antique language and ethnocentrism, as having raised issues of enduring relevance that more political philosophers should address today.

5. In recent decades, much of political philosophy has focused on principles, while real-world politics revolves around the effort to create, strengthen, and reform institutions. I do not doubt the importance of principles, but I think the relative neglect of institutions has been a mistake. Because politics is a collective enterprise, principles take on meaning as they are crystallized in institutions that channel collective decisions and activities. Some apparently worthy principles may

not be amenable to institutionalization; if so, their action-guiding force is questionable. As Stephen Elkin has argued in his recent book *Reconstructing the Commercial Republic*, political philosophers should relearn the art of thinking constitutionally. As they do, they may discover connections between the principles/institutions dyad and Williams' distinction between political moralism and political realism.

6. While contemporary political philosophers have not entirely neglected other forms of relations and associations, I think it is fair to say that their principal focus has been on the nation-state. (I'm as guilty of this as anyone.) We must now begin to ask whether phrases such as the "international community" are mere pieties or rather point toward emerging realities that we should take seriously. Many of us share a vague sense that while the international lawyers go too far in equating domestic and international legal regimes, "realist" theorists of international relations go too far in the other direction when they argue that politics in the absence of a sovereign who possesses the force needed to overawe others is necessarily anarchic. Is this zone between (crudely) Kant and Hobbes just a conceptual morass, or is there something that we can do to characterize it more precisely as a distinctive form of human association? The issue is too important for us not to try.

7. As good children of the Enlightenment, most contemporary political philosophers have taken it for granted that their enterprise is to be conducted within the bounds of human reason. Many have tacitly assumed the validity of Max Weber's proposition that modernization brings secularization. Recent events, domestic and international, have made it clear that the relation between faith and rationality is back on the agenda of practical politics. It should be back on ours as well.

What are the most important unsolved questions in political philosophy and/or related disciplines and what are the prospects for progress?

Mathematical problems are solved. Scientific puzzles are resolved. Political philosophy is not like that. According to one view of political philosophy, the evidence of the unchanging questions is clearer than the answers to them will ever be. According to another view, historical contingency and change will always create new problems for which the old answers do not suffice. There are other views as well. Despite their differences, they mostly converge on the conclusion that political philosophy is an inherently open-ended venture.

To be sure, progress is possible. We know more about the theory and practice of constitutionalism than we did when Locke wrote. We have learned, painfully, that efforts to forcibly impose unitary conceptions of the good society can unleash extremes of human brutality. And we have learned that human affairs are more malleable than was once supposed—for example, that new political norms and arrangements can alter age-old relations between men and women.

For the most part, however, we will have to content ourselves with whatever clarity, most of it local and temporal, our efforts can yield. And if what we write is read by our great-children, I suspect it will be more for the questions we raised and the challenges we posed than for the answers we offered.

Selected publications

Books

The Practice of Liberal Pluralism (Cambridge, 2004).

Liberal Pluralism (Cambridge, 2002).

Liberal Purposes (1991).

Justice and the Human Good (Chicago, 1980).

Kant and the Problem of History (Chicago, 1975).

Articles

"Contending with Liberalism," in Margaret O'Brien Steinfels, *American Catholics and Civic Engagement* (Rowman & Littlefield, 2004).

"Value Pluralism and Liberal Political Theory," *American Political Science Review* 93, 4 (December 1999).

"Two Concepts of Liberalism," *Ethics* 105, 3 (April 1995).

"Political Theory in the 1980s: Perplexity Amidst Diversity," in Ada W. Finifter, *Political Science: The State of the Discipline* (American Political Science Association, 1993).

"What is Living and What is Dead in Kant's Practical Philosophy?" in Ronald Beiner and William James Booth, *Kant and Political Philosophy* (Yale, 1993).

"Practical Philosophy and the Bill of Rights," in Michael J. Lacey and Knud Haakonssen, *A Culture of Rights* (Cambridge, 1991).

"Pluralism and Social Unity," *Ethics* 99, 4 (July 1989).

"Community, Democracy, Philosophy: The Political Thought of Michael Walzer," *Political Theory* 17, 1 (February 1988).

"Socratic Reason and Lockean Rights: The Place of the University in a Liberal Democracy," *Interpretation* 16, 1 (Fall 1988).

"Liberal Virtues," *American Political Science Review* 82, 4 (December 1988).

"Moral Personality and Liberal Theory: John Rawls's 'Dewey Lectures'," *Political Theory* 10, 4 (November 1982).

5

Amy Gutmann

President of the University of Pennsylvania

Professor of Political Science in the School of Arts and Sciences at Penn, with secondary faculty appointments in the Philosophy Department in Arts and Sciences, at the Annenberg School for Communication, and at the Graduate School of Education.

University of Pennsylvania, PA, USA

Why were you initially drawn to political philosophy?

Early in life, I was drawn to political philosophy without realizing that I would grow up to become a political philosopher! My avid interest in justice evolved from having a father who fled Nazi Germany as a Jewish college student in 1934 and who brought his entire family – including four older siblings – to join him in India.

In high school, I exhorted my fellow graduates in 1967 to action. "Involvement," I said, "must uproot complacency. It must be a continuous ideal throughout our lives, not just the ideal of ambitious youth—for involvement is as realistic a solution to world problems as it is an idealistic, moral solution. It is the chance for our generation to put into action all that we have spent years learning, for what is education if it is not the foundation for living?"

While I felt the stirrings of my inner political philosopher, I began my undergraduate studies at Radcliffe Harvard as a mathematics major during the cataclysmic year of 1968. Student activism and opposition to the Vietnam War, already at fever pitch, had metastasized into hostile confrontations with university administrators on several campuses.

While I was opposed to the war, I also opposed the extremist rhetoric and violent tactics directed against innocent individuals. I pursued the questions that stood at the basis of the social movements at the time: What makes government legitimate? When does government cease to be legitimate? What justifiable and effective means are available to resolve conflicts?

Out of intellectual curiosity I enrolled in Gov 106b, Michael Walzer's legendary course on the history of political theory. The course not only helped me begin to develop my thinking about these questions, but also furnished in Walzer himself a role model of the kind of teacher and scholar that I aspired to become.

Public political philosophers like Walzer had several attributes in common:

- They displayed the moral courage of their convictions.

- They stood within, not apart from, the society they criticized.

- They wrote and spoke in lucid, accessible language with which they connected to their fellow citizens.

- They did not demonize their adversaries or idealize their allies. They did not toe party lines or pitch the rhetoric of dangerously seductive myths.

- They prized intellectual integrity and practiced mutual respect and responsibility. They constantly put their own ideas to the test.

- And they pledged their foremost allegiance to social justice understood as a *practical* pursuit of improving the lives of real - *not hypothetical* - people.

I switched to an interdisciplinary social science (honors) major (with the inauspicious name of 'social studies') and began devouring the canonical works in political philosophy—beginning with Plato's *Republic*.

Although I rejected the content of Plato's philosophy, I could not escape Plato's conclusion that public action must be partly philosophical to be justified:

> Unless either philosophers become kings in their countries, or those who are now called kings and rulers come to be sufficiently inspired with a genuine desire for wisdom; unless, that is to say, political power and philosophy meet together, there can be no rest from troubles for states, nor yet, I believe, for all mankind.

Against the backdrop of campus confrontation and upheaval, this notion of tempering political power with philosophical wisdom planted seeds in my own philosophical thinking. I began to chart a middle ground between the solitary path that a lot of philosophers took (then and now) and mass protest: Deliberating with other people as equals on the decisions that bind us all. I reasoned that we are more likely to arrive at better policies and produce a more civil society by deliberating with one another in the spirit of mutual respect.

I also was fortunate to have as my mentors four of the most influential political philosophers of our time. John Rawls admitted me into his graduate seminar while I was still an undergraduate. I was also challenged by Robert Nozick's original insights and brilliant libertarian response to Rawls' *Theory of Justice*. Michael Walzer would become one of my two dissertation advisers. The other was Judith Shklar, a generous mentor and powerful role model who managed to overcome gender discrimination to pursue a brilliant career.

These four scholar-teachers further fueled my passion for political philosophy, for teaching and scholarship as do – in a very different way – the ongoing challenges of our troubled times.

What do you consider your own most important contribution(s) to political philosophy, and why?

The first important contribution I made to political philosophy was the systematic analysis of the importance of democratic education for democratic politics. My early book *Democratic Education* opened new conversations in political philosophy and education, and provoked both scholars and practitioners to rethink the role that education plays in a democracy. Now in its second revised edition, the book has been translated into about a dozen languages, and it is widely taught in schools of education and liberal arts curricula throughout the world.

The book addresses the central questions in the political theory of education: How should a democratic society make decisions about education? What should children be taught? How should citizens be educated? The book also takes on some contemporary scholarly debates: What is the appropriate response of democratic education to the challenge of multiculturalism? Should schools try to cultivate patriotic or cosmopolitan sentiments among students?

Democratic Education has been the touchstone both for my subsequent work on deliberative democracy and for the values that

I have aspired to advance as a scholar and university president: liberty, opportunity and mutual respect. It is a work that bridges philosophy and policy in ways that have sparked productive inquiry and education.

A second contribution to the field is my work with Dennis Thompson in developing the theory of and conceptual framework for deliberative democracy—which has been widely researched and hotly debated since *Democracy and Disagreement* was published 10 years ago. We proposed deliberation not as a panacea, but rather as an antidote and alternative to the coarseness, intransigence, and extremism that had degraded and debased our politics and public discourse. By demonstrating how deliberation and mutual respect could elevate the quality of moral debate, we presented a model for putting moral reasoning and moral disagreement back at the center of everyday politics.

Here is the gist of our argument: Deliberation helps us understand other people's points of view, their interests and values, and encourages us to take them into account when we make up our own minds, as we must do. Deliberation is not a substitute for decision making. It is not endless discussion without decision. Deliberation is action-oriented; it is intended to inform decision making, and to develop our collective capacity to pursue justice while finding mutually acceptable terms of social cooperation—even when we continue to disagree.

By deliberating, we defend our positions with reasons while expressing the respect we owe to other reasonable people, especially when we disagree with them or cannot concede their main points. By hearing people out and responding to the substance of their arguments, we treat people with dignity, Kant would say as ends in themselves, Mill would say as individuals, Rawls would say with respect, not as mere means to our ends.

Most fundamentally, deliberative democracy affirms the need to justify decisions made by citizens and their representatives. In a democracy, leaders should therefore give publicly accessible reasons for their decisions, and respond to the reasons that citizens give in return. The reasons that deliberative democracy asks citizens and their representatives to give should appeal to principles that individuals who are trying to find fair terms of cooperation can reasonably accept. They are reasons that can and should be accepted by free and equal persons seeking fair terms of cooperation.

By valuing mutual respect over agreement and by showing how

citizens and their representatives can live with moral disagreement in a morally constructive way, this conception of deliberative democracy is both more idealistic than other theoretical conceptions and more realistic.

A third contribution to the field of political philosophy is my discussion of group identity and its intersection with justice. In democratic politics, most people are most influential in groups, and identity groups are a manifestation of a basic freedom of association. I have sought to demonstrate the ways in which a politics that depends in no small part on identity groups can work to better secure equal liberty, opportunity, and civic equality for all individuals, not only for the most privileged or the most powerful members of disadvantaged groups.

The relationship between group identity and democratic politics is far more complex than blanket critiques and defenses of identity politics suggest. A democratic perspective attends to the interplay between group identities and democratic politics and assesses their relationship on the basis of broadly defensible principles of justice.

I argue that identity groups as such are neither friends nor enemies of democratic justice. They pose distinctive challenges that have been neglected by political theorists who overlook the advantages of organizing on the basis of mutual identity in democratic politics and by political scientists who lump all politically relevant organizations together under the rubric of interest group politics. To overcome both kinds of neglect, I presented a democratic view that recognizes the legitimate but also problematic parts played by group identity in democratic politics and therefore the importance of distinguishing between the good, the bad, and the ugly of identity group politics.

A fourth and – I hope – foremost contribution to political philosophy is my work in helping many students become outstanding, original scholars in their own right, specifically by mentoring and directing their research toward engaging the important questions that arise in the intersection of political philosophy and public policy. I was fortunate to be mentored by four eminent political philosophers. I have been mentoring young women and men ever since I left graduate school in 1976. Many former students have become great political philosophers in their own right, with the widest range of perspectives and contributions to the field. Their scholarship and teaching is by far my most important and satisfying accomplishment in political philosophy.

5. Amy Gutmann

What is the proper role of political philosophy in relation to real, political action? Can there ever be a fruitful relation between political philosophy and political practice?

The proper role of political philosophy, plain and simple, is to speak truth to power in defense of human rights, freedom and other important political values, and in opposition to corruption, tyranny, cruelty, and oppression.

The substance of the political philosopher's critique of political power and/or public policy should be informed by reasoned arguments and evidence that are open to challenge over time.

Political power necessarily generates the need to compromise. Those in politics and government can be pressured to shade the truth or conceal facts that do not conform to a party line. While politics is the art of the possible, political philosophy should aim to extend and expand the boundaries of the possible, and to push politics as close as possible toward the realm of the desirable. This is one of the primary reasons why meaningful political philosophy in the public sphere is best advanced by people who hold no direct positions of political power.

We therefore should be wary of a direct relation between political philosophy and political practice. History offers countless examples of corruption in the translation of political philosophies into practice by publicly unaccountable intellectuals who attain political power. Political philosophers can have a beneficial, but far less direct impact on political practice. The main role of political philosophy in relation to political power is to provide moral direction.

One model of an influential political philosopher serving as a moral guide is Michael Walzer. No one can seriously debate the morality of warfare and within war without taking into account Walzer's arguments. It is significant that Walzer does not conform to any party's political agenda. For example, in his *Dissent* essay, "Can There Be a Decent Left?" which appeared in the spring after 9/11, Walzer took many left-wing critics fiercely to task for "their knee-jerk anti-Americanism, old left dogmatism, and the rejection of any fellowship larger than the sect of the politically correct and the morally pure." What Walzer called "the politics of guilt and resentment" blinded these critics to the need for moral balance, intellectual perspective, and a justified military response after the 9/11 attacks. He then issued a *cri de couer* to his fellow leftists "to put decency first."

In my judgment, political philosophy practiced and expressed honestly can influence political practice (and thus change the world). But it must not sacrifice principles and truths to political expediency.

What do you consider the most neglected topics and/or contributions in post-Rawlsian or late 20th century political philosophy?

A topic that would benefit from far more systematic philosophical treatment is the intersection between our identity and interests. The conceptualization of decision-making too long has been split between those who presume that both the process and the people involved are rational and interest-based, and those who presume (to the contrary) that irrational (or non-rational) identities are what drives politics. The advocates of rational decision-making put too much emphasis on the supposed ability of policy makers to weigh the consequences of choices and make decisions in a calculated fashion, as purely interest-driven individuals. The advocates of identity tend to be too deterministic in viewing individuals as committed to the values and traditions of the dominant groups with which they affiliate. Political philosophy has the capacity to bridge the two perspectives, which – when integrated – can together offer more accurate and important insights into how and why individuals choose and act, and about how policy is shaped by interests and identities (note the plural in both instances).

Another neglected topic is the accountability of elected representatives. Given the enormous complexity and importance of issues addressed by government (not to mention the vast warmaking powers of national governments), and given the vast sums of taxpayer money spent on vital services (such as health care, crime control and education) and on programs and policies that large number of citizens might oppose on moral grounds, I find it troubling that our field has done so little to produce a well grounded and developed theory of accountability. If public officials are ultimately accountable to citizens, then we need a more fully developed understanding of the ends and means of constitutional democratic accountability.

Another field that deserves more attention by political philosophers is communication and politics. How are politically relevant ideas most (or at least more) effectively communicated? What should we think of the ever growing sources of information to which citizens are exposed? Here is a very specific theoretical and practical question worthy of attention by political philosophers who are willing to extend their expertise in my direction: What can mass media do about our deliberative deficit? Answers to all these questions would greatly improve our critical understanding of democracy.

What are the most important unsolved questions in political philosophy and/or related disciplines and what are the prospects for progress?

"What is a just society?" "How much – and what kinds of – freedom is enough?" "Are human beings equal? If so - In what sense of the term?" "What is the best defense of constitutional democracy?" "What are the strengths and weaknesses of different forms of government?" "To what extent do the answers to these questions depend on particular historical contexts?" The list of important unsolved questions goes on...

As a child, I became so fascinated with solving math puzzles that I began to design them. Among the challenges that drew me to political philosophy were its unsolved puzzles, which had implications for understanding the practical world of ethics and politics. Problems in political philosophy afforded me the continuous opportunity to investigate more, to reconsider, to elaborate issues that make a real difference in the world. On the way I missed the opportunity to write 'QED' and close the notebook. The questions in and of themselves always remain open to more adequate answers—and do not lend themselves to final solutions.

What are the prospects for progress? The prospects are great; the certainties (or even near certainties) for proofs, however, are few. Progress must not be measured by consensus. In fact, in light of the importance of human freedom, one measure of progress (although not the only one to be sure) is the degree of reasoned debate that surrounds important questions. Furnishing another set of standards of progress are the criteria by which we typically would measure any intellectual endeavor: logic of argument, soundness of evidence, breadth and depth of understanding. In short, the prospects of progress are great but the likelihood of closure is small. Indeed, premature closure on the big questions of our time would be a symptom of political repression or cultural conformity. And so, the debate goes on—and our understanding grows.

Selected publications

Democratic Education; Color Conscious: The Political Morality of Race (co-authored with K. Anthony Appiah).

Identity in Democracy; Democracy and Disagreement; and *Why Deliberative Democracy?* (both co-authored with Dennis Thompson).

6
Chandran Kukathas

Neal A. Maxwell Professor of Political Theory,
Public Policy and Public Service
Department of Political Science
University of Utah, USA

What drew me to political philosophy?

My father was a writer in Malaysia, and at a very young age I decided I wanted to be a writer too. When I was nine, we studied History as a school subject for the first time and I decided then that I would become an historian. We moved to Australia when I was 11, and after I finished my secondary education I enrolled at the Australian National University, intending to become a high school history teacher who would also write great works of history, and maybe some novels along the way. But the rest, in this case, is not history.

In my first year at college I read Plato's *Republic* and Hobbes' *Leviathan*, in a course taught by a PhD student, Mr Craddock Morton. (I had originally planned to work for a year before attending university, but conversations with my father over the summer of 1974–75, in which he talked at length about the *Republic*, made the prospect of going to university too exciting to postpone.) I read Hobbes again when I studied the English Revolution, and yet again the following year when I took a course in Modern Political Thought. It was reading *Leviathan* and the *Republic*, more than anything else, which drew me to political philosophy. The attraction was not ideological but a mixture of intellectual and aesthetic. Politically, I was a moderate socialist who thought it might be a good thing to become a Marxist, and this tendency was strongly encouraged by some of my history teachers, who had been trying to persuade their students that Marxist theory offered the best guide to writing good history. I read as much of Marx as I could and found it invigorating and, on occasion, compelling. (I had since high school been contemptuous of conservatism, and becoming a Marxist seemed like a good way of expressing that contempt.) In my final year I wrote a thesis on Australian Aboriginal protest movements and planned to go on to a career as a Marxist historian. But in the second half of the year I was introduced to the philosophy of science, and to the writings of Karl Popper. My Marxist convictions were subjected to challenge for the first time and did not stand up. This did not have much impact on my ideological views, at least to begin with, but it did make me much more interested in philosophical questions and less interested in historical ones.

I graduated at the end of 1978 and decided I wanted to study political theory in the United States. I did not have much idea of how to go about it so took a job as a research assistant at the Australian Institute of Aboriginal Studies to earn money. When a better job came along a few months later, teaching political science at the Royal Military College, I decided to work on an MA part-time. My proposed thesis on the idea of human nature in the thought of Hobbes, Hume and Mill was deemed far too ambitious so I worked on Hume for the next three years—at a time when there was very little scholarship on Hume's politics. My own politics began to change at this point. A close friend I had graduated with had begun to work on his own Master's thesis on Hayek and Nozick, and we started to discuss these very surprising ideas—surprising, that is, to us as people of the left. Over the next two years we both shed most of our earlier political convictions. Becoming a libertarian made political philosophy even more compelling. After being rejected by several American universities I won a scholarship to Oxford. At first I thought I might continue to work on Hume; but by the time I got to England in 1982 I was enough of a libertarian to want to write about Hayek.

John Gray was appointed my D.Phil supervisor but I had already approached David Miller to ask if I could work with him. As it turned out, I was advised by both, and benefited from their very different styles and views. John was always an enthusiast, who wanted to talk not so much about the structure of a chapter or an argument I had put forward as about how the material related to other ideas, other thinkers, and the state of the world. He was ferociously critical of views he had come to reject, particularly if they were views he had once held himself, and full of enthusiasm for ideas he thought promising. His eagerness to look at the big picture was infectious, and made writing political theory seem like an adventure. David's manner was very different, and he looked much more critically at everything I wrote, picking to pieces arguments that didn't work or that begged the question. He more than anyone else made me a more careful philosopher. But his most significant influence on my thinking was to make me more ambitious intellectually. Having arrived in Oxford with a young family and a three-year scholarship, I was determined to finish on time and find a job, and thought the best thing to do was to choose a manageable topic on which to write. David persuaded me not to sell myself short, and convinced me to be more ambitious in my thinking.

My interest in political philosophy does also have its origins in a long-standing interest in politics. My political awakening came with the election in December 1972 of the first Australian Labor government in twenty-three years. I was 14 and in my fourth year of secondary school. The Whitlam government was a disaster but I was a passionate defender of it, and was drawn to many left-wing causes because I identified with Labor. Like many students, I became actively involved in campaigns to discredit Apartheid South Africa and end its sporting ties with Australia; I sympathized with the Aboriginal struggle for land rights; and I was horrified when the Governor-General sacked the Prime Minister in 1975. But my political thinking was also shaped by family history. Growing up in Malaysia as a member of the Sri Lankan Tamil minority, I learnt that in our schooling, and in employment, preference would be given to members of the indigenous Malay community. My parents thought it would be better to move to Australia where their children would be treated as equals. Even though my father was careful to explain that the point of the Malaysian "bumiputra" policy was to equalize the condition of the Malays, who were the poorest members of the community, I felt dissatisfied with the policy and its justification. In school I was friends with boys from all races—Indians, Chinese, Malays, Eurasians—and could not see any justice in treating us differently because of our racial differences. My observation of Malaysia's political history over the years has hardened my dislike for all racial politics.

In summary, my answer to the question of what drew me to political philosophy is that I drifted into it. I was politically engaged and wanted to be a writer. Reading political philosophy introduced me to works of great beauty, and made me want to write such works of my own.

6. Chandran Kukathas

My most important contributions to political philosophy

Any answer to this question presupposes some understanding of what political philosophy might be. In my view, political philosophy – and, for that matter, philosophy – is not a practical endeavor but a theoretical one. Its purpose, ultimately, is description: to try to present an account of the world that makes sense of the confusion that confronts us when we look at it unthinkingly, or when we understand it through the claims of those who interpret the world as it suits them. Political philosophy does not try to find a view from nowhere, but it does try to describe the world from a single, consistent, point of view. The world it tries to describe is not the world or the universe as a whole—doing that is the job of metaphysicians—but the world of politics: that realm in which we find humans struggling to order their collective affairs and deal with their conflicting and converging interests. Political philosophy, above all, is not advocacy. Political philosophers may themselves be advocates, and some have gained prominence, and even success, in this respect: John Stuart Mill in the nineteenth century and Peter Singer today are obvious examples. But philosophy is not advocacy, and political philosophy is not a form of political action. I will return to this point in the next section.

The contribution I have made that I would most like to see recognized is the critique of justice and social unity as values through which we should try to understand political life and the idea of the good society. Among the oldest questions in political philosophy is the question of how the many can live as one, and the most venerable answer is that justice describes that form of social unity that we seek, and to which we should aspire. Yet while there is nothing wrong with the question, many of the answers political philosophers have given have been wanting because they have exaggerated the desirability and the possibility of social unity. The many can live as one to a very limited degree, and if we look at political life what we will find is not so much unity as plurality. Such unity as we do find is not enduring but unstable and changeable.

I have tried to elaborate this view in my book, *The Liberal Archipelago*. The main thesis of that work is that we should understand the good society not as a single political community but as a loose network of associations whose members are free to move and to associate with those whose thinking and practices they find congenial. Such a society is not a body governed by a single standard of justice but rather one in which accommodation among plural values is constantly being worked out in the compromises that are struck. A good society is a kind of system of mutual toleration.

This is not a particularly novel idea. On the contrary, an appreciation of the importance of toleration can be traced back to the beginnings of liberal thought. What is less well recognized, however, is how demanding an idea this is, for the defenders and advocates of toleration have always been fairly quick to insist that toleration has its limits. For many, those limits are circumscribed by justice. What I have tried to emphasize in my own writings is how taking toleration seriously requires being willing to put up with much more than we generally believe. It sometimes means putting up with what we regard as injustices.

Taking such a position does not mean embracing skepticism about morals more generally. It only means taking the view that politics is about working out how to accommodate moral difference rather than trying to achieve substantive moral ideals. It is not about trying to bring about a just distribution of goods or promoting equality or creating autonomous beings. There is a range of competing views on offer about which ethical ideals should govern a good society. It would be hard to expect people not to have opinions about what values should inform public policy or govern institutional arrangements. Citizens—including moral philosophers—will often be advocates of one set of values or another. Taking toleration seriously, however, means giving priority to allowing differing ethical views to co-exist, for dissenting views are not to be suppressed.

I think of this as an impeccably liberal position, drawing from it the conclusion that a liberal society will accept within it even highly illiberal elements. Aside from in my book, I have tried to defend this view in a number of papers, some dealing with the issue at an abstract liberal, but others looking at concrete issues such as euthanasia laws, gay rights, and the treatment of women in minority communities. My difference with many other liberal philosophers is that most are not willing to tolerate illiberalism to the degree that I am. If I have made a contribution to contemporary debate about liberalism it is probably that I have tried to push liberalism to its logical limits on the basis of one particular interpretation of its fundamental premises.

I regard the position I hold as a libertarian one, and I consider much of my work as a contribution to libertarian theory. While it shares something in common with much of libertarian thought, however, it also differs from a good deal of it because my thinking does not begin with assumptions about self-ownership or individual rights. I think of libertarianism as a kind of theory of value pluralism: a solution of the problem of accommodating conflicting moral values. For me, the most compelling part of Nozick's *Anarchy, State and Utopia* was not the theory of justice but the theory of utopia. The libertarian utopia is an accommodating ideal which recognizes that there are many different understandings about how human beings should live—not only individually but also collectively. In a way, my work has been an attempt to explore the implications of a Nozickian idea of utopia.

Political philosophy and political action

There is no connection between political philosophy and political action, any more than there is a connection between statistical analysis and political action or accountancy and political action. Political philosophers can certainly engage in political action, and reflection on the nature of political practice may well produce interesting and insightful political philosophy. But philosophy is essentially an academic exercise aimed at uncovering the truth about how to understand the world. The important thing may well be to change the world rather than merely to interpret it, but the philosopher qua philosopher is an interpreter rather than an activist.

For this reason, I don't see political philosophy as having much to contribute to political practice. One would no more seek the advice of a political philosopher in designing political institutions or crafting public policy than one would consult a moral philosopher if one were confronted with an ethical dilemma. Political philosophy is not about providing practical guidance, though it can provide insight into the nature of political life and help us better understand (or see through) the many political claims that are made everyday.

In this regard, I think John Rawls was seriously mistaken in thinking that political philosophy is public discussion taken to a higher level of abstraction. Rawls's thought was that political philosophy would "uncover how citizens might, on due reflection, want to conceive their society." In so doing, it would have some practical impact on the workings of society, resolving tensions in thought that created tensions in practice. In reality, philosophy plays no such role. Indeed, the more abstract it becomes the less it has to do with politics and the less it contributes to political life. The more it contributes to politics, the less philosophical it becomes. I think Michael Oakshott was right to suggest that politics is essentially deliberative, while philosophy is demonstrative. The philosopher elaborates concepts through which we can view the world, crafting lenses that bring matters into sharper focus, or enable us to see things that might otherwise have eluded our notice. But the philosopher will be ignored by those whose business is political action—unless a kind of philosophical theory can be pressed into service of some practical goal.

I don't by this mean to suggest that ideas play no part in politics. They do. But in politics ideas are powerful when they are capable of motivating action. In politics what matters, then, is that the ideas in question are attractive or inspiring or practically useful. Coherence is a minor or subordinate virtue. In philosophy, however, coherence is vital, for philosophy cannot tolerate anomalies. Because politics is a goal-directed activity, the "philosophical" ideas that are adopted will be the ones that political activists think will further those ends.

Some years ago I served on a government advisory body whose task it was to report on the state of multi-culturalism in Australia and make general recommendations for future policy. We were asked to write a report that, among other things, set out a public philosophy whose terms would justify multicultural policy. As a member of the sixteen-person council, I concluded early on that there was not much point in trying to persuade everyone of the merits of a libertarian perspective on the world, but I nonetheless thought I should try to influence the direction our report took. I was concerned by the number of members of the council who thought about multi-culturalism as mandating support, including public funding, of ethnic organizations, and also by the number of members who wanted to write an aggressive report criticizing anyone who was not sufficiently supportive of multiculturalism. Like a number of others, I thought a more temperate report would be less damaging in a political climate in which the ruling party and its supporters were wary of—and, at the extreme, hostile to—the idea public policies accommodating cultural diversity. Consequently, we argued (successfully) that we should produce a report that presented multiculturalism as an idea that grew out of Australia's traditions of democratic equality. I myself commended in particular Will Kymlicka's ideas of "multicultural citizenship", even though these were ideas of which I had been highly critical. As a political activist, it seemed to me that these ideas would prove more congenial than some of my own theories, and that in this context my differences with Kymlicka were less important than the beliefs we shared. (My suggestion that we consider "toleration" a central Australian value met with little enthusiasm. Indeed, all of the council members of Chinese origin were very unhappy with the idea of toleration, which they regarded as having negative connotations. To them it meant not so much refraining from repressing others as being willing to suffer repression oneself. In that arena, the most coherent arguments for toleration as a fundamental value were never going to get anywhere.)

I offer this case as an example of the way in which philosophy gives way to the demands of political action. If I were a political activist I would choose to advance not those ideas that were most coherent philosophically but ones that served those practical ends to which I was committed. In this respect, the best political philosophy seems to me to be generally of little practical relevance. In politics in the broadest possible sense, *A Theory of Justice* is about as useful as the *Mona Lisa*—though no less beautiful and awe-inspiring.

What are the most neglected topics in late twentieth century political philosophy?

It is hard to imagine that any philosophical subject is neglected today when there are more philosophers than ever writing and publishing. If anything, the problem may be that on many topics there is more work than is really necessary.

Nonetheless, if I had to nominate some areas into which political philosophy might go I would make two suggestions. First, it seems to me that we are living in an era in which the idea and nature of the state is undergoing a profound transformation. One might speculate about all kinds of reasons for this, ranging from population movements to the growth of international trade to the emergence of a variety of international regimes embodied in international conventions or represented by international organizations. The dominant theories of the modern state, from, say, Hobbes and Bodin to Hegel and Mill, are no longer capable of adequately describing the states of the twenty-first century. I don't mean by this to suggest that the modern state is disappearing, though many have advanced such a view. I simply think that it is a different kind of entity to that theorized by Mill in the late nineteenth century, or even by Oakeshott in the late twentieth.

Second, I think it would be good if more political philosophy were self-consciously philosophical and if we saw a return to a greater emphasis on conceptual analysis. I agree with Jeremy Waldron that too many people think that political philosophy is about what one would "allow" according to one's lights. Yet Plato is interesting not because of what he would or wouldn't allow but because of the way in which he tried to elucidate concepts through which we could see the world more clearly.

In light of both of these suggestions, the contribution to political philosophy that I think is most neglected by philosophers is that of F.A. Hayek. Having begun his career as an economist, Hayek turned to political philosophy when he turned into an advocate. His great worry was the threat to modern civilization posed by the ideas of Nazi and Stalinist totalitarianism, and he thought that to combat these notions it was important for scholars to turn their attention to the task of articulating and defending liberal political ideals. His success as an advocate, however, has tended to obscure his achievements as a philosopher. Contrary to what I have suggested in this interview, Hayek thought that successful advocacy depended on getting things right philosophically, and he directed a great deal of his intellectual energy to trying to develop concepts that would describe a modern liberal social and economic order. Whether or not he was successful—and I have in my own studies of Hayek tried to argue that there are serious weaknesses in his philosophical enterprise—the scope and ambition of Hayek's work is impressive. Perhaps when some of the ideological fog has lifted, and Hayek is regarded as a social thinker rather than an advocate, his ideas will be subjected to more careful scrutiny.

What are the most important unsolved problems in political philosophy and what are the prospects for progress?

The bad new is that the prospects for progress in political philosophy are poor, but the good news is that there are no unsolved problems. The reason there are no unsolved problems is that, if one thinks of political philosophy as having a stock of standard questions—such as "what is justice?" or "what is the basis of our obligation to obey the state?"—there is no shortage of solutions. We have a plethora of answers bequeathed to us by the history of political thought, but we do not all find the same answers compelling. To some extent, we continue to debate the same questions, making the same moves, raising the same objections, and coming to the same competing conclusions. If progress is measured by the level of philosophical agreement, the prospects for advancement are dim.

But then, the point of political philosophy is not to solve problems. If we think political philosophy offers us a kind of knowledge, it is not knowledge of the kind science provides. So scientific models of the growth of knowledge are not appropriate. Political philosophers do not by their efforts add bricks to a growing wall or to a tower that will eventually reach the heavens. Nor do they even expand our understanding by criticizing past theories and supplanting them with better ones. If that were so, we would long since have given up reading Aristotle and Rousseau, secure in the knowledge that they had been superseded.

If we need a model of political philosophical knowledge, I would suggest that the political philosopher as a kind of tour guide. Every tour guide requires a certain amount of knowledge. Some possess only a little bit of very local knowledge and can conduct us across only a small stretch of terrain, though if they are to do their jobs well they would have to have some idea of the contexts in which their particular patches of turf are located. Other guides, however, are able to show us more of the landscape, maybe even to take us to summits from which to survey the entire valley—convincing us, perhaps, that this is really the only place from which to see the whole as it really is. But every guide is a guide to a changing landscape, and a good guide must understand what has endured, though in changed shapes and locations, what is new, and what routes and passages no longer exist.

Political philosophers possess, to varying degrees, knowledge of this kind. Their subject is the politics of a landscape rather than its geography. Their aim is to show how different parts relate to one another, or to the whole; or to show how differently things would look if viewed from another perspective or under a different aspect. Of course, like all tour guides, political philosophers have their disagreements about the best way to go about their enterprise. No two political philosophers are likely to show you the same city. But it would be wrong to conclude from this that they do not possess a kind of knowledge, just as it would be a mistake to disparage the learning of a tour guide because he does not contribute to scientific discovery.

Select Bibliography

'The Mirage of Global Justice', *Social Philosophy and Policy*, 23(1), 2006, 1-25.

Pierre Bayle's Philosophical Commentary on the Words of Jesus Christ: Compel Them to Come In, Indianapolis: Liberty Fund (co-edited with an introduction with John Kilcullen, 2005).

'Immigration', in Christopher Wellman and Andrew Cohen (eds.), *Contemporary Debates in Applied Ethics*, Blackwell, 2004.

The Liberal Archipelago: A Theory of Diversity and Freedom, Oxford University Press, 2003.

'Responsibility for past injustice', *Politics, Philosophy, and Economics*, 2 (2), 2003.

'The Cultural Contradictions of Socialism', *Social Philosophy and Policy*, 20 (1), 2003, pp.165-190.

'Islam, Democracy, and Civil Society', *Journal des Economistes et des Etudes Humaines*, 13 (2/3), 2003, 325-340.

'Equality and Diversity', *Politics, Philosophy and Economics*, 1 (2), 2002, pp.185-212.

'Classical liberalism and ethical pluralism', in Richard Madsen and Tracy B. Strong (eds.), *The Many and the One: Attitudes Toward Ethical Pluralism*, Princeton University Press, 2002.

'Can a Liberal Society Tolerate Illiberal Elements?', *Policy*, 17 (2), 2001: 39-44.

'Is Feminism Bad for Multiculturalism?', *Public Affairs Quarterly*,15 (2), April 2001, pp.83-98.

'Liberalism and Multiculturalism: The Politics of Indifference', *Political Theory* 26 (5), 1998, pp.686-699.

'Cultural toleration', in Will Kymlicka and Ian Shapiro (eds), *Ethnicity and Group Rights* , *NOMOS* 39, New York, New York University Press, 1997, pp.60-104.

'Multiculturalism as Fairness', *Journal of Political Philosophy* 5 (4) 1997 pp.406-427.

'Are there any cultural rights?', *Political Theory*, 20, 1992, pp.105-139.

Hayek and Modern Liberalism, Oxford University Press, 1989.

7

Andrew Mason

Professor of Political Theory
University of Southampton, UK

Why were you initially drawn to political philosophy?

As a teenager, I was interested in normative issues about how one should live, and what makes a society just, the latter largely as a result of a concern with inequalities of opportunity. I started to pull philosophy books off the shelves in my local public library, but my interest was for the most part separate from what I studied at school, where I specialised in the natural sciences. When I decided to go on to higher education I wasn't brave enough to make the decision to study Philosophy. Instead I chose to study Chemistry at Bristol University in the UK. But I took Philosophy as an optional subject and loved it, especially the courses on moral and political philosophy. I admired the clarity of thought philosophers achieved, and I began to understand better the normative issues which had engaged me in an inchoate sort of way before. I changed degree course at the end of my first year of study and never looked back.

After finishing my first degree, my interest in philosophy remained as strong as ever. After a year out, I decided to continue in higher education and took an opportunity to study for a Masters degree at the University of Minnesota in Minneapolis. I joined a lively postgraduate community there, with several graduate students working on topics in political philosophy. Some of them were working from perspectives that were already familiar to me (libertarian, left-liberal, and socialist), but others were developing socialist-feminist and radical feminist theories which I had not encountered much before, and which influenced my thinking in various ways. At the end of my Masters programme, I returned to the UK to study for a doctorate at Oxford, entering what was in many ways a much more conservative environment, dominated by the liberal-communitarian debate.

What do you consider your own most important contribution(s) to political philosophy, and why?

I think my best contributions have been made in two areas: first, liberal nationalism, and second, egalitarianism. My contribution to the study of liberal nationalism involves a critique of two ideas: first, the idea that the stable realisation of various values, such as respect for individual rights, democratic participation, and social justice, requires citizens to share a national identity; second the idea that a shared national identity is a source of special obligations that fellow nationals owe to each other.

Liberal nationalist ideas came to the fore in the wake of the communitarian critique of liberalism which preoccupied many political philosophers during the 1980s. Some liberals came to think that liberalism needed a more robust account of what was required to bind citizens together in a stable polity and concluded that it was important in practice for citizens to share a national identity. They argued that a shared national identity not only provides people with the motivation to participate politically, and to support redistributive policies on grounds of social justice, but is also the source of special obligations that fellow nationals owe to each other. Though I would deny that 'liberal-nationalism' is an oxymoron, I think that it is nevertheless the wrong direction for liberalism to take. The kind of policies that liberal nationalists would have us adopt in order to foster and sustain a shared national identity have moral costs even if they are not oppressive, and they stand in the way of more radical conceptions of global egalitarian justice.

Central to the liberal nationalist argument is the idea that the realisation of values such as democratic participation and social justice requires citizens to share a sense of belonging together. By a sense of belonging together, I mean a belief amongst them that there is some special reason why they should associate together which appeals to something other than, say, the fact that they happen to live in the same polity. (A shared history or culture, or a common first language, are the obvious possibilities here.) In response I distinguish between a sense of belonging *together* and a sense of belonging *to a polity*, and argue that the latter may be achieved in the absence of the former, and that it may be enough in many circumstances to facilitate the realisation of liberal values. A person has a sense of belonging to a polity if and only if she identifies with most of its major institutions and some of its central practices, and feels at home in them. My proposal is that it may be possible to foster a widespread sense of belonging to a polity amongst diverse citizens by accommodating their demands in various ways and giving them various forms of legal and political recognition (see my 'Political Community, Liberal-Nationalism and the Ethics of Assimilation', *Ethics*, Vol. 109, 1999; *Community, Solidarity and Belonging*, Cambridge University Press, 2000, Chapter 5).

I also question whether co-nationals are bound together by special obligations in the way that liberal nationalists maintain. Liberal nationalists contend that we have special obligations to fellow nationals that have their source in the national identity we share. In response I argue that we can make sense of the idea that we owe special obligations to compatriots, but that these are best understood as grounded in the value of citizenship rather than in the existence of a shared national identity. Indeed I contend that these special obligations are partially constitutive of citizenship as well as being justified by the intrinsic value of this relationship (see 'Special Obligations to Compatriots', *Ethics*, Vol. 107, 1997; *Community, Solidarity and Belonging*, Ch. 4)

The other contribution I have made which I would highlight is to debates over egalitarian justice. In a recent book (*Levelling the Playing Field: The Idea of Equal Opportunity and its Place in Egalitarian Thought*, Oxford University Press, 2006), I have tried to develop a pluralist account of egalitarian justice which includes a conception of equality of opportunity, that has a principled commitment to open competition for advantaged social positions, and to the provision of fair access to the qualifications required for success in these competitions, but which also involves principles which aim to mitigate (rather than fully neutralise) the effects of differences in people's circumstances whilst at the same time holding them appropriately accountable for their choices.

My account is distinctive in giving a role to what I call quasi-egalitarian principles. These principles do not regard equality as non-instrumentally valuable, nor do they suppose that inequality as such is objectionable. On the other hand, they differ from a doctrine of sufficiency, and from principles that merely give priority to the worse off. Quasi-egalitarian principles are essentially concerned with comparative advantage. They regard inequalities of a particular degree or kind as objectionable, not (merely) because of their effects on the realisation of other values, such as equal citizenship, but as such.

I argue for two specific quasi-egalitarian principles that are designed to place limits on the degree of inequality that can permissibly emerge from differences in people's circumstances. The first of these is an educational access principle, which is grounded in the idea that the effects of differences in people's social circumstances should not be such that some but not others possess (or can reasonably be expected to acquire) the resources necessary to obtain a good that is important in general for a person's access to overall advantage. The second is an accumulation of wealth principle, which holds that the effects of differences in people's circumstances should not be such that some but not others can acquire the resources that are necessary in order to be able to lead a decent life whilst choosing not to work to earn an income. My proposal is that these principles work together with others, including a sufficiency principle, to constrain the effects of differences in people's circumstances on their access to overall advantage.

What is the proper role of political philosophy in relation to real, political action? Can there ever be a fruitful relation between political philosophy and political practice?

My view of these matters is similar in some respects to G.A. Cohen's (see his 'Facts and Principles', *Philosophy and Public Affairs*, Vol. 31, 2003). He insists that we need to distinguish fundamental principles from principles of regulation, which I think is important in this context. He also believes that fundamental principles are fact insensitive. I'm not sure he's right about this, but I do think (as he does) that fundamental principles may be unrealisable in practice. Indeed I think it is perfectly coherent to defend a particular principle of justice whilst conceding that it would be impossible ever to realise it given the inevitable limits of human knowledge or human nature (see my 'Just Constraints', *British Journal of Political Science*, Vol. 34, 2004). If this is right, there is a level of inquiry that is independent of issues of feasibility, and which does not directly address the question of what should be done or what institutions we should adopt. But there are also other levels of inquiry that are no less important and which are tied more closely to political practice. These other levels involve, first, the identification of feasibility constraints that prevent us from realising fundamental principles; second, an account of the second best when a fundamental principle is unrealisable, whether wholly or in part; third, an assessment of the costs of implementing fundamental principles when it is feasible to do so. Consider each of these in turn. When identifying feasibility constraints, we will need to investigate what is possible given our current historical circumstances and what we know about human nature, and we will also need to take account of limits on institutional design. None of this can be done without an interdisciplinary study of history and society. When identifying the second best, we need to be aware that what counts as second best may be very different from the arrangements which would be required to realise the fundamental principle, were that possible. When identifying costs of implementation, we should be concerned with moral as well as non-moral costs. Trying to implement a principle of justice may be counterproductive. It may make matters worse viewed in terms of that principle, or it may make matters worse from the perspective of another principle of justice, or from the point of view of the realisation of some other value.

So I think there can be a highly fruitful relationship between political philosophy and political action, but it will have to involve an engagement with other disciplines as well. We do not need to suppose that political philosophy, properly so called, is restricted to the most abstract level of analysis concerned with the discovery of fundamental principles; we might have a broader conception of it which includes levels of inquiry that involve identifying feasibility constraints and assessing costs of implementation. But however we understand the content of political philosophy, identifying fundamental principles will only be a short step towards answering the question of what kind of political action is required in response to these principles. The move from fundamental principles to political action has to be made via an investigation of feasibility constraints, largely an empirical study, and by an assessment of the costs of implementing principles and how they should be balanced against each other, which requires both empirical inquiry and further normative analysis.

What do you consider the most neglected topics and/or contributions in post-Rawlsian or late 20th century political philosophy?

There are two areas that I would highlight that I think have been neglected but are now receiving increasing attention: first, the proper role of responsibility within a theory of justice, in particular the issue of when people can legitimately be required to bear the costs of their behaviour; second, the issue of global justice (including the relevance of the effects of environmental degradation to that issue), and the moral significance or otherwise of national boundaries or state borders. Although progress has been made on these issues, I think there is much work still to be done on them.

Another issue that I think is important but which is still largely neglected is that of how we should proceed in the face of disagreement over principles of justice. Like Jeremy Waldron, I think that disagreement over these principles is constitutive of politics as we know it (they are part of 'the circumstances of politics'), so we need an account of how we should proceed in the face of this disagreement (see J. Waldron, *Law and Disagreement*, Oxford University Press, 1999). In my view, this requires an account of what gives us the authority to implement one set of principles rather than another in the context of disagreement over them.

The most obvious solution to this problem is to say that it is legitimate procedures that provide this authority. But what makes a procedure legitimate? Some would say that a procedure is legitimate if and only if it is justifiable to all; others hold what appears on the surface to be a different position, that a procedure is legitimate to the extent that it includes or involves, in some appropriate way, all citizens rather than a subset of them. Each of these accounts would seem to leave open the possibility that coercive power may be exercised legitimately but unjustly. But what limits, if any, does justice place on legitimacy? Outcomes which undermine the legitimacy of procedures might with good reason be regarded as both unjust and illegitimate (for example, those which undermine the equality of opportunity to participate in these procedures), but what about outcomes that are unjust but do not adversely affect the operation of these procedures, for example, violations of religious liberty? Are these outcomes nevertheless legitimate? If the idea of legitimacy is bound too tightly to ideas of justice, it will not be able to provide a solution to the problem posed by the circumstances of politics, that is, the problem of how we should proceed in the face of disagreement over principles of justice. Indeed, we would be confronted by a regress, for disputes over principles of justice would generate disputes over the legitimacy of procedures, and the question would arise of how we are to proceed in the face of disagreement over which of these procedures provides us with the authority to implement one set of disputed principles of justice. On the other hand, when the connection between legitimacy and justice is too loose, we will be left with the possibility that legitimate exercises of political power may be deeply unjust. This would again raise doubts about whether we have really found a solution to the problem posed by the circumstances of politics, for we would have to confront the possibility of deep and pervasive conflicts between justice and legitimacy, with no easy answer to the question of how, as individuals at least, we should proceed in the face of this conflict. It will be implausible to suppose that we should always side with legitimacy, and correspondingly hard to avoid the conclusion that sometimes the legitimate exercise of coercive power may be justifiably resisted.

What are the most important unsolved questions in political philosophy and/or related disciplines and what are the prospects for progress?

Political philosophy rarely, if ever, solves problems once and for all. Old problems usually persist despite attempts to resolve them, and even when they are successfully resolved, new ones arise from the ashes of the old. In my view, however, it would be a mistake to conclude from this that political philosophy makes no progress. We should not measure progress in terms of problems solved or questions answered, but rather in terms of improved understanding. Progress occurs through clarifying the question that is being asked and by coming to a better understanding of which answers to that question are coherent. I think considerable progress has been made in the study of justice, in the sense that we understand the issues much better, though there are still many that we do not understand very well, for example, issues to do with the moral significance of national or state boundaries, and the issue of when justice requires people to bear the costs of their behaviour. I do not doubt that progress, in the sense of improved understanding, will be made on these issues as they come to the forefront of political philosophy.

Selected publications

Books

Explaining Political Disagreement (Cambridge: Cambridge University Press, 1993).

Community, Solidarity and Belonging: Levels of Community and Their Normative Significance (Cambridge: Cambridge University Press, 2000).

7. Andrew Mason

Levelling the Playing Field: The Idea of Equal Opportunity and its Place in Egalitarian Thought (Oxford: Oxford University Press, 2006).

Journal Articles

'Autonomy, Liberalism and State Neutrality', *The Philosophical Quarterly*, Vol. 40, 1990, 433–452.

'Politics and the State', *Political Studies*, Vol. 38, 1990, 575–587.

'Workers' Unfreedom and Women's Unfreedom: Are They Analogous?', *Political Studies*, Vol. 44, 1996, 75–87.

'Special Obligations to Compatriots', *Ethics*, Vol. 107, 1997, 427–447.

'Imposing Liberal Principles', *Critical Review of International Social and Political Philosophy*, Vol. 1, 1998, 98–116. Also in Richard Bellamy and Martin Hollis (eds.) *Pluralism and Liberal Neutrality* (Ilford, Essex: Frank Cass, 1999). Reprinted in G. W. Smith (ed.) *Liberalism: Critical Concepts in Political Science*, Vol. IV, *The Limits of Liberalism* (London: Routledge, 2002).

'Political Community, Liberal-Nationalism and the Ethics of Assimilation', *Ethics*, Vol. 109, 1999, 261–286.

'Equality, Personal Responsibility and Gender Socialisation', *Proceedings of the Aristotelian Society*, Vol. 100, 2000, 227–246.

'Egalitarianism and the Levelling Down Objection', *Analysis*, Vol. 61, 2001, 246–254.

'Equality of Opportunity, Old and New', *Ethics*, Vol. 111, July 2001, 760–781.

'Just Constraints', *British Journal of Political Science*, Vol. 34, April 2004, 251–268.

'Equality of Opportunity and Differences in Social Circumstances', *The Philosophical Quarterly*, Vol. 54, July 2004, 368–388.

8

Martha Nussbaum

Ernst Freund Distinguished Service Professor of Law and Ethics

Department of Philosophy, Law School, and Divinity School

The University of Chicago, IL, USA

Why were you initially drawn to political philosophy?

Politics fascinated me from a very early date. I was too young to play an active role in the Civil Rights Movement, but it played a large role in my thinking, especially since my father, originally from the deep South, remained a racist, and we had many quarrels on that account. My role in the anti-war movement was not a radical one; it consisted of licking stamps for Gene McCarthy. I was somewhat skeptical of the Marxian movements of my time, and had then basically the same political views I do now: redistributionist, social-democratic, but liberal rather than corporatist or perfectionist. By the time the women's movement got going, I had both a baby and a job, so I didn't have time to go to meetings, but I knew all too well the issues that the movement was about, through experiences of workplace discrimination, deficient support for child care, and sexual harassment. So it was probably inevitable that, sooner or later, I would turn to political philosophy.

Early in my academic career, I did not work on political questions, and yet, I think that there is a close relationship between the questions that preoccupied me then and the questions in political philosophy that preoccupy me now. The focus of my early work, both in Greek and Roman philosophy and in philosophy and literature, was on the scope and significance of human vulnerability to events beyond human control. I felt that the role of events beyond people's control in the structure of the good human life had not been sufficiently appreciated in modern moral philosophy. I turned to the Greek tragedians and philosophers for a better understanding of such matters. (Although I was working on these issues before I was ever in a seminar taught by Bernard Williams, he had a major influence on me, above all by giving me a sense of permission and possibility. Questions that many thought outside the boundaries of philosophy could now be approached, as I wished to, within it.)

I became particularly interested in analyzing the structure of emotions, because they are our ways of appraising the way things are with important elements of our good life that lie beyond our control. I felt that the Stoic analysis of emotions as appraisals of valued "external goods" was promising, though in need of philosophical modification. I did not, however, agree with the Stoics' normative thesis that the good life is one that avoids all emotional and evaluative investment in the uncertain world beyond the boundaries of our wills. I turned to Aristotle to recover a balanced conception, which ascribes great importance to our own moral efforts, and yet acknowledges the damages of luck.

Thinking about the good life and its deep needs from the world (for food, movement, health, political activity, the conditions of love and friendship, the conditions of equal respect) led me to political philosophy. Obviously enough, one job of political arrangements is to bring these essential goods more within the reach and control of people, so that more of them can lead flourishing lives. I began to see that Aristotle's political conception contained the roots of such ideas, and I felt that it supplied, with its emphasis on human capability and functioning, some elements that were either absent or insufficiently stressed in the political philosophy of the late twentieth century. Amartya Sen's critique of the Rawlsian idea of primary goods in favor of a rich idea of human capabilities seemed to me very much like what Aristotle had articulated. In 1986 I began a collaboration with Sen at the World Institute for Development Economics Research that has lasted to the present day (though the connection with the Institute ended in 1993).

Being at that Institute (run by the United Nations, but located in Finland), associating every day with people from many developing countries, and, in 1988, traveling to India in connection with our work, I saw the huge problems faced by the poor in developing countries. I became particularly fascinated by the problems, and also the resourcefulness, of poor women. This experience completely transformed me, and my work. The intellectual ideas that were percolating already took on a practical urgency, and I began to ask myself what these ideas could offer to that world of political reality. It appeared to me that they could offer a great deal. Amartya Sen had already worked on the measures of capability that went into the Human Development Reports of the UN Development Programme, and yet I felt that there was more philosophical work to be done, defending this universalistic conception against forms of cultural relativism and working with its concepts to map out a theory of social justice.

From that time on, I have devoted a good part of my energy to work in political philosophy, although I have continued, as well, to work on the emotions. Increasingly, I try to connect the two domains, talking about the "political psychology" of a decent society and a decent world culture, and writing, as well, about the emotions behind religious violence and extreme nationalism.

What do you consider your own most important contribution(s) to political philosophy, and why?

There are four contributions that I think worth mentioning. The first, and perhaps the best known, is my development of the "capabilities approach" as a basis for an account of minimum social justice. Sen has used this approach only for comparative purposes, but I have thought it possible, and promising, to use the idea of a set of interrelated human capabilities as the basis for an account of minimum social justice, in connection with the idea of human dignity and a life in accordance with human dignity. I argue that if we ponder the idea of human dignity, we see that this dignity requires, for its support, various forms of material and institutional assistance, and that we can at least make a start toward describing these conditions by arguing that a minimally just society will secure to all its citizens a threshold level of ten valuable capabilities, which I then go on to enumerate. There is much more to be said about the conception, the role of equality and equal respect in it, the role of the idea of the threshold level of each capability, and the role of the concept of capability itself. The conception is a form of "political liberalism" in Rawls's sense: that is, the capabilities are introduced not as a complete Aristotelian account of a flourishing life, but as an account of key political goods, concerning which we hope we can attain an overlapping consensus. I spend a lot of time trying to show that this conception is respectful of diverse "comprehensive doctrines."

The conception has been refined over time and will go on being refined. In *Women and Human Development*, I employed the approach to analyze the prerequisites of gender justice. There, I also argued that the approach supplies better guidance overall than that supplied by preference-based Utilitarian conceptions. Recently, in *Frontiers of Justice*, I have argued that it can supply good answers to questions posed by the problem of justice between nations, the problem of justice for people with disabilities, and (suitably extended) the problem of justice for nonhuman animals. In that book I compare the approach in detail to a variety of approaches stemming from the classical doctrine of the social contract, with particular attention to Rawls.

Meanwhile, there has been for four years an international organization, the Human Development and Capability Association, dedicated to further work on the approach (in both Sen's and my versions) and to its practical implementation. We currently have about 700 members from about 40 countries. So it appears that this conception has generated a lot of interest, as an alternative to simplistic growth-focused conceptions that tend to dominate in development economics.

The second contribution, which overlaps a good deal with the first, is the development of a capability-based theory of sex equality. My interest in philosophical feminism is broad and multifaceted. The work on women and capabilities lies at its core, but I have also written about sexual orientation, rape, sexual harassment, and other issues, both in the American context and in the Indian context. Working on my capabilities approach, I got to know India as well as I could, and I felt that there were some interesting problems in philosophical and legal feminism that I wanted to approach in that context, partly because I think the whole world can learn from the Indian constitutional tradition, and partly because I had an intervention to make in particular debates. So I've written on the law of religion and gender, on rape, and on domestic violence, as well as on the subordination of poor women through discrimination in the workplace.

There are many fine feminist philosophers, but I suppose I think that there is need for more feminist philosophy that has an international focus and that is based on detailed knowledge of other nations. In addition, there is need for continued work on feminism from within the liberal tradition of political philosophy, particularly after the premature death of Susan Okin. Much of the best feminist theory issues challenges to traditional liberal theories of justice. I believe that those challenges can be answered by a theory that is still in key respects liberal, with a large role for both freedom and equality. I argue, however, that liberalism has to change in important respects to respond to the feminist critique. (Mill understood this, and I consider my views to be, in many respects, further developments of a Millian approach.) I think of my feminism as both radical and liberal, and as showing (I hope) how a radical critique of sex-based inequality can be articulated within liberalism.

The third contribution is my work on emotions. Again, this overlaps a good deal with the other two, and it will overlap even more in future work that I am planning. The great political philosophers of the past in the Western tradition have often been distinguished thinkers about the emotions. Plato, Aristotle, Seneca, Aquinas, Spinoza, Rousseau, and Adam Smith are only a few of the many examples one might mention. Today, however, the role of emotions in political societies has been relatively neglected, and I have tried to address that lack, starting out from an overall analysis of the structure and function of emotions that is as refined and precise as I can make it. I analyze emotions that can at least potentially support the aims of a decent political culture (compassion), but also at those that are more problematic (disgust and shame). Increasingly, I am addressing the problem posed by the emotions for moral and political education, and trying to work out an account of the cultivation of appropriate emotions in connection with the capabilities idea.

Connected to all of these contributions, and in effect a fourth contribution, has been a focus on education for world citizenship. In *Cultivating Humanity*, focusing on higher education in the United States, I argued that three abilities that we associate with the humanities are crucial to the development of good citizenship in an increasingly interconnected world: the ability to think Socratically, questioning one's own beliefs; considerable knowledge of non-Western cultures and their history; and the ability to use the imagination to cross boundaries of class, race, gender, and sexuality. I am currently planning more work on this sort of issue, in light of the horrible rush to a focus on technology and the other "profitable" forms of education, with its concomitant neglect of the arts and humanities, which supply essential ingredients for decent democratic citizenship.

8. Martha Nussbaum

What is the proper role of political philosophy in relation to real, political action? Can there ever be a fruitful relation between political philosophy and political practice?

Good political philosophy, I believe, begins from a grasp of the world and the most urgent problems in it. At the same time, it should be good as theory: refined, analytically precise, responsive to the best historical texts, and, to a certain degree abstract. Let me elaborate these conditions further.

Theories of social justice should be abstract. They should, that is, have a generality and theoretical power that enables them to reach beyond the immediate political conflicts of their time, even if they do have their origins in such conflicts. Even political justification requires such abstraction: for we cannot justify a political theory unless we can show that it can be stable over time, receiving citizens' support for more than narrowly self-protective or instrumental reasons. And we cannot show that without standing back from immediate events.

On the other hand, theories of social justice must also be responsive to the world and its most urgent problems, and must be prepared to alter their formulations and even their structure in response to a problem that is new, or to an old problem that has been culpably ignored.

Most theories of justice in the Western tradition, for example, have been culpably inattentive to women's demands for equality and to the many obstacles that stood, and stand, in the way of that equality. Their abstraction, though in some ways valuable, concealed a failure to confront one of the world's most serious problems. Attending adequately to the problem of gender justice has large theoretical consequences, since it means acknowledging that the family is a political institution, not part of a "private sphere" immune from justice. Correcting the oversight of previous theories is therefore not a matter of simply applying the same old theories to a new problem; it is a matter of getting the theoretical structure right.

Although people can certainly engage in practical politics on all these issues without such a detailed philosophical investigation, I believe that the detailed investigation is helpful. First, we find ourselves, today, in a world dominated by theory, only it is a rather crude and unhelpful type of theory. (I am thinking of the crude normative theories associated with neoclassical economics, which portray the goal of society as utility- or wealth-maximization. At other times in history, philosophers have had other theories to contend with, such as the theory of the divine right of kings.) It is no use to go to the World Bank with the refined practical intuitions of an activist; theorists only listen to other theories, and the capabilities approach, by supplying a counter-theory to the economic approaches, serves as an ally of the good activist, by finding theoretical ways of making that person's practical intuitions salient. Second, close theoretical work shows respect for the people one is criticizing. One could write an op ed saying that economists have crude perceptions of human development, but it seems worth doing something more respectful and detailed, confronting the other conceptions with carefully worked-out arguments. Third, theory is helpful because it is always helpful to see exactly where the problem kicks in, so that one can change the right thing rather than the wrong thing. For that we need a well worked-out conception that covers the ground in a systematic way. In fact, I am skeptical that a less detailed philosophical investigation has much practical relevance, when the questions are complex and the theoretical structures elaborate. If we go too quickly to the "bottom line," we lose the characteristic type of illumination that philosophy is able to provide. Certainly the great practical works in political philosophy are not great because of lack of detail. John Stuart Mill's *On Liberty* is great despite its frustrating lack of detail, and would have been even better had it spent more time working out foundational issues, such as the account of harm, or the relationships between liberty and preferences, liberty and rights. Rawls's two great books supply especially valuable practical guidance because they do try to answer hard foundational questions with rigor and pleasing detail.

Suppose we have a theory that has relevance to practical issues: what then? If philosophers are to influence political practice, they need avenues of connection. Philosophers are usually not good politicians, so one has to think how their complex conceptions might come to influence practice. One such avenue is supplied by teaching, especially when one teaches students who are not only specialists in one's own subject, but are going to go on to influence society in very different ways. The American liberal arts system brings one into contact with future politicians, journalists, lawyers, business leaders, many other people who will influence society, and one may at least hope that they do so with a memory of what they have learned from a good class in political philosophy. The primary reason I wanted an affiliation with a law school was to be able to teach students who would be clerks for judges, who would argue important court cases, and so on.

Another avenue of influence is through writing for the general public. Unfortunately, that kind of writing is particularly difficult to do in the US today, because the media are so dominated by corporate interests that there is very little hope of an intellectual's getting before a general public. Few non-fiction books are reviewed in general media, and almost no books of philosophy. Philosophers are not asked to write for such media, and a person who tries to get an op ed published has a hard time. In the past I've been able to get book reviews published and to address general ideas that way. But it is getting more and more difficult.

Fortunately, not all countries are like this: in Holland, for example, philosophy plays a respected role in popular culture, serious books of philosophy are widely reviewed and discussed, and large public audiences gather for lectures about philosophy. I would put Holland, India, and Italy at one end of a spectrum, the US at the other end, and nations such as Canada and Germany somewhere in the middle, in terms of the ease of an intellectual's addressing a general public. I don't know what one can do to change this situation in the US.

A third avenue of influence is through connections to people who actually make policy. The capabilities approach has had a good deal of influence on development agencies, on policy makers (not in the US), and, increasingly, on leaders and their thinking. In general, it is usually easier to get some contact with experts appointed to administrative agencies than with politicians, who, at least in the US, are running as hard as they can away from intellectuals, even if they began as academics themselves. Americans are suspicious of academics, and don't like people who hang out with them too much. On the other hand, the modern administrative state has a need for expertise, so it contains a good number of intellectually sophisticated people who are open to new ideas.

I agree with Kant: a "secret condition" of a perpetual peace among nations is that the rulers of the world would take seriously what the philosophers say. But Kant said that this condition had to be secret, because he knew that political leaders didn't want to admit their need for anything that the philosopher can provide. So, says Kant, they should at least protect the freedom of speech so that the philosopher *can* make recommendations – whether they publicly admit their need for them or not! Well, we tenured academics in America do much better than Kant where free speech is concerned, but that has not meant that the *soi-disant* rulers of the world think it important to listen to us. Again: it's much easier for me to talk to political leaders in India than in my own country. The situation in India and Holland shows us that human beings are not by nature averse to political philosophy: indeed, they can be very fond of it, and give it a real place in their lives. Unfortunately, cultural forces militate against this happening in any stable or widespread way, where the US is concerned.

It was not always so: the framers of our Constitution (like the framers of India's constitution much later) were quite influenced by philosophical ideas. James Madison, in particular, was a very good philosopher himself, and all were much influenced by Thomas Paine. Between that generation and the present has come lots of anti-intellectualism. It's lucky for us (people who care about justice in the United States) that our Constitution was made when it was, and that the Constitution cannot easily be changed.

The most exciting and, to me, hopeful avenue for public engagement that has come my way has been the creation of the Human Development and Capability Association, which I mentioned before. This Association was founded by a group of excellent younger economists and philosophers, from nations including Brazil, Japan, Italy, Pakistan, and Holland, who believed that the work Sen and I had been doing was important for the world and who wanted to foster further work on both theory and implementation. Our annual meetings bring together theorists in economics, philosophy, political science, and other disciplines, and it also includes development practitioners. The average age of participants is very young, and many, isolated in their own countries, derive support from the contacts they make. We hope that the work this Association generates will influence international agencies, as well as the academy. The very existence of this association shows the importance of luck in a human life: Sen and I did not seek its creation, and we are utterly dependent on the hard work, the integrity, and the excellence of the people who fortunately came our way.

My experience in the Association has made it clear to me that philosophy has to be academically rigorous and high-quality if it is to make any worthwhile contribution to public life. It is very easy for idealistic young people to move too quickly to the "bottom line," neglecting the hard analytical work that is needed to make good on a claim. But if they write that way, they are not contributing anything distinctive: they are neither politicians nor philosophers, and they will not make a difference. On the other hand, there is no reason why philosophers have to write badly and obscurely. So many great philosophers (Plato, Seneca, Rousseau, Mill) wrote extremely well, showing that philosophical quality and good writing are not incompatible. One should emulate these examples.

What do you consider the most neglected topics and/or contributions in post-Rawlsian or late 20th century political philosophy?

The topic of emotions in political life is an old one, but it went through a period of neglect, and now it is fortunately being revived. The topic of gender justice was simply not addressed for a very long time, but it is not neglected now. The topic of justice for people with disabilities was utterly neglected in the long tradition of Western political philosophy, but it is now being creatively addressed. The topic of justice for non-human animals was boldly raised by Jeremy Bentham and John Stuart Mill, and it had been a prominent theme in late Greek Platonism. (It was also prominent in Buddhist and Hindu philosophy.) Today, this topic, and related issues of environmental justice, are attracting renewed attention, although I believe that it is important to address them with good theorizing, not just eloquent practical writings. What I would like to see is a lot of different approaches, all well argued, and a lively increasingly refined discourse about them, just as happened in the area of social justice after Rawls's book was published, and thanks to his influence.

The topic of justice between nations, and global justice generally, has been on Western philosophy's agenda ever since Cicero, but we have not made as much progress on this topic as we should have. Theories of social justice that take the nation-state as their basic unit have been very thoroughly worked out, and refined alternatives are now available. Theories of a just world order are in their infancy, and some of the ones that are available are unhelpfully distant from the current world and the entities that are actually powerful within it (including multinational corporations, international agencies and agreements, nongovernmental organizations of many kinds). One problem in working on such theories is that it is hard to do it well if one does not know very much about the world, and many young philosophers have a deplorable level of ignorance. It would be nice if the generally required part of an undergraduate education (for all students, not just philosophers) acquainted students with the basic facts of the global economy, the main world religions, the postcolonial history of developing nations, and much more. My own education was lamentable in this regard, and I have spent a lot of my time playing catch-up. Fortunately, I've had some very good opportunities for learning.

Another neglected topic is that of education. As with the emotions, so here: this was a central topic in mainstream Western political philosophy, engaging the attention of Plato, Aristotle, the Stoics, Locke, Rousseau, Kant, and many others. In the twentieth century, John Dewey made a distinguished contribution to thought about democratic education, and he did so in connection with a profoundly influential reform of primary and secondary education in the United States. Meanwhile, in India, philosopher Rabindranath Tagore was both writing about education (in a way closely related to Dewey's, emphasizing the role of imagination and the arts) and pioneering a progressive school that focused on the pupil's own creative involvement in the learning process, particularly through the arts.

Today, however, leading political philosophers simply don't write about education. I think what happened was that education became hyper-professionalized and generated its own separate professional schools. The work done in these schools was, unfortunately, rarely any good, so philosophers got contempt for the whole area, and stopped thinking about it. John Rawls was different: he saw the importance of the topic, and, in his own abstract way, he did make a contribution. But we need something less abstract and more engaged with what's going on in schools and universities. It's a crucial time, because the pressure for success in the global market has made many nations drop humanities and arts in favor of an emphasis on science and technology alone, and pedagogy is also slipping away from the progressive tradition exemplified by Dewey and Tagore, toward a reliance on force-feeding and rote learning. Philosophers, however, are nowhere to be found protesting these changes. I wrote about higher education because I felt I had a responsibility as a citizen of the academy, and a beneficiary of the security it confers, to talk to the public about why good citizenship in a diverse world requires new forms of learning. But that book focused on what I knew best, higher education in America. I now feel that it is urgent to write about the education of children, and to address the issues in a global way. I feel that we need many more voices contributing to this debate. Philosophers have forgotten how exciting the topic is, when approached by the likes of Seneca and Rousseau, and they therefore don't bother with it. This is one area where I feel philosophers have an urgent social responsibility.

Another such issue is religion. Philosophers often hate religion, and so they don't write about it, they just ignore it. Those who don't hate it often write about the classics issues in philosophy of religion, epistemological and metaphysical. Good writing in political philosophy about religion is relatively rare. Again, there is a strong tradition here in Western thought, including Roger Williams, Thomas Hobbes, John Locke, Spinoza, David Hume, Immanuel Kant, Moses Mendelssohn (whose writings ought to be much better known than they are), and John Rawls. But we need to start working on this topic with an eye to the problems that vex our world today, problems of religious fear and loathing spawned by the fear of global terrorism.

To do this work well, we need to learn much more about non-Judeo-Christian religions, and, most obviously, about Islam. We ought to be teaching every undergraduate philosophy major courses on Islamic philosophy, but to do that we first have to educate ourselves! I would like to see a vigorous conversation about religion and political philosophy across national, cultural, and religious lines. It would help if philosophers participating in these conversations didn't show contempt for people who hold religious beliefs. I urge young philosophers to go spend some time in distant nations to develop their sense of these issues. I have a former graduate student teaching in Beirut, another in Dubai, and I am about to visit East Jerusalem, where a fine Palestinian philosopher, Sari Nusseibeh, the son-in-law of J.L. Austin, is President of Al-Quds University, and teaches a course in critical reasoning that he has required of all undergraduates. Contacts that are fraught in the diplomatic sphere may possibly be eased through the academy, but we need to educate ourselves if we are to participate well in such discussions.

What are the most important unsolved questions in political philosophy and/or related disciplines and what are the prospects for progress?

I have answered the first part of this question already, so let me turn to the second part. I think that the modern academy supplies working conditions that are unprecedentedly favorable to good philosophical work: tenure, strong protections for academic freedom, decent pay, and a reasonable teaching load. (As the placement officer for our job candidates in philosophy for many years, I know that it is increasingly difficult getting into one of these secure slots, so I am talking only about a lucky few.) When we look at the conditions that philosophers had to endure in so much of the history of Europe, we should feel that we have an unparalleled chance to make progress, especially as the life span continues to lengthen. Philosophy is an old person's profession (fortunately, for those of us who are getting old), and so the advances in health care that make the years between 60 and 80 better years for people in wealthy nations are favorable for the production of good philosophy.

Our good working conditions have their drawbacks. Philosophers can be remarkably isolated from life outside of the academy, and can avoid knowing much about countries other than their own. If they don't take active steps to overcome this isolation, they will not make useful contributions to political philosophy, because that subject, as I've said, is responsible to an ever-changing world and its problems. So it isn't inevitable that philosophers will address the world's most urgent problems well. On the other hand, as an editor of *Ethics*, I see more and more work coming in that does manifest a serious interest in the world, whether it is work on corporate responsibility, or work on animal rights, or work on global justice.

Any feminist is very likely to be an optimist, because there has been so much progress for women over the course of the past century—both practical progress and theoretical progress. When we compare the thriving field of feminist philosophy to the void that existed until around 1970, we see that a passion for justice, combined with philosophical talent, can change a field. So I'm optimistic that the same sort of progress will be made on the other problems I have named. I'm also optimistic that this work will make a difference to the world. As Kant said, so long as one does not know that progress is impossible, one has a duty to hope for it, since only that hope will motivate one's best practical efforts.

Selected publications

Books

The Fragility of Goodness: Luck and Ethics in Greek Tragedy and Philosophy, Cambridge University Press, 1986.

The Therapy of Desire: Theory and Practice in Hellenistic Ethics, Princeton University Press, 1994 (paper 1996).

Poetic Justice: The Literary Imagination and Public Life (The Alexander Rosenthal Lectures, 1991), Beacon Press, 1995, paper edition 1997

For Love of Country: A Debate on Patriotism and Cosmopolitanism (lead essay mine, with responses): Beacon Press, 1996.Updated Edition, 2002.

Cultivating Humanity: A Classical Defense of Reform in Liberal Education, Harvard University Press, 1997.

Sex and Social Justice, Oxford University Press, 1999.

Women and Human Development: The Capabilities Approach, Cambridge University Press, N.Y., 2000.

Upheavals of Thought: The Intelligence of Emotions, Cambridge and New York: Cambridge University Press, 2001.

Hiding From Humanity: Disgust, Shame, and the Law,. Princeton: Princeton University Press, 2004.

Frontiers of Justice: Disability, Nationality, Species Membership. Cambridge, MA: Harvard University Press, 2006.

The Clash Within: Democracy, Religious Violence, and India's Future. Cambridge, MA: Harvard University Press, 2007.

Liberty of Conscience: The Attack on America's Tradition of Religious Equality. New York: Basic Books, summer 2007.

Articles

"Non-Relative Virtues: An Aristotelian Approach," *Midwest Studies in Philosophy* 13 (1988) 32–53. Expanded version in M. Nussbaum and A. Sen, eds., *The Quality of Life* (Oxford: Clarendon Press, 1993).

"Aristotelian Social Democracy," in *Liberalism and the Good*, ed. R. B. Douglass, G. Mara, and H. Richardson (New York 1990) 203–52.

"Human Functioning and Social Justice: In Defense of Aristotelian Essentialism," *Political Theory* 20 (1992) 202–46.

"Aristotle on Human Nature and the Foundations of Ethics," in *World, Mind, and Ethics: Essays on the Philosophy of Bernard*

Williams, ed. J. E. G. Altham and Ross Harrison, Cambridge University Press 1995, 86–131.

"The Good as Discipline, the Good as Freedom," in *Ethics of Consumption: The Good Life, Justice, and Global Stewardship*, ed. David A. Crocker and Toby Linden (Lanham: Rowman and Littlefield, 1998), 312–41.

"Public Philosophy and International Feminism," *Ethics* 108 (1998), 762–96.

"Duties of Justice, Duties of Material Aid: Cicero's Problematic Legacy," *Journal of Political Philosophy* 7 (1999), 1–31.

"The Costs of Tragedy: Some Moral Limits of Cost-Benefit Analysis," *Journal of Legal Studies* 29 (2000), 1005–36.

"The Future of Feminist Liberalism," *Proceedings and Addresses of the American Philosophical Association* 74 (2000), 47–79.

"Rawls and Feminism," in *The Cambridge Companion to Rawls*, ed. Samuel Freeman (Cambridge: Cambridge University Press, 2003), 488–520.

"Compassion and Terror," *Daedalus* Winter 2003, 10–26.

"Capabilities as Fundamental Entitlements: Sen and Social Justice," *Feminist Economics* Vol. 9, Number 2 and 3 (July/November 2003), 33–59.

"'Don't Smile So Much': Philosophy and Women in the 1970s," in *Singing in the Fire: Stories of Women in Philosophy*, ed. Linda Martín Alcoff (Lanham: Rowman and Littlefield, 2003): 93–108.

"Women's Bodies: Violence, Security, Capabilities," *The Journal of Human Development* 6 (2005), 167–83.

"Education and Democratic Citizenship: Capabilities and Quality Education," *Journal of Human Development* 7 (2006), 385–95.

"Radical Evil in the Lockean State: The Neglect of the Political Emotions," *Journal of Moral Philosophy* 3 (2006), 159–78.

9
Philippe Van Parijs

Chaire Hoover d'éthique économique et sociale
Université catholique de Louvain, Belgium
Visiting Professor of Philosophy, Harvard University, MA, USA

Why were you initially drawn to political philosophy?

When I was 11, I started reading many history books. By the time I was 14, I had decided, possibly as a consequence, that I would go into politics, and hence needed to study law. At 16, however, after having read Emmanuel Mounier's *Introduction aux existentialismes*, I got engrossed in Nietzsche. My earlier convictions were shattered—about what politics should aim at, indeed about what mattered in life. I hitch-hiked to Sils-Maria, to Rapallo, to Portofino, some of Nietzsche's fetish destinations. But it did not help much. When the time came to go to university, I decided to play it safe and did several degrees at the same time, but philosophy was central. As Kafka put it in his *Forschungen eines Hundes* (*Investigations of a Dog*, English ed.: 1922), which I read and reread at the time, the priority was "to sort out the ultimate ends". Philosophy was supposed to help. And it did.

Once "ultimate ends" were sorted out as much and as little as I thought was possible, my intention was to return eventually to the political questions in which my philosophical interests originated. But before going into political philosophy, I felt a substantial detour was in order, with two main components: philosophy of science and economic theory. After having briefly believed, under French post-68 influence, that Louis Althusser was the next-plus-ultra of philosophical rigor, I was easily persuaded by my Louvain supervisor, Jean Ladrière, that the analytical tradition was a better place to turn to for what I was looking for. My two undergraduate theses were devoted, respectively, to the philosophical foundations of mathematical statistics and to the formal structure of a variety of theoretical models used in the social sciences.

9. Philippe Van Parijs

My Oxford DPhil thesis, which took off from my Louvain doctoral dissertation on functional explanation and became my first book, was devoted to evolutionary explanation in the social sciences. Along the road, especially during the three semesters I spent at Bielefeld and at Berkeley, I devoted much time to economic theory, neo-classical, Keynesian and Marxian alike.

By the time I returned to Belgium in 1980, the detour was over. I finally read Rawls's *Theory of Justice*, which I had discovered and bought six years earlier when first arriving in Oxford as a graduate student but not read beyond the first page. I then organized, with Jean Ladrière, what was probably the first French-language seminar about contemporary Anglo-American political philosophy and edited the first French-language book about Rawls. Although I found Nozick's *Anarchy, State and Utopia* and Roemer's *General Theory of Exploitation and Class* more exciting, I soon realized that Rawls's theory had provided me with a base camp which I was unlikely to ever leave.

What do you consider your own most important contribution(s) to political philosophy, and why?

One thing I think I have done – at least this is how I understand now what I did – is to propose an alternative framework for formulating a liberal-egalitarian conception of distributive justice. The most common framework, shared, among others, by Ronald Dworkin and Amartya Sen, makes distributive justice a matter of correcting unfair inequalities in *endowments*. In Rawls's framework, distributive justice is a matter of access to *social positions* and of expectations of social and economic advantages associated with these positions. In the framework I proposed in my *Real Freedom for All*, distributive justice is a matter of fair distributions of the *gifts* we receive very unequally in the course of our lives, most of them, under contemporary conditions, through the jobs we occupy. Framing distributive justice in this third way naturally generates a prima facie case for an unconditional basic income. Each of the three frameworks relies on a stylized picture of the world which has advantages and drawbacks. The third one, I believe is the most appropriate one for the world into which we are moving.

Another thing I have been trying to do is provide a systematic treatment of the issues of justice that arise from linguistic diversity. The spreading of a world-wide lingua franca is consistent with justice as fair cooperation, and called for by justice as equal opportunity. Yet the diversity of native languages must be defended, not because, all things considered, it can be relied upon to serve the general interest, let alone because it may constitute a value in itself. If linguistic diversity is to be defended, essentially through a firm implementation of a linguistic territoriality principle, it can only be as a by-product of what is required by justice as equal dignity. So, at least, I am trying to argue in a book in progress under the title *Linguistic Justice for Europe and for the World*.

What is the proper role of political philosophy in relation to real, political action? Can there ever be a fruitful relation between political philosophy and political practice?

Yes, I believe in the possibility and importance of such a fruitful relation. Among people who are politically active, whether in a partisan or non-partisan mode, among civil servants, among journalists, among students, and in the educated public at large there is, in my experience, a strong need and explicit demand for a discourse that combines a well-informed synthetic interpretation of what is happening in our societies and in our world with an articulate formulation of the principles that should guide us in assessing alternative feasible options for the future.

This is of course a big job. Philosophers cannot hope to accomplish it by constructing far-fetched objections and counter-objections to each other's arguments in the well-insulated rooms of their ivory towers. Doing it properly requires that scholars whose core business is to reflect critically on normative propositions and arguments should interact intensively with demographers and geographers, economists and sociologists, political scientists and lawyers, even biologists and climatologists, in order to understand interdependencies and assess feasibilities and thereby offer a robust interpretation of the present and the past and a vision of the future that stands a chance of not being too naive.

Doing the job properly also requires from political philosophers that they should use a language that can be understood by the audience addressed. This means using plenty of examples drawn from real life — having a "real life" oneself makes them easier to find and more effective to use. It means unfolding philosophical puzzles as the logical destination of trips which have actual debates as their point of departure. It means avoiding all jargon that could not be clearly explained to one's grandmother. It means taking the trouble and the risk of spelling out, be it conjecturally or illustratively, the policy implications of the principles under discussion. It means having both the modesty to stress that political philosophy will not offer political actors a ready-made optimal policy-package and the boldness to claim that it will offer crucial guidance for some of the most difficult choices.

My feeling is that there is a growing demand for political philosophy so practiced—by no means the exclusive preserve of professional political philosophers. Indeed, political philosophy so practiced must beware of not becoming too successful. This fear was on my mind, for example, when in January 2004, in Brasilia's presidential palace, I had to publicly give my philosophical blessing to Brazil's official adoption, unprecedented at a national level, of a universal basic income proposal, just a few minutes before President Lula signed it into law.

What do you consider the most neglected topics and/or contributions in post-Rawlsian or late 20th century political philosophy?

Up to the very end of the 20th century, the bulk of political philosophy was conducted with reference to "a society". It took for granted that the nation, the state, the country, constituted the appropriate level. Political philosophy, today, needs to be conceived and practised in the first instance at the global level.

True, most topics relevant at the domestic level are also relevant at the global level and conversely. But some will become far more salient as political philosophy shifts its focus from the domestic to the global level. Migration and language issues are among them and are for this reason in my view, relative to their emerging importance, among the "most neglected topics" of late 20th century political philosophy.

What are the most important unsolved questions in political philosophy and/or related disciplines and what are the prospects for progress?

I find it hard to talk about "unsolved problems in political philosophy", but I have no difficulty identifying questions which I see as serious problems in my own effort to reach reflective equilibrium.

One of them, perhaps the most serious one, is how to combine a notion of justice as equality of opportunity (whether framed in the language of endowments, social positions or gifts) with a notion of justice as equal dignity. Could one not best be understood as a dimension or precondition of the other? If they need to be kept distinct, which should yield to the other if and when they clash? Maybe other people – including Rawls through the role he ascribes to the social bases of self-respect – have solved these problems to their own satisfaction. I have not solved them to mine. Can anyone help?

Selected publications

Evolutionary Explanation in the Social Sciences. An Emerging Paradigm, Totowa, NJ, Rowman & Littlefield ("Philosophy & Society") & London, Tavistock, 1981, xvi + 255 p.

Le Modèle économique et ses rivaux. Introduction à la pratique de l'épistémologie des sciences sociales, Genève & Paris, Droz, 1990, 243 p.

Qu'est-ce qu'une société juste? Introduction à la pratique de la philosophie politique, Paris, Le Seuil ("La Couleur des idées"), 1991, 316 p.

Marxism Recycled, Cambridge & New York, Cambridge University Press (*Studies in Marxism and Social Theory*), 1993, x + 252 p.

Real Freedom for All. What (If Anything) Can Justify Capitalism?, Oxford & New York, Clarendon Press (*Studies in Political Theory*), 1995, xii + 336 p., Oxford paperback, 1997.

Sauver la solidarité, Paris: Editions du Cerf ("Humanités"), 1995, 104 p. Expanded Dutch edition: Leuven & Apeldoorn, Garant, 1996, 140 p.

Refonder la solidarité, Paris: Editions du Cerf ("Humanités"), 1996, 120 p.

Ethique économique et sociale, Paris: La Découverte ("Repères"), 2000, 2nd ed. 2003, 124p. (with C. Arnsperger)

What's Wrong with a Free Lunch?, Boston: Beacon Press ("New Democracy Forum"), with a preface by R. Solow and comments by B. Barry, E.S. Phelps, E. Rothschild, H.A. Simon and others, edited by J. Cohen & J. Rogers.

Hacia una concepción de la justicia social global, Medellín: Fundación Confiar, 2002, 148p.

L'allocation universelle, Paris: La Découverte ("Repères"), 2005, 124p. (with Y. Vanderborght).

Redesigning Distribution, London: Verso ("Real Utopias"), 2005, 320p. (with Bruce Ackerman and Anne Alstott, edited by Erik O. Wright).

A Basic Income for All (expanded English edition of *L'Allocation universelle*, Cambridge (Mass): Harvard University Press, is now in progress (with Y. Vanderborght).

10
Philip Pettit

L.S.Rockefeller University Professor of Politics
and Human Values
Affiliate Professor of Philosophy
Princeton University, USA

Why were you initially drawn to political philosophy?

As with many philosophers, I tend to get theoretically engaged with questions, even practically important questions, only when I find them intriguing, puzzling, perhaps downright paradoxical. From early on I found issues in political philosophy intriguing because of their connection with more basic questions in the philosophy of mind and society. This theoretical interest in political philosophy was sharpened enormously by the heady experience of what seemed like a cultural revolution in 1968 and 1969. As a young, pre-doctoral lecturer at University College, Dublin I was swept up in the student revolution in March 1969 and edited a collection of pieces by the student leaders and their faculty sympathizers.

I got into philosophy originally through becoming possessed by the work of Jean Paul Sartre; I wrote a short dissertation on the notion of bad faith in his philosophical and literary work for an L.Ph degree, when I was still in my teens. Later I came to see Sartre as mistaken in his exceedingly atomistic picture of the human subject, especially in his earlier work, and having found that bias in Sartre, I began to find it everywhere, particularly among moral and political philosophers. That was a recurrent theme in my lectures at University College, Dublin. It ushered in a period in which I searched for an alternative, less atomistic picture of the mind and for the new angle I was sure it would provide on political and also ethical questions.

One body of literature I explored was associated with French structuralism but I became disillusioned with this approach and was quite critical of it when I wrote a short book, *The Concept of Structuralism*, in the mid 1970's. While working on structuralism, which I did as a post-doctoral fellow at Cambridge University, I became more and more interested in Wittgenstein, and in what I took to be his very non-atomistic view of how rule-following, and so thinking itself, is possible. This interest matured in the course of working my way into more analytical traditions in the philosophy of mind and language. I did that work in collaboration with Graham Macdonald, my colleague at the University of Bradford, which led to the publication of our book on 'Semantics and Social Science' in 1981.

The appearance of Saul Kripke's book on Wittgenstein on rule-following in 1982 had a big impact on me and on my continuing obsession with working out a non-atomistic picture of the mind and exploring its implications for moral and political philosophy. In 1983 I moved from Europe to Australia, fleeing Margaret Thatcher's England, and over the following decade I was able to benefit from that wonderfully robust philosophical culture in developing this idea. The line I argued on rule-following laid the basis for the non-atomistic theory of mind presented in a number of articles and in my book, *The Common Mind*, which appeared in 1993. In that book I developed this view of the human subject and used it to argue for an associated complex of approaches in the philosophy of social science and in political philosophy.

The key idea in that book is that while individualism is sound, atomism is not. Individualism argues rightly that whatever forces are operative in society, they do not undermine our conception of ourselves as imperfect but more or less autonomous subjects. Atomism is mistaken, so I maintained, in suggesting that all the central aspects of the human mind are fixed in place without anything more than causal dependence on social relationships. I argued that the capacity of humans to reason in a mutually accessible way presupposed a process of triangulation on common meanings in which more than one person had to be involved. No one could become capable of reasoning, then, without relying on others; and this, for more than contingent, causal reasons. Being able to reason without any history of reliance on others would be like being able to applaud with one hand.

What is the significance of non-atomism for political philosophy? In *The Common Mind* I argued that it made it possible to think that the most basic political values might presuppose human society, rather than being values that would have persuaded solitary individuals to enter society. I was struck by the fact that on the standard account of freedom as non-interference, the solitary individual would be the very exemplar of freedom, not having to live with anyone who might interfere in his or her life. And this led me to think about how freedom would be most naturally conceptualized, assuming that it is essentially an ideal for social beings. The clear answer, so it seemed to me, was that freedom would have to be conceptualized as a social status: one of relating to others within constraints that ensured – and more or less obviously ensured – that you were not subject to anyone else's dictate; you were your own man or woman.

Scarcely had I begun to explore that idea when I became aware of recent work by my Cambridge friend, Quentin Skinner, on the tradition of thinking about freedom in the long republican tradition. He had argued against the standard view that this conceptualization of freedom did not support the positive conception of freedom as participation in political life and I became quickly convinced, primed by his observations, that what it supported was precisely an idea of freedom as a certain social status. This was the status of not living *in potestate domini*, in the power of a master; not living under a culture or law or economy where others could push you around at will and with relative impunity. I later described this notion of freedom as an idea of non-domination. It played the central role in my 1989 book with John Braithwaite, entitled *Not Just Deserts: A Republican Theory of Criminal Justice*, and was developed more fully in my 1997 book, *Republicanism: A Theory of Freedom and Government*.

Not only did I find this ideal of freedom philosophically rich as well as politically suggestive, I became drawn into the intriguing history of its demise in the late eighteenth century in favor of the alternative ideal of freedom as non-interference. I argued, and am still persuaded, that it was the weaker demands of the new ideal that made it attractive, ironically, for reformers like Bentham and Paley. They expanded the compass of political concern to include workers and women, at least in principle, and they and their progeny would have found it easier to argue for freedom for all in this weaker sense, rather than for freedom for all in the sense in which this would allow no one to live in subjection to others.

What do you consider your own most important contribution(s) to political philosophy, and why?

Importance is hard to adjudicate, and embarrassing. But I can certainly address the question of the ideas that continue to seem sound to me, and that still give me a buzz. The non-atomistic emphasis on the social nature of the reasoning mind – the emphasis on the extent to which we are conversational, co-reasoning animals – is at the core of much of my work and the contributions I would like to mention all connect with this. A first is the conception of what it is to be a person, in particular a person possessed of the capacity for free will and free thought; a second is the interpretation of what it is to be socially and politically free, developed in republican terms; a third is the associated normative ideal, ethical and political, that is naturally supported from the viewpoint of human beings as co-reasoners; and a fourth is the opening that that viewpoint provides for thinking of groups as capable of incorporating in the guise of persons..

The conversable, orthonomous person

There are two ways of thinking about what it is to be a person. One characterizes persons by the stuff of which they are constituted; this approach is implicit in Boethius's famous definition of a person as an individual substance of rational nature. The other characterizes persons by the capacities and roles they can exercise. Michael Smith and I implicitly argued for an approach in the second category when, assuming that persons are creatures possessed of free will and free thought, we suggested that such capacities should be conceived of as aspects of conversability: aspects of the ability to be engaged in the give and take of reasons. We coined a name for this capacity to respond to reason — to respond to what is right according to reason — dubbing it 'orthononomy': the rule of the 'orthos' or right.

On the emerging conception, full functional persons are agents who are able to engage in the give and take of reasons, whether with others or with themselves, whatever the neural infrastructure that makes such engagement possible. I tried to develop this conception further, and connect it with political themes, in my 2001 book on *A Theory of Freedom: From the Psychology to the Politics of Agency*. In a forthcoming book entitled *Made with Words: Hobbes on Language, Mind and Politics*, I argue that the germ of the idea is to be found, surprisingly, in Hobbes.

Smith and I also outlined an associated ideal of personal life, building on this conception of the capacities of free will and free thought associated with personhood. What will it be to exercise such capacities fully? It will consist in making yourself sensitive to the reasons that are available in any area of thought and action and in responding effectively to the demands of those reasons. It will involve the exercise of the capacity of orthonomy, an achievement that may itself be described as becoming orthonomous. The ideal of orthonomy is distinct from that of 'autonomy' in the literal sense of that word — the sense in which the self rather than the right is supposed to rule — but it is closely connected with the Kantian line of thought that lies in the background of many discussions of autonomy.

Freedom as non-domination

The idea of freedom as non-domination continues to intrigue and engage me, for two reasons. First, I think that it is philosophically very rich, especially in comparison with rival approaches to freedom. And secondly, I think it has a raft of congenial implications for practical politics; more on this later.

While it is intuitively fine for human beings to influence one another by co-reasoning, it is objectionable for them to seek control by means that undermine co-reasoning. Domination is defined as control of this alienating kind. Dominating control may be enjoyed, not just when the controller practices hostile coercion or force; it is also available in a virtual way when the controller has access to hostile interventions, however unlikely he or she may be to intervene. Whatever the controlled agent does in such a case will be done only so far as the controller allows it: only by the controller's leave, only *cum permissu*, as republicans would have put it. Thus freedom as non-domination requires protection against the possibility of hostile intervention: protection against others having access to such interference in one's life. It requires more than just the absence of such interference, which might come about by sheer luck, and more than not just a reduction in the probability of interference; such a reduction might come about while the controller retains access to interfering options, as when the victim is wily or charming or servile enough to win favor.

Does freedom as non-domination require protection against all coercive and forceful interference? No: not against the interference of those agents who are themselves virtually controlled by the person who is subject to the interference, as in the case of Ulysses. Whatever the interferer does in this sort of case will be done with the permission of the controlled. As there can be dominating control without interference, then, so there can be interference without dominating control. The conception of freedom as non-domination comes apart in two important ways from the rival interpretation of freedom as non-interference. More on the significance of this rupture below.

Normative ideals

Because human beings may reason with one another, eschewing resort to dominating forms of control, there is a natural ideal available for the conduct of human life. This is associated with the practice of relating to one another under limits, imposed from without or within, that sideline the possibility of dominating control. In such a practice of mutual interaction persons will enjoy respect at one another's hands, in the intuitive sense in which respect goes with giving and taking reasons: being on speaking terms. They will command this respect as a matter of effective right, not enjoy it just by the grace or gift of others—if indeed that were possible. And they will typically command it as a matter of common awareness, with each person being conscious of the resources they each have, and conscious that each shares in this consciousness. In the regime envisaged, each person will be able to walk tall, look others in the eye, and make overtures of trust and love at will, not under any sort of duress.

This normative ideal is inscribed in the very co-reasoning practices that distinguish human beings from other species, to echo a theme from Jürgen Habermas, and it has an ethical and a political side. Ethically, it argues for fidelity to the norms of respect, at least in the absence of those perverse circumstances that might make fidelity counter-productive. In insisting on that proviso, I display my consequentialist commitments. Although I cannot defend the approach here, I am one of those who thinks that at the ultimate level of justification, the important thing is be able to show that one's behavior serves to promote the good, as that good can be understood by all. The norms of respect represent the guidelines that must be generally followed if people are each to enjoy the good of respect but those norms are only binding in circumstances where following them is truly productive of that good. When the would-be murderer asks after the whereabouts of a potential victim, there is no doubt as to which course of action is likely to promote the enjoyment of respect overall and no doubt about how you ought to behave. Here the red lights go on and the very value of respect argues for suspending ordinary fidelity to the norms of respect.

There is a political as well as an ethical ideal associated with co-reasoning practices, however, and this underlines the political significance of freedom as non-domination. We might fully respect one another, in the sense of relating under the give and take of reasons, living on speaker terms, yet not do anything for those who are poor and needy and unable, because of their dependency, to command respect. As a consequentialist I believe that we ought to do something about this but I don't think that there is a lot that we can do individually. We may each help out the poor and needy but the fact that they depend on us for such grace means that they do not command our respect and do not truly enjoy freedom as non-domination. The only way in which the problem can be put right is by the sort of collective provision that the state is uniquely positioned to supply. Hence I see a case here for the sort of state that would empower and protect the weakest as part of a project for facilitating practices of co-reasoning and promoting freedom as non-domination.

The problem with which this leaves us, however, is the oldest problem in republican philosophy. *Quis custodiet ipsos custodies?* Who will guard us against our guardians? The problem is to devise institutions such that it becomes plausible that while the republican state promotes freedom from domination amongst its citizens, guarding each against others, it does not itself perpetrate such domination. I will return to this problem below.

Groups as persons

Given the functional or performative conception of a person as a conversable subject – an agent who can participate in the give and take of reasons – it becomes possible to represent certain group agents as persons. The point was emphasized by Hobbes, drawing as he did on medieval traditions of legal thought. Suppose that a number of people embrace certain common purposes and a method for revising those purposes; endorse certain common judgments on how to pursue those goals, and a method for updating those judgments; and organize to have whatever actions are required for the satisfaction of the purposes, according to the judgments. And suppose, moreover, that the group does all of this via practices of reasoning, both within its own ranks and in explaining itself, committing itself, and justifying itself to others. Such an incorporated group will constitute a person, according to the functional criterion, having all the capacities associated with conversability and orthonomy.

But will the group be a person that is truly distinct from its members? Will it be more that a *persona ficta*, a fictional person, in the medieval usage? Or will the recognition of group persons be quite consistent with 'singularism': the doctrine, as I think of it, that there are only individual persons, no persons of a collective sort? Many people have argued that group persons are fictional, and singularism is basically sound, on the grounds that the attitudes they endorse – their purposes and judgments and so on – are just constructs, usually majoritarian constructs, from the corresponding attitudes among members, among elites, or in a sovereign dictator.

As I reject atomism, so I reject singularism; and all of this, within a broadly individualist frame. The reason for doing so derives ultimately from a puzzle that I called 'the discursive dilemma' in my 2001 book, *A Theory of Freedom*; this is a generalization, as I showed there, of 'the doctrinal paradox' in the reasoning of collegial courts. The dilemma shows that if a group tries to organize its attitudes, say its judgments, on the basis of the majority views of its ordinary or elite members, as non-dictatorial groups are generally assumed to do, then it will almost certainly fail as an agent; it will end up with inconsistent judgments on matters where its purposes require it to form opinions.

The point can be illustrated with a group of just three people, A, B and C, trying to make majority judgments on three propositions, 'p', 'q' and '$p\&q$'. A and B may vote for 'p', B and C for 'q', in which case the group will believe that p and that q. But if the group also forms its view on whether $p\&q$ by majority vote, then it will judge, inconsistently, that $not\text{-}p\&q$. A and C will vote against '$p\&q$': A because of rejecting 'q', C because of rejecting 'p'. If the group is to do its business satisfactorily, then, it will have to agree to hold by a set of views, say that p, that q and that $p\&q$, where one element in that set is rejected by a majority of members. Given that any plausible group agent is going to confront discursive dilemmas over time, as it builds up its body of attitudes, it follows that no satisfactory, non-dictatorial group agent is going to have attitudes that are just majoritarian constructs from the attitudes of members.

This point is deepened and strengthened by an impossibility result that Christian List and I proved in 2002, and that has been followed by a spate of similar theorems. What these show, in one formulation, is that if over time a group confronts a set of logically connected issues on which to form judgments, as any group agent will; if it forms its judgments on the basis of the views of more than one member; and if it succeeds in maintaining consistency, then its views cannot be a function, majoritarian or otherwise, of the corresponding views among its membership. Intuitively, it will have to constitute an agent with a distinct, novel set of attitudes. The group will have to have a mind of its own.

This result, which is as demonstrable as anything in philosophy, raises a host of interesting questions and possibilities, and I am trying to come to terms with these in my current work, including a joint project of work with Christian List. It need not imply that group persons deserve respect, except so far as this is required by respect for its members. But it does imply, I believe, that they can and should be held responsible for what they do as corporate entities; this is defended in a recent paper on 'Responsibility Incorporated' in *Ethics*. Corporate responsibility of this kind complements the individual responsibility of corporate agents and is essential for avoiding the responsibility deficit that occurs when the individuals all have excuses that mitigate the degree to which they are personally subject to blame.

The approach raises a host of interpretive and normative questions in politics. How far can any unincorporated group – the founders or the people or, by some accounts, the legislators – be ascribed common intentions or other attitudes; how far can it prove interpretable or contestable? And how far, say on grounds of being made interpretable and contestable, should various political and legal bodies be required to incorporate in such a manner? These questions connect with issues that are currently at the foreground of political theory. One is Ronald Dworkin's question as to the status of integrity as an interpretive principle in the law. Another is the issue highlighted in John Rawls's work on the law of peoples as to how far well-ordered states can be seen as representing peoples, and as deserving of mutual respect in an international community that resembles a community of persons. And yet another set of issues, related to republican concerns, bears on how far domination becomes a more threatening prospect, both for individuals and for groups, in the presence of powerful group agents: powerful states, multinational corporations, and international religious and other networks.

What is the proper role of political philosophy in relation to real, political action? Can there ever be a fruitful relation between political philosophy and political practice?

My own personal experience in political action is limited. Apart from my involvement as a young lecturer in the student revolution of the late 1960's, I have had two other direct engagements with politics. One was in 1998, when I headed a small committee that reported, ten years after its establishment, on how the system of self-government in the Australian Capital Territory was working. I had full access to those in parliament and the bureaucracy while pursuing this review and learned enormously from the experience. The other engagement with politics is more recent, and more indirect. It springs from the commitment made by the Spanish President, Jose Luis Rodriguez Zapatero, to following the principles in my book 'Republicanism'. Mr. Zapatero invited me to give a public lecture on republicanism in Madrid, soon after his 2004 election, and in his response he invited me publicly to review his government, shortly before the next election, on how far it has measured up to those principles. This has kept me in touch with Spain and I have had one extended meeting with Mr. Zapatero, discussing his performance in government.

These two experiences have convinced me that if a political philosophy can be presented in a unified, vivid manner, and in such a way that the main implications are clear, then it can serve well in public forums. My own distillation of republicanism involves presenting it as a philosophy that has a radical policy agenda, directing government to promote freedom as non-domination, but a restrictive constitutional message, insisting that government should be curtailed and challenged in such a manner that it itself is not dominating. The constitutional message, as I argued in my book, supports an approach under which government is not only democratically elected, and restricted by the rule of law, the separation of powers, and a provision for basic rights, but is also exposed to contestation, formal and informal, at the hands of an elected opposition, statutory oversight bodies, an independent media, and effective civic movements.

I argued on the basis of this approach for a variety of reforms in ACT government, many of which were adopted. And, very strikingly, Mr. Zapatero has been assiduous in seeking to push a republican or 'civicist' agenda, and to gain an understanding for this agenda among citizens. On the constitutional front, he has been prepared to distribute power away from Madrid to the regions, as in the new Catalan constitution, and he has taken a principled stance on making the national broadcaster independent of government influence, on the model of the BBC. On the policy front, he has taken serious steps to guard against what he himself sees as the domination of women, introducing domestic abuse legislation and measures for increasing the presence of women in politics and business; he has introduced legislation giving homosexual couples the right to marry and to enjoy the symbolic and other privileges of that institution; and he is promoting a law of dependency that would increase welfare rights, in particular for those who are disabled, and for those who may have to provide home help for the disabled or otherwise dependent.

The republican philosophy with which I identify appeals on a number of fronts. One is that it has a solid and indeed engaging philosophical core, in the notion of freedom as non-domination. A second is that it is not a novel creation of mine or anyone else's but a long and well-tested tradition, albeit a tradition that has gone underground in the past century or more. And a third relates precisely to the capacity it has to bring into a single, eye-catching package the sorts of policy and constitutional proposals at which I have been gesturing. I belong on the left and republican theory appeals to me for the fact that it makes it possible to present left policies, not as the hodge podge that they sometimes appear to be, but as expressions of a coherent, unified vision.

What do you consider the most neglected topics and/or contributions in post-Rawlsian or late 20th century political philosophy?

Let me mention three topics on which I would love to see more work. The first is in the political philosophy of criminal justice, where discussion has often been limited to discussions of retributivist versus utilitarian conceptions of punishment. The way in which criminals are treated in most democratic societies today is barbarous, reflecting what Montesquieu called the tyranny of the avengers. This trend has worsened over the past few decades, as politicians have learned that it makes good politics to use every occasion of outrageous crime as an opportunity for demanding ever more stringent responses. Political philosophers need to spend much more energy on questions in the area of criminal justice, exploring the myriad questions to do with what should be criminalized, how crime should be monitored and investigated, how charges should be brought and adjudicated, and what sorts of responses should be explored for dealing with convicted offenders. There are now many social movements, such as the restorative justice movement, that are actively exploring alternative approaches but they receive little or no support from work among political philosophers.

A second area that I would like to see at the center of philosophical concern bears on institutional design, as it is sometimes called. Many of the classic texts in political theory, from Machiavelli's *Discourses* to Montesquieu's *Spirit of the Laws*, to Mill's *Considerations on Representative Government* deal with how institutions should be ordered in the real world of parochial bias, limited resources, and institutional and psychological pathology. I think it is little short of scandalous that this area of work is hardly ever emulated by political philosophers today. As criminal justice is left to the lawyers and criminologists, so institutional design is left to regulatory theorists and economists. Philosophers are happy to talk about democracy, for example, without ever exploring the rival merits of the Washington versus the Westminster system.

A third area where I would like to see more philosophical work connects with these laments about the neglect of criminal justice and institutional design. The theory of the second best is largely ignored in political philosophy, being left again to economists and political psychologists. This is the theory as to how things should be organized, not under idealizing assumptions of full compliance, but also under assumptions of only partial compliance and, more generally, under assumptions of imperfections on all sides. I see my 2004 book with Geoffrey Brennan on *The Economy of Esteem* as a venture into this field. The idea there is to see how far institutions may be organized so that even if people's virtue fails in some measure, their presumptive concern with enjoying the esteem of their fellows, and avoiding their disesteem, may keep them on the straight and narrow.

10. Philip Pettit

What are the most important unsolved questions in political philosophy and/or related disciplines and what are the prospects for progress?

The jazz musician, Humphrey Lyttleton, was once asked where he thought jazz was going and his reply, so it is reported, was: "If I knew where jazz was going, I'd be there already". To be important yet unsolved, I assume that a question has to look likely to yield to inquiry and research. And most of us who identify such questions in our field are likely to want to work on them; we will want to be there already.

That said, I hope it won't appear to be self-serving if I say that from my own perspective the most pressing problems arrange themselves around the topics of my current concern. The complex of issues that I am currently focused on in political philosophy connects both with the republican project, as I think of it, and with the analysis of group agency and belongs, broadly, in the theory of democracy. Here is a set of questions on which I would love to see my way more clearly than I currently do.

Democracy involves the idea of popular control. But control requires a controller, levers of control, and a control target. What is the democratic controller? What, in other words, is the people? A mere aggregate, no more unified that those who live on earth at the same latitude? Or a corporate agent, akin to Hobbes's 'company of merchants'? Or something in between, if indeed there is something in between? What are the democratic levers of control? The inputs to electoral process? The inputs of popular protest and demonstration? Or also inputs of a less popular kind, such as the constraints imposed by a constitution, the restrictions supported by statutory oversight bodies, the decisions of the courts? And what is the target of the control process that democracy is supposed to implement? The realization of the people's will, whatever that is? Conformity to the people's opinion, if that represents something more tangible? The satisfaction, so far as possible, of people's preferences? Or conformity to those public reasons that the people recognize as relevant considerations in collective decision-making, however differently they weight them?

These are the broad questions in political philosophy with which I am currently struggling. I dwell on them, think I make a little progress, get stalled and migrate temporarily to questions in some other area of philosophy. When I come back and try again, I may find a little more traction, but in the normal event I will bog down once more. And so the rondo goes on in a shuttle pattern to which

I have worked all of my career. I hope I may make progress and contribute to the conversation in which we each play only a small and very temporary part. But, much more importantly, I hope that sooner or later, in whatever corner of debate, the conversation will generate the image of democracy that I seek. This image would rescue democracy from the cynicism of those who reduce it to a purely electoral ideal and from the romanticism of those who cast it as an impossible ideal of relentless participation and debate.

Selected publications

Not Just Deserts: A Republican Theory of Criminal Justice, with John Braithwaite, Oxford University Press, 1990, pp. viii and 228. Pb 1992.

The Common Mind: An Essay on Psychology, Society and Politics, Oxford University Press, New York, 1993, pp. xvi and 365. Second, paperback edition, with new chapter, 1996, pp. xvi and 381.

Republicanism: A Theory of Freedom and Government Oxford University Press, Oxford, 1997, pp..x and 304.Paperback edition, with new postscript, 1999.

Three Methods of Ethics: A Debate, with Marcia Baron and Michael Slote, Oxford: Blackwell, 1997, pp.vi and 285.

A Theory of Freedom: From the Psychology to the Politics of Agency Polity Press, Cambridge and Oxford University Press, New York, 2001, pp 193.

Rules, Reasons, and Norms: Selected Essays Oxford University Press, Oxford, 2002

Frank Jackson, Philip Pettit and Michael Smith *Mind, Morality, and Explanation: Selected Collaborations* Oxford University Press, Oxford, 2004, pp xii and 427. (Reprints sixteen of my co-authored pieces.)

Geoffrey Brennan and Philip Pettit *The Economy of Esteem: An Essay on Civil and Political Society*, Oxford, Oxford University Press, 2004, pp. xii and 339. Included in Oxford Online Scholarship 2004. Paperback 2006.

Penser en Societe: Essais de Metaphysique Sociale et de Methodologie, P.U.F., Paris, 2004, vi and 184. A selection and translation, with a new introduction, of five papers on social metaphysics and methodology.

Made with Words: Hobbes on Language, Mind and Politics, Princeton, Princeton University Press, 2007.

Joining the Dots, in Michael Smith, H.G.Brennan, R.E.Goodin and F.C.Jackson, eds, *Common Minds: Themes from the Philosophy of Philip Pettit,* Oxford, Oxford Unviersity Press, 2007, pp 215-344. A monograph-length statement of my overall views, organized around responses to other papers in the volume.

11
John E. Roemer

Elizabeth S. and A. Varick Stout Professor
of Political Science and Economics
Yale University, New Haven, USA

Zig-zagging toward political philosophy

As a freshman at Harvard in 1962, I took the first and last philosophy course of my career, a general education course in the great ideas of philosophy. It became the last course due to an argument I had with my section leader about Zeno's paradox. He (and, I believe, the professor of the course, whose identity I have forgotten) maintained that, despite modern mathematics, the paradox remained: I contended that anyone who understood infinite series would conclude that no paradox existed. I received a low mark on my paper which argued this position, and, disgusted with the innumeracy of philosophers, never entered Emerson Hall again, until, many years later, I visited John Rawls there. I majored in mathematics, and indeed, to my later regret, took only the necessary minimum of courses outside of mathematics.

I entered graduate school in mathematics at Berkeley in the fall of 1966, where I chose to attend in part because of its political activism (the Free Speech Movement had culminated in 1964). My parents were socialist intellectuals, and I had considered myself a socialist since adolescence, or before. (I remember thinking, as a child, that the good guys were the workers, the [Brooklyn] Dodgers, and the Democrats, and the bad guys were the bosses, the Yankees and the Republicans.) During the 1950s, our family lived abroad for five years, because of McCarthyist persecution of my parents; socialism was one of the most important themes in our family life. Although, as an undergraduate, I was not politically active, I was very much involved in intellectual discussions of socialism and imperialism, and had decided to become active in the anti-Vietnam War movement at Berkeley.

After two quarters of studying graduate mathematics at Berkeley, the contradictions in my personal life came to a head: I was spending as much time as possible in anti-war activity, but not as much as I wanted to spend, because of the demanding mathematics curriculum. Furthermore, I could not come to terms with continuing to do abstract mathematics as a career, when the world was aflame. I wanted, however, to remain an intellectual. Transferring to economics seemed an obvious move—for there I could use my mathematical training and work on politically important questions. My application to economics was quickly accepted: at that time, students with mathematical talent were at a premium in economics.

Indeed, the economics Ph.D. program took much less of my time than mathematics had taken; a mathematically sophisticated student could more or less sail through the graduate program at Berkeley in the late 1960s, without (unfortunately) learning much economics, and that is what I did. In my fourth quarter of graduate work in economics (October 1968), there was a student uprising at Berkeley, centered around our accusations of administrative racism. (The details involved struggles for a Black Studies program, and the relationship of the university to the struggle of the Black Panthers in Oakland, among other things.) I, and some 70 others, were arrested for occupying a university administration building. (We eventually spent two weeks in the county jail and paid 'restitution' for the damage the police did when they trashed the building during the process of arresting us.) At the campus faculty-student hearings to which we were subjected, those who behaved abjectly and admitted their behavior had been wrong were put on university probation. Those, however, who said that the occupation of the building had been a legitimate tactic in protest of the university's role in US imperialism were suspended. Being among the latter, I was suspended from school for a year. It may be of note that the philosopher John Searle was the vice-chancellor at Berkeley in charge of student discipline during this period; he had an intransigent attitude toward student protest. Consequently, I lost my student deferment from the draft, and so to avoid being drafted and sent to Vietnam, I took a job teaching mathematics in the San Francisco secondary schools; math and science teachers, being at a premium, were deferred from the draft. I taught junior-high and high-school mathematics for five years in San Francisco. During this period, I became involved in struggles around racism in the schools (my first assignment was to Pelton Junior High School, which served the Hunters' Point ghetto in San Francisco, and whose student body was at least 90% black).

With other liberal and left-wing teachers, we took our struggle to the teachers' union (AFT), building a Teachers' Action Caucus, which challenged the leadership to make student concerns, and racism in particular, a more central focus of the union's program. In 1973, I decided to try to return to academia. A small, *gauchiste* political party to which I belonged had concluded that, with the winding down of the Vietnam war, the next major international struggle would be inter-imperialist rivalry between Japan, the up- and- coming power, and the United States. I had completed my graduate course work before my expulsion at Berkeley; the economics department generously allowed me to continue where I had left off, and to write a dissertation on US-Japanese competition in international markets and investment, a theme inspired by Lenin's *Imperialism: The highest stage of capitalism.*

There were no courses in Marxist economics in the major American universities in those days; what I knew of the subject came from reading the classics, and modern Marxists such as Paul Baran, Paul Sweezy, Harry Magdoff, and Harry Braverman. There was one Marxist on the Berkeley economics faculty, Richard Roehl, an economic historian. He consented to be my advisor, although my topic was far from his interests. (Richard was subsequently denied tenure at Berkeley.) During my period of course work, I had taken courses in mathematical economics, planning, and economic theory. I knew nothing about international trade, the area in which I had chosen to write.

Consequently, my dissertation was naïve—a piece of statistical journalism. I put forth a theory of how capitalist economies pass through four stages; according to it, Japan was in the (rising) second stage, and the United States was entering the (declining) fourth stage. But the theory was not explicated with the sophistication that modern economic theory requires, nor was it tested with the sophistication of modern econometrics. It was neither fish nor fowl.

The defense of the thesis turned into an argument between two members of the examining committee: Jagdish Bagwhati, who maintained that it was sub-par, more or less for the reasons I have given, and Benjamin Ward, an iconoclastic senior member of the faculty, who praised its boldness. Ward was dissatisfied in a major way with the turn that economics was taking in the United States, and saw me as a dissident, both with regard to my interests, and to method. I was passed, thanks to Ward, and went onto the job market. Having in fact been away from school for five years (I wrote the dissertation while continuing to teach in San Francisco), I was not terribly confident, due to my own (objectively correct) estimate concerning my paltry knowledge of economics. But, once again, mathematical credentials carried me through; I was hired as an assistant professor at the University of California at Davis and began teaching there in the fall of 1974. I had no plan to try to teach a course in Marxian economics. My assignment at Davis was to teach a mathematical methods course for graduate students, and to teach undergraduate courses in intermediate theory and international trade. There were, however, two tenured faculty, Richard Cornwall and Ross Starr, who were microtheorists, and encouraged me to try to apply economic theory to Marxian economics. Michio Morishima, a respected micro-theorist, had recently published a book entitled *Marx's Economics,* in which he presented the ideas of a school of Japanese Marxist economists that had been, for some years, applying techniques of linear algebra and input-output analysis to Marx's economic ideas. I spent the summer of 1975 studying Morishima's book, was very much taken with it, and taught a graduate seminar the next year on the topic. It was this suggestion of Cornwall and Starr that reoriented my path, and helped me to align my political interests with my mathematical background, something that I had been struggling to do since 1966.

I began working on Marxian economics in earnest. Morishima's work eschewed general equilibrium theory, the topic in mathematical economics that I considered to be the most beautiful one. I had learned general equilibrium at Berkeley from the master, Gérard Debreu. I naturally thought in those terms. My first efforts were not very interesting—finger exercises, more or less, that got me back into practice after so many years away from mathematical economics. (These were published in Roemer (1981).)

My next project, however, was more mature. Marx had proposed a theory of exploitation, with three historical cases: slavery, feudalism, and capitalism. The nature of exploitation varied with the specifics of property relations. Could one propose a general theory of exploitation, of which these would be special cases, and which would also include a variant of socialist exploitation? Perhaps the latter could explain, I thought, the contradictions in socialist societies.

In 1981, I completed my manuscript *A general theory of exploitation and class*, which proposed that general theory, using the concept of characteristic-form games, and the core. In standard economic theory, individual agents are endowed with skills, resources, and commodities. They engage in trade, and an equilibrium allocation of labor and commodities ensues. Such an allocation is said to be in the core of the economy if no coalition of agents could withdraw with its own endowments and arrange an allocation for itself, using the endowments of its members, that would improve the utility of all its members (over the utility they were receiving in the large economy). An important theorem states that any competitive (Walrasian) equilibrium allocation is in the core—meaning that all possibilities for gains from trade among all possible coalitions have been exhausted at a competitive equilibrium. (Conversely, for economies that are 'large,' the *only* core allocations are their competitive equilibria.) I proposed that, by varying the rules stating what assets a coalition could leave the large economy with (as a thought experiment), one could characterize different kinds of exploitation.

The neoclassical core concept characterized, in fact, *feudal* exploitation. That is, the coalition of serfs would be better off if the serfs could withdraw from feudal society with their own skills and their family plots of land. A coalition was *capitalistically exploited*, I proposed, if it could improve the welfare of all its members by withdrawing from the large economy with its skills and with its *per capita share* of the alienable assets of the entire economy. I demonstrated that, in a number of simple models, this definition was equivalent to *Marxian exploitation*: the statement that an individual is exploited (under capitalism) if the labor embodied in the bundle of commodities he can purchase with his income is less than the labor he expended in production. Finally, a coalition was *socialistically exploited* if it would be better off by withdrawing from the economy with its per capita share of alienable and inalienable assets (i.e., skills.)

The importance of this general theory was that it provided a characterization of exploitation directly in terms of a counterfactual thought experiment that altered property relations from their existing state. Marx's definition of exploitation, in terms of labor accounts, was quite indirect. Why is it so obviously bad (a state of *exploitation*) to be able only to purchase commodities embodying less labor than one had expended oneself in production? Could not this be an innocuous consequence of the complex division of labor in society? The property-relations definition that I gave highlighted exactly what the ethical problem was with a particular system: feudalism was wrong because serfs could do better with their own property than they were doing under the lords, and capitalism is bad, so Marxists say, because, morally speaking, everyone should have an equal entitlement to society's produced assets (means of production.)

The general-theory book did something else as well. It provided microfoundations for the class stratification of capitalist society. In the general-equilibrium model it proposed, every agent enters trade with certain assets—skills and property. Every agent maximizes a utility function subject to the constraint imposed by his endowment. At equilibrium, agents sort themselves into different class positions—some hire others, some only sell their labor power, some work for themselves, some hire others and work for themselves, and so on. I showed that the historical class stratification that the classical writers (Marx, Lenin, Mao) had identified, emerged in equilibrium solely from a model of optimizing agents with differential endowments who face competitive markets.

This claim gave rise to a debate among Marxists. In my model, class stratification and exploitation arose under perfect competition. Alternatively put, these phenomena would exist in a world with perfectly enforceable and complete contracts. But the phenomena summarized under the phrase 'struggle at the point of production' are ones that exist only in a world of incomplete contracts. If workers and capitalists could write complete contracts for exactly what would happen in the labor process, on the factory floor, there would be no need for foremen, strikes, speed-up—in a word, no direct and proximate oppression of workers by bosses. These phenomena are ones of an incomplete contract world. Thus, I claimed, exploitation and class were entirely the consequence of the distribution of property, and that the nasty and daily oppression of workers by bosses, so characteristic of the history of capitalism, was an epiphenomenon.

One might appreciate that this view would raise hackles among Marxists, given the prominence at the time of Harry Braverman's book, *Labor and Monopoly Capital*, which argued that the essence of capitalism was the struggle between workers and bosses over the labor process.

There is a fine point here. Marx claimed not by making any ethical judgments about capitalism. This issue was discussed exhaustively in the 1970s and 1980s in the literature. I and many others think that, despite his apologia, Marx was condemning capitalism on grounds of justice.

While working on my general theory, in 1980, I read G.A. Cohen's *Karl Marx's theory of history: A Defence*, which had been published in 1978: I was swept off my feet. Here was a magisterial attempt to put the theory of historical materialism on a rigorous foundation. Cohen had done, using analytical philosophy, what I was attempting to do, using mathematical economics: to study Marxism in a non-dogmatic way, asking which theses would survive a modern analysis. I sent Cohen several chapters of my manuscript, and he replied with enthusiasm. In the spring of 1981 I went to London, spending three months at University College with Cohen. Thus began my tutorial in political philosophy.

I had been working on the distinction between the Marxian definition of exploitation and the property-relations definition that I had proposed. I wrote above that, in some simple models, these definitions were equivalent. But there were also models where they made opposite diagnoses. Consider the case of a young, able farmer who owns 10 acres, and an old, infirm farmer who owns one acre. The young farmer works up all his own acreage, but wants to earn more, so he sells his labor power to the old farmer, who makes a small profit from his labor. The Marxian definition would say the old farmer exploits the young one, but the property-relations definition does not. Indeed, one can construct examples like this even when both individuals have the same preferences. Which concept is 'right'? I published my first philosophy paper expounding these puzzles (Roemer (1982b)). Several years later, I argued that it was not exploitation in the Marxian sense with which egalitarians should be concerned, but rather the unequal distribution of assets in capitalist society (Roemer (1985a)). Marx, I said, had located the injustice of capitalism in the unequal distribution of ownership in the means of production, but had proposed an inadequate proxy for it, with his labor accounting definition of exploitation.

Having convinced myself that the ethical interest of Marx's attack on capitalism lay not in what occurred in the labor process, but in the inequality of the distribution of the means of production, I began a more serious engagement with political philosophy and, in particular, its egalitarian variant. Ronald Dworkin's (1981 a,b) two papers on equality were squarely in my path—doubtless, I was directed to them by Jerry Cohen. In particular, Dworkin had proposed a way of conceptualizing what 'equality of resources' required. The problem is that some resources can be transferred between people at will, and some, like skills and talents, cannot. So how should one conceptualize or characterize the allocation of transferable resources that would constitute an equalization of *all* resources across persons? What allocation of transferable resources would properly compensate people, from an egalitarian standpoint, for their non-transferable resource endowments? Dworkin provided an answer with his insurance scheme behind a veil of ignorance.

Dworkin did not know the economic theory necessary to model his proposal, which is the theory of contingent claims, or the general equilibrium theory of insurance. I applied this theory to Dworkin's environment, with its thin veil of ignorance (Roemer (1985b)). The somewhat surprising result was that the Dworkinian insurance market, properly modelled, could actually *hurt* those who were poorly endowed with talents, exactly those whom it was designed to help. It could end up transferring alienable resources *from* the untalented *to* the talented—and this in a world where all individuals had the same preferences, so differential ambition (in Dworkin's sense) could not be to blame. The upshot was, that although I was sympathetic with Dworkin's aims, and his implied ethic of equalizing resources, I concluded that his particular mechanism for implementing that goal did not work. Indeed, it could do just the opposite of what was intended.

The next question was: Is there a mechanism, which would work for any given stipulation of an economic environment, for 'equalizing resources,' in the sense of recommending an allocation of transferable resources that properly compensated people for their inalienable endowments? In Roemer (1986), I argued that the only such mechanism was the one which allocates transferable resources so as to *equalize welfare*—so Dworkin's attempt to argue *against* equalizing welfare and *for* equalizing resources was incoherent. That paper is an axiomatic demonstration: it postulates a set of axioms that an allocation rule must satisfy for it to qualify as a resource-equalizing rule, and then deduces that the only rule satisfying the axioms, on a sufficiently rich domain of possible environments (or worlds) is the one that distributes alienable resources to equalize welfare. I now think those axioms are too strong; there is room for a conception of equalizing resources that is distinctive from equalizing welfare. I stand, however, by my claim that Dworkin's insurance mechanism is not the right one, for the reason given earlier: in non-pathological two-person environments, it can allocate less than half of the alienable resource to the individual with fewer internal resources. (If two individuals have identical preferences, but one is handicapped, then she should be compensated with more than half of the alienable resource, for the allocation of resources to count as equal, all things considered. But Dworkin's insurance scheme will not always do this.)

In the later 1980s, several philosophers, in particular Richard Arneson and G.A. Cohen, wrote critiques of Dworkin's theory. Arneson argued that Dworkin was correct in arguing that equality-of-welfare as an ethic was unsustainable because it ignored the issue of responsibility, but he was incorrect to move from there to an advocacy of equality of resources. The right move, said Arneson, was to advocate equality of *opportunity* for welfare. Cohen argued, similarly, that Dworkin had done a great service by bringing responsibility into the theory of egalitarianism, but he had placed the cut incorrectly, between preferences and endowments; rather, it should be placed between what one is rightly responsible for and what one is not. In particular, a person might not be responsible for her preferences, if they were induced in her during childhood, for example. Exactly what one should be held responsible for is an open question, but it generally cannot be one's preferences.

I studied Arneson's paper, and tried to provide a model of how to equalize opportunities for welfare. I concluded that the proposal he outlined was in general not feasible (see Roemer (1996, chapter 8)). So I tried to construct an algorithm which, given a conception of personal responsibility and a stated objective of human accomplishment, would find the allocation of resources that equalized opportunities for achieving that objective (Roemer (1993)). I refined the idea over the 1990s, and published a short book on the subject (Roemer (1998)).

In brief, the language of my algorithm has five words: objective, circumstance, effort, type, and policy. The objective is a concrete form of welfare or advantage. Circumstances are those aspects of a person's environment for which we deem he or she should not be held responsible. A type is the set of all persons with similar circumstances. Effort is the set of actions for which we deem the person is responsible. The policy is an intervention that allocates some resource to persons, or, more generally, influences the actions and/or outcomes of individuals (such as a tax policy). The equal-opportunity policy (if there is one) is that policy that makes it the case that the value of the objective finally achieved is a function only of one's effort, not of one's circumstances—that is, its aim is to nullify the effect of circumstances on outcomes in the society in question. Absent such a policy, the algorithm finds the policy that minimizes the effect of circumstances on outcomes, according to a certain metric.

My purpose, in proposing this algorithm, was not to solve the philosophical problem of what people should be held responsible for. The algorithm begins with any conception of responsibility, summarized in the delineation of circumstances and effort, and finds the policy that equalizes opportunities for the objective with respect to that conception. Indeed, in collaboration with others, I have carried out several applications of the algorithm: Julian Betts and I (in press) have calculated how educational finance should be allocated in the United States among secondary school students to equalize opportunities for acquiring wage-earning capacity, where the circumstances comprise the socio-economic status of the individual's parents and/or his or her race, and effort comprises the entire residual that explains outcomes. With a team of labor economists, we have calculated the extent to which income taxation, in eleven countries, equalizes opportunities for income acquisition among workers (Roemer et al, 2003). A number of other applications of the theory have been made by others (e.g., Peragine (2004), Lefranc et al (2006)). The World Development Report issued by the World Bank, entitled "Equity and Development," elaborates the theme that equality of opportunity should be taken as the metric (or at least *a* metric) for judging economic development (World Bank (2006)). See as well my comments on the Report (Roemer (2006c)).

One of the significant aspects of this theory of equal opportunity is that it is *nonwelfarist*. By welfarism, a social-choice theorist means a specific feature of a theory of justice: it is that species of theory in which justice is some function of the levels of 'welfare' achieved by society's members. (I place 'welfare' in quotes, because the proper word is really 'outcomes.') Welfarism is consequentialism: all that matters, for social evaluation, is knowledge of the pattern of outcomes. Utilitarianism is an example of a welfarist theory: so is equalization of welfare, or maximization of the minimum welfare in society. The two most notable attacks on welfarism in modern political philosophy are those of Rawls and Robert Nozick. (Rawls said that the distribution of primary goods, not welfare, is what matters for justice; Nozick said it's the procedure, not the outcome, that matters.) Dworkin's theory is also non-welfarist. The equal opportunity approach is non-welfarist:

one must know not only the outcomes, but how hard people tried – how much effort they expended – to evaluate whether a distribution of outcomes conforms to justice. One must know what the definition of circumstances – that is the typology of society – is. I believe that one of the important aspects of the equal- opportunity proposal is its formalization of a broadly held popular view. If one asks the proverbial man on the street whether a certain unequal distribution between persons is just, he might well reply, it depends on how hard they each tried. A second important aspect is that, taking even a minimal conception of what circumstances comprise, the resource allocation, in actual applications, is often far more compensatory than current policy implements. (For instance, in the Betts-Roemer calculation, we show that equalizing opportunities for wage earning capacity would require spending about four times as much per student on students whose mothers have less than a high school education, as on students whose mothers have a college education.)

My most recent work in political philosophy concerns the veil of ignorance. There are, I think, two quite precise proposals for how the veil of ignorance should be modelled, and therefore, what distribution of worldly resources that thought experiment recommends: these are due to John Harsanyi (1953) and Dworkin (1981b). (I do not include Rawls's proposal, for it is insufficiently precise and, I think, is as well an inconsistent implementation of his ideas.) Neither Harsanyi nor Dworkin, however, properly completed his proposal, something I have already indicated with respect to Dworkin. In Roemer (2002 and 2006a), I propose how to complete these two models of the veil of ignorance, and I show that, in each case, the completed models not only make inegalitarian recommendations, but are even non-prioritarian: that is, they tend to give priority in resource allocation to the talented instead of to the untalented. I indicated earlier what this means in discussing Dworkin's insurance mechanism; it turns out the same pathology afflicts the (completed) Harsanyi model.

Consequently, not only should egalitarians not attempt to base their ethics on veil of ignorance arguments: more strongly, neither should mere prioritarians. Now some might respond that the veil of ignorance is an appealing conceptualization of the ethical problem, and so one must conclude that the right ethics cannot be prioritarian. I resist this proposal, but I lack, as of now, a clear a priori argument against the veil of ignorance as a thought experiment.

In recent years, I have been concentrating less on political philosophy and more on understanding the relationship between democracy and the achievement of justice. To what extent can we expect democracy to bring about equality of opportunity, over the long term? This is not an ethical question, but a positive one. In Roemer (2006b), I ask whether competition between political parties, which represent different coalitions of citizens partitioned by income, will bring about the implementation of a regime of educational financing that will, eventually, eliminate the differences in human capital (or wage-earning capacity) associated with different family dynasties. In the model I study, children from more poorly educated families will, *ceteris paribus*, develop less human capital than other children, and the question is whether democratic politics will engender sufficiently compensatory financing of education to rectify these family effects. The answer is complicated, but in a word, there is no guarantee that this will occur, if dynasties are purely self-interested. So democracy should not be enshrined as the egalitarian's panacea.

The editors have asked us to comment on what we believe the pressing questions are in political philosophy. I cannot think much farther ahead than my next project, and so I will beg off on this question. I would not be surprised, however, if neurophysiology transforms quite radically our ideas about responsibility. I cannot believe that philosophers have already taken into account all the possibilities, the surprises which brain science has in store for us. There is a good deal of ferment today on questions of international justice; these are subtle questions and I expect progress on them in the coming period. I am deeply interested in a question of psychology: to what extent can we expect people to be liberated from material greed as a motivator and material acquisition as a goal, if markets continue to be used (as I think they must) to allocate resources? But as I advise students not to present half-baked ideas in seminar, I shall resist the temptation to do so here myself.

References

Braverman, Harry. 1973. *Labor and monopoly capital: The degradation of work in the 20th century,* New York: Monthly Review Press 13.

Cohen, G.A. 1978. *Karl Marx's theory of history:A defence,* Oxford University Press.

Dworkin, Ronald. 1981a. "What is equality? Part 1: Equality of welfare," *Philosophy & Public Affairs* 10, 185–246.

–1981b. "What is equality? Part 2: Equality of resources," *Philosophy & Public Affairs* 10, 283–345.

Harsanyi, John. 1953. "Cardinal utility in welfare economics and in the theory of risk-taking," *Journal of Political Economy* 61, 434–435.

Lefranc, Arnaud, Nicolas Pistoles, and Alain Trannoy, 2006. "Equality of opportunity: Definitions and testable conditions, with an application to income in France," Working paper.

Peragine, V. 2004. "Ranking income distributions according to equality of opportunity," *Journal of Income Inequality* 2, 11–30.

Roemer, J. 1981. *Analytical foundations of Marxian economic theory*, Cambridge University Press.

– 1982a. *A general theory of exploitation and class*, Harvard University Press.

– 1982b. "Property relations vs. surplus value in Marxian exploitation,"*Philosophy &Public Affairs* 11, 281–313.

– 1985a. "Should Marxists be interested in exploitation?" *Philosophy & Public Affairs* 14, 30–65.

–1985b "Equality of talent," Economics and Philosophy 1, 151–188.

– 1986. "Equality of resources implies equality of welfare," *Quarterly J. of Economics* 101, 751–784.

– 1993. "A pragmatic theory of responsibility for the egalitarian planner,"*Philosophy & Public Affairs* 22, 146–166.

– 1996. *Theories of distributive justice,* Harvard University Press.

– 1998. *Equality of opportunity*, Harvard University Press.

– 2002. "Egalitarianism against the veil of ignorance, " *Journal of Philosophy* 99, 167–184.

– et alia. 2003. "To what extent do fiscal systems equalize opportunities for income acquisition among citizens?" *Journal of Public Economics* 87, 539–565.

– Roemer, J. 2006a. "Impartiality, solidarity, and distributive justice," in *The egalitarian conscience: Essays in honour of G.A. Cohen*, ed., Christine Sypnowich, Oxford UP 14.

– 2006b. *Democracy, education and equality*, Cambridge University Press.

– 2006c. "Review essay: The 2006 World Development Report," *Journal of economic inequality* 4, 233–244.

World Bank, 2005. *World Development Report: Equity and development*, Oxford University Press.

12

George Sher

Herbert S. Autrey Professor of Philosophy
Rice University, USA

Why were you initially drawn to political philosophy?

My interest in political philosophy began as a visceral reaction to the relatively insignificant policy of Affirmative Action. I am the first-generation son of immigrant parents, refugees from Hitler and his minions, and from my parents I inherited an abiding belief in the value and virtue of hard work. From them I inherited, too, an enduring admiration for an America in which the rules are the same for everyone and success is a relatively straightforward function of effort plus talent. I still have these attitudes—as much as anything, they define me. Given my meritarian leanings, I naturally found Affirmative Action repugnant, and my first foray into political philosophy – I had previously worked in action theory and the philosophy of mind – was an attempt to explain why.

Although the issue seemed simple at first, it didn't stay that way for long. As I tried to make clear the basis for my opposition to (what was then called) reverse discrimination, questions emerged, divided, ramified, and divided again. From my initial concern with the claims of the best-qualified and of the victims of injustice, I soon graduated to broader questions about the nature and grounds of desert and the scope and rationale of compensatory justice. These in turn gave rise to even broader questions about the role of time and personhood and responsibility in our moral thought and the role of the state in structuring and regulating our lives—questions that will without doubt occupy me for the rest of my life. This illustrates, I think, how much political philosophy (and, indeed, just philosophy) is all of a piece. It doesn't matter much where you begin—any trail, conscientiously followed, will eventually take you down into the same depths.

An interesting thing happened as I was writing that first essay: as I burrowed deeper into the issues, I found myself compelled by the force of the arguments to change my position. From an outright opponent of Affirmative Action, I moved to being a hedged and reluctant defender. The essay was well received and has been widely reprinted, and I remain convinced that it owes much of its appeal to the intellectual tension that marked its beginning. Although I've tried to remain as open to competing intellectual forces as I'm proud of having been at that early stage, I've never again had the experience of having to abandon a position to which I was viscerally committed. I'm honestly not sure whether this is because I used up all my candor back in 1973, whether it's because I've steered away from the issues that matter too much to me to talk about (I do that in class sometimes), or whether the more foundational issues to which I've increasingly gravitated are less emotionally pressing.

What do you consider your own most important contribution(s) to political philosophy, and why?

I view myself as having made three main contributions to political philosophy, the first of which was to (help to) restore to philosophical respectability the important notion of desert. When I began writing my book on that topic, the idea that the way an individual ought to fare can be straightforwardly determined by his own behavior or character was in eclipse. Where goods such as wealth, opportunity, and positions were concerned, the prevailing paradigm was Rawlsian: justice and injustice are properties of large-scale sets of social institutions, and what any individual can lay claim to is simply a function of what the rules of those institutions dictate and what they lead him reasonably to expect. The achievement of *Desert* (1987), as I see it, was to reinsert the individual himself back into this picture by showing, for an important range of specific goods and bads, how his own acts and traits can directly determine the ways he ought to be treated and the things he ought (or ought not) to have. Some have found the book unsatisfying because it does not show desert to be either a strongly unified normative notion or a notion that ought to play a central role in shaping of our social and economic institutions. These implications, and especially the second, bother me too sometimes. However, on balance, I'm quite satisfied with the fact that mine is the comprehensive account beyond which anyone who seeks greater unification, or who wishes to assign desert a more central role in guiding the design of social institutions, must go.

The second contribution that I think is worth mentioning is more diffuse: it is the creation of a body of work on a range of "applied" issues that includes, but is not exhausted by, compensatory justice, diversity in the education and the workplace, role morality, nuclear deterrence, subsidized abortion, moral compromise, and punishment. Such topical issues often elicit sloppy and emotional thinking, and one of the good things that philosophy has done in recent years has been to show that they can be also approached in a more orderly and rigorous manner. Although applied philosophy can all too easily degenerate into political apologetics, it is, at its best, a vehicle for exposing hidden normative premises, revealing new argumentative strategies, and in general illuminating dark and chaotic sectors of the intellectual terrain. I hope I am among those whose work has provided this form of illumination.

My third and most recent contribution to political philosophy is to explore, in clearer and more systematic manner than had yet been done, the merits and defects of the familiar thesis that it is inappropriate for governments to take a position on the question of what constitutes a good life. That thesis had for some time been influential in liberal thought – Ronald Dworkin once referred to it as the "nerve" of liberalism – but there was little consensus either about its exact content or about the best way to defend it. In my book *Beyond Neutrality: Perfectionism and Politics* (1997), I clarified the interpretive possibilities along a number of crucial dimensions, laid out the most important ways of defending the thesis, and worked systematically through the resulting defenses, arguing against each. I also defended a positive theory of perfectionism that I took to be worthy of promotion by the state. This is one of a very small number of theories that actually seek to explain why (instead of simply declaring that) certain traits and forms of activity are good just in themselves, and I view it as a significant contribution in its own right. Unfortunately, the theory is buried near the end of the book, and so has received far less attention than the book's more critical sections.

Beyond Neutrality took a long time to write. When I began, the thesis that the state should be neutral toward different conceptions of the good was in the ascendent, while by the time I was finished, it was already beleaguered. Thus, I certainly can't take credit for bringing the thesis down, though I can perhaps take credit for delivering the *coup de grace* (if the thesis is in fact dead).

12. George Sher

What is the proper role of political philosophy in relation to real, political action? Can there ever be a fruitful relation between political philosophy and political practice?

There are several questions here, the easiest question of which is whether political philosophy should answer to ideology or to truth. The right response is, of course, is that it should answer to truth. (I think, in fact, that there is a truth of the matter – or, if the phrase sounds more soothing, a right answer – about questions of justice, political legitimacy, and the like, but what I'm saying here doesn't depend on that. If instead some version of noncognitivism or relativism is true, then it will itself be part of the truth to which political philosophy should answer.) This point would hardly be worth making if so many in the academy – including, disgracefully, many in philosophy departments – did not see it as their mission to convert students to their own political views and agendas. Although persons of this stripe often insist that they are only trying to inculcate the beliefs that *are* true, the quality of their allegiance to truth is called into question by the rigidity of their convictions. As a test for whether someone is committed to truth in the right sort of way, I propose this question: Is it more than logically possible that he could change his mind?

A very different question about theory and practice is whether work in political philosophy can play a useful role in guiding the decisions of (e.g.) voters, legislators, or the body politic. As my previous remark about illuminating dark sectors of the intellectual terrain may suggest, my answer here is again "yes." However, that answer must be tempered by the recognition that just as few political decision-makers are trained philosophers, so have few philosophers come closer than the voting booth to the pressures and constraints of actual politics. Because the academy is quite sheltered, and also because many philosophers (myself included, I'm afraid) are not eager to dirty their hands with empirical data, the fit between theory and practice is bound to remain imperfect. However, even an imperfect fit seems far better than no fit at all.

The last theory/practice question I'll mention is how the political philosopher should think of his own contribution to political life. The reason there's a question here is that the effect of what any given theorist says on what actually goes on in politics is hopelessly murky. With rare exceptions, scholarly books and articles are read mainly by other scholars who at most react to them by modifying the ideas in their own books or articles. These books and articles are then read mainly by yet other scholars, who in their turn react by modifying the ideas in yet further books and articles. This busy world of scholarly influence is hardly sealed off from the popular consciousness – its ideas are constantly bubbling to the surface – but they usually work their way up as broad tendencies of thought rather than as the discernible products of discrete individuals. Viewed abstractly, this model of highly mediated influence seems quite respectable; but viewed more personally, the idea of affecting the world only as a member of the theorizing beehive – or, to vary the simile, only as a contributor to the great mulch-pile – can be a bit deflating.

What do you consider the most neglected topics and/or contributions in post-Rawlsian or late 20th century political philosophy?

I think political philosophers have done a pretty comprehensive job of exploring the main normative and conceptual issues that arise in connection with existing social practices and institutions. Indeed, in some areas, the coverage has been overinclusive: the demand for professional ethicists has spawned a breed of professional head-scratchers for whom *everything* is morally problematic. What philosophers have done less well, however, is to recognize large-scale social changes that compel us to rethink our familiar practices, structures, and moral categories. (One notable exception is Samuel Scheffler, whose illuminating essay "Responsibility in a Global Age" (*Social Philosophy and Policy* 12 (1995): 219–36) calls attention to a mismatch between our traditional concept of responsibility, which is tailored to a world in which the effects of people's actions are local, relatively small-scale, and comparatively easy to discern, and a modern world in which most significant occurrences are the indirect and composite results of many different actions performed by many different individuals occupying many different social roles.) Two very important tendencies whose impact has not been sufficiently appreciated are, first, the changes in human life and thought that have resulted from recent technological developments and, second, the increasingly dangerous fragmentation of the international order.

The importance of technological change is that it alters aspects of human life that give rise to the problems that politics seeks to solve. Our political structures take the form that they do because our lives have certain general features—because we experience the world in characteristic ways, form relationships marked by characteristic structures, share a common range of aims, aspirations, and fears, and engage in standard forms of practical and theoretical reasoning. Thus, if the cumulative effect of our technologies in these areas is great enough, it is bound to have a significant impact on the sorts of political structures that are possible and desirable.

And, in fact, technology's impact on these aspects of our lives is quite pervasive. Here are a few examples, chosen more or less at random. Human interactions from courtship to commerce are now marked far less than they used to be by physical interaction, with all of its subtle cues, and far more by electronically mediated meetings of minds; the constantly accelerating pace of innovation confounds the formation of stable expectations, and the confidence they bring, by rendering our ability to envision even the near-term future increasingly uncertain; information (and misinformation) is becoming both more and more easily available and more and more fragmented, modular, and unintegrated, with uncertain effects on both thought in general and political discourse in particular. These effects, and many others like them, are surely altering the ways in which we understand and communicate with each other, the sorts of collective deliberation and planning of which we are capable, the things that we aspire to and enjoy, and the conditions under which we can flourish. Just how all this affects either the problems of political philosophy or the resources available for solving them is a question that analytic philosophers have hardly raised. (Philosophers working in the continental tradition, influenced by Heidegger, have been more attuned to the importance of technology, but their methods and approach are so much not mine that I have not gotten much that I found useful from them.)

The other important tendency that I want to mention – the fact that many of the most important problems of governance, broadly construed, transcend national boundaries – is in one respect not underdiscussed at all. That all nations comprise a "global village," that the world's economy is becoming increasingly integrated, and that environmental degradation and terrorism are common threats, are all clichés. Unfortunately, our general awareness of these facts has yielded little constructive thinking about the sorts of political structures that might be appropriate to their management. The models currently at our disposal are pretty clearly inadequate. The traditional Hobbesean world of independent self-interested states is the problem rather than the solution. Regional confederations, to be effective, would have to centralize decision-making power to a degree that conflicts with the democratic principle of self-government and, if the European Union is any guide, would threaten to smother much that is distinctive and good in the traditions of their member nations under vast layers of bureaucracy. A world government, if conceived as a kind of souped-up United Nations with full legislative and executive power, would have each of these vices to a far greater degree. In addition, any global political unit would have to be composed of member states a distressing proportion of whose current governments are thugocracies and many of whose populations harbor long-standing hostilities and (real and imagined) grievances toward one another. Given the magnitude of these problems, the task of envisioning – and *a fortiori* of seeing how to implement – an effective set of supranational political arrangements may simply be beyond our capacities. It is therefore not surprising that philosophers with an interest in global affairs have tended to concentrate on more manageable problems such as distributive justice between the world's rich and poor, secession, citizenship, and just war theory. However, as understandable as it is, the absence of high-level theoretical work on trans-national governance remains a major (and highly regrettable) gap in the current literature.

What are the most important unsolved questions in political philosophy and/or related disciplines and what are the prospects for progress?

Before I can address the question, What are the most important unsolved questions of political philosophy?, I must say something about how I view philosophy's aim. Although I do think there is a truth of the matter about many normative and metaethical questions, I take philosophy to be less concerned with the bald assertion of true propositions than with uncovering the reasons for believing what is true at as deep a level as possible. Because there are good reasons on both sides of most disputes, those who engage in philosophical inquiry cannot reasonably aspire to anything resembling deductive proof. Instead, they must content themselves with persuasively marshalling the considerations that support the positions they favor and that pose problems for their competitors. There's certainly progress in philosophy, but it generally takes the form of a clearer or more comprehensive appreciation of what can be said for and against various positions and what accepting them would commit us to. Although such progress sometimes does lead to a position's being abandoned – witness the verifiability theory of meaning and analytical behaviorism – the more usual effect is the continuation of the dispute at a different level.

Because I see political philosophy this way, I think very few of its problems have definitively been solved. Thus, I take the question of which unsolved problems are most important to be just about equivalent to the question of which problems *are* most important. Here are a few candidates, as measured by the urgency of the practical problems from which they arise.

As we all know, a distressingly large proportion of the world's population lives in conditions of appalling poverty, and even in the affluent United States, there are vast disparities between the rich and the poor. Because each person's life prospects are greatly influenced by factors over which he lacks control (the wealth or poverty of his parents, the quality and amount of education he receives, the economic opportunities available in his society, and so on), many of the inequalities among members of the same societies, and virtually all inequalities among members of different societies, are undeserved. Although there is wide agreement that much inequality is unjust, there is far less agreement about what distributive justice does require. Thus, despite all that has been written on the topic – it is surely among the most-discussed in political philosophy – the questions it raises are still of the first importance.

Intertwined with these questions are a second set, which arise because every aspect of the way things now are has its roots in innumerable prior events. Each individual's current situation can be traced both to many previous decisions that he and others have made and to the many complex social arrangements that structured their options; the world's current political boundaries can be traced partly to wars, invasions, and conquests, partly to continuous patterns of occupancy through the centuries; and so on. Of the prior occurrences that shaped the current situation, some seem morally significant because they created legitimate expectations, others because they were sources of desert or entitlement, and still others because they involved wrongs or injustices whose current effects require rectification. One philosophical problem is how to organize the various historical considerations that seem relevant to who should have what; another is to assess the moral force of each candidate consideration; yet a third is how to apply the resulting assessments when we lack (and can never hope to obtain) the relevant detailed historical information.

The problems just mentioned concern the distribution of goods and opportunities, broadly construed. By contrast, another class of urgent problems concerns the shape of our political institutions and the relations among these institutions. One such set of problems – those of transnational governance – was sketched above and so does not require further discussion, but a closely related set requires independent treatment. These are the problems that arise when we try to adapt key elements of our cherished political morality – the liberal notions of religious toleration, civil rights, and privacy, for example, or our traditional ideas of what is permissible in the conduct of war – to the current struggle with Islamic totalitarianism. Although various elements of this struggle have been seen before – we have had opponents who were illiberal and antidemocratic, who sought world domination, who intentionally targeted non-combatants and ignored other moral constraints, who sought to infiltrate our society, and so on – the current combination of these elements seems to me to be unprecedented both in its savagery and in the destructiveness of the weapons to which our enemies potentially have access. We are now seeing the beginning of a necessary public debate on how to adapt our beliefs and values in the service of preserving our nation and our cultural ideals, but philosophers have not yet had much of a presence in that debate. It is high time that we did.

There is one further point that I want to make. Philosophical inquiry as we know it requires certain background conditions. It requires a stable environment, a society prosperous enough to support a class of thinkers, and a culture that prizes the free play of the intellect. These conditions cannot be taken for granted. Although our social and economic systems are multiply redundant, and although they contain many resources for self-repair, their complexity and interdependence also renders them vulnerable to cascading and mutually reinforcing failures. Because our systems are in this way fragile, and because our enemies are resourceful and implacably hostile to our deepest values, the struggle with Islamic totalitarianism has a practical as well as a theoretical dimension. It is relevant to political philosophy not only as a source of interesting and difficult normative questions but also as a threat to bring down the very civilization that makes the whole enterprise possible. Some view this threat as overblown; I do not. I hope I'm wrong.

Selected publications

Books

Desert, Princeton University Press, 1987; paperback 1989.

Beyond Neutrality: Perfectionism and Politics, Cambridge University Press, 1997.

Approximate Justice: Studies in Non-Ideal Theory, Rowman and Littlefield, 1997.

In Praise of Blame, Oxford University Press, 2006.

Articles

"Justifying Reverse Discrimination in Employment," *Philosophy and Public Affairs*, Winter, 1975.

"Effort, Ability, and Personal Desert," *Philosophy and Public Affairs*, Summer, 1979.

"Compensation and Transworld Personal Identity," *The Monist*, July, 1979.

"What Makes a Lottery Fair?" *Nous*, May, 1980.

"Ancient Wrongs and Modern Rights," *Philosophy and Public Affairs*, Winter, 1981.

"Subsidized Abortion: Moral Rights and Moral Compromise," *Philosophy and Public Affairs*, Fall, 1981.

"Moral Education and Indoctrination," *The Journal of Philosophy*, November, 1982 (co-author William J. Bennett).

"Our Preferences, Ourselves," *Philosophy and Public Affairs*, Winter, 1983.

"Educating Citizens," *Philosophy and Public Affairs*, Winter, 1989.

"Three Grades of Social Involvement," *Philosophy and Public Affairs*, Spring, 1989.

"My Profession and Its Duties," *The Monist*, October, 1996.

"Diversity," *Philosophy and Public Affairs*, Spring, 1999.

"But I Could Be Wrong," *Social Philosophy and Policy*, Summer, 2001.

"Blame for Traits," *Nous*, March 2001.

"Effort and Imagination," in Serena Olsaretti, ed., *Essays on Justice and Desert*, Oxford University Press, 2003.

"Transgenerational Compensation," *Philosophy and Public Affairs*, Spring 2005.

"Kantian Fairness," *Philosophical Issues* (*Nous* annual supplementary volume), 2005.

"Out of Control," *Ethics*, January 2006.

13
Larry S. Temkin

Professor of Philosophy

Rutgers, The State University of New Jersey, USA

Why were you initially drawn to political philosophy?[1]

I don't really think of myself as a political philosopher, *per se*. I think of myself more as a moral philosopher, or normative theorist. But much of my career has addressed topics of central concern to political philosophy. In this interview, I shall mainly discuss my interest in, and contributions to, one of those topics: equality.

Like much of one's life, how I came to write on equality is largely a matter of luck; though no doubt those who believe in Fate (as I do not) would say that I was destined to do so.

The roots of my interest in equality lie deep in my youth. But were it not for several serendipitous events during graduate school, I might never have addressed the topic professionally. Let me comment on each of these factors, and how they combined to generate my research on equality.

Personally, I have been concerned about equality – and related notions like justice and fairness – as long as I can remember. Mostly, this had to do with my upbringing and heritage. My father, Blair Temkin, worked seven days a week when I was young, and was a man of enormous personal integrity. My mother, Leah Temkin, worked for many years teaching reading to adults; mostly to the poor, people of color, and immigrants. In both word and deed my parents conveyed to me the importance of treating all people respectfully, as equals. Moreover, in numerous ways—from volunteering locally to sponsoring poor children in distant lands— my parents taught me that one had an obligation to benefit the less fortunate, both at home and abroad.

---

[1] I am very grateful to Jeff McMahan, Jacob Ross, and Mikhail Valdman for their comments and suggestions on an earlier draft of this interview.

My parents' lessons were informed, and strengthened, by my Jewish heritage. All of my grandparents' families immigrated to the United States around the beginning of the 20th century. The persecution of the Jews was a reality for my grandparents, whose families had lived in *shtetls* – Jewish ghettos on the border of Poland and Russia – subject to the pogroms, and forced conscriptions, of Tsarist Russia. As importantly, when I was born, in 1954, the horrors of the Holocaust were still fresh in everyone's minds. The trials of the Jews were especially impressed upon me by my grandmother, Faye Sigman, who had founded the first Jewish Sunday School in the small – virtually all Christian – town of Appleton, Wisconsin. As a child, I knew the sting of being called a "dirty Jew" or a "kike," and the stories I heard about centuries of persecution filled me with a deep sense of righteous indignation. Bigotry, hatred, and discrimination were not only dangerous; they were terribly unfair and unjust. Correspondingly, they should be condemned wherever and whenever they occurred. Thus, from an early age, I took seriously the importance of treating *all* people as equals, regardless of their race, creed, religion, nationality, or gender. (Sexual orientation had not yet entered my consciousness!)

On a lighter note, like most children I had an inflated sense of my being "different." I was, in fact, short, scrawny, buck-toothed, pigeon-toed, and freckle-faced—plus I wore glasses, my ears stuck out, and many of my peers thought me "too brainy." When, inevitably, I was teased for my attributes, I was not only hurt, I was deeply offended. I was keenly aware of being teased for features beyond my control, and this struck me as patently unfair. Moreover, I felt similarly when others were teased for factors not their fault. Such teasing dominates playgrounds, but its prevalence never deadened my acute sense of its unfairness.

So, my egalitarian sensibilities were already well-developed as I became a teenager, in the turbulent times of the late 1960s and early 1970s. Like many of my generation, I questioned my country's role in the Vietnam War; but I was even more taken by the Women's Liberation and Civil Rights movements. (Indeed, David Feldman's Civil Liberties class was the most powerful, scary, and important class I ever took. Its portrayal of the systematic mistreatment of America's downtrodden, and especially blacks, was deeply disturbing.) Similarly, I felt a personal sense of shame and guilt that my country, and family, should possess, and squander, *so* much, while millions, globally, suffered or perished from poverty, famine, disaster, or disease. And to this day, I remember a bitter argument with an uncle over a government regulation requiring wheelchair access to the small foundry which he and my father had founded. My uncle thought it was stupid, inefficient, and objectionably intrusive for the government to require them to install a $10,000 ramp, when no handicapped person had ever shown up at the foundry, and none was ever likely to. To my eye, extra expense seemed clearly warranted to give those who were *already worse off than the rest* an opportunity to participate in as full a range of life plans as was possible. More particularly, it seemed patently unfair that the able-bodied should have access to a workplace, but the handicapped should not. Thus, from middle school through college, I was greatly disturbed by pervasive inequalities: between men and women, whites and blacks, rich and poor, developed and developing nations, healthy and handicapped, etc.

So I have long been concerned about inequalities. But, like many, I often compartmentalize my personal and academic concerns, and when I went off to graduate school my aim was to pursue philosophy of language. Fortunately, I arrived at Princeton one year after John Rawls's great work, *A Theory of Justice*, appeared, and there was enormous excitement about the rebirth of ethics, and of social and political philosophy. I took courses with Tom Nagel, Tim Scanlon, and Gil Harman, and soon decided to work in value theory.

In my third year of graduate school, two chance conversations changed my life. The first convinced me to audit a seminar with a young visiting philosopher of whom I had never heard. The second convinced me to take an extra year before going on the job market. The seminar was Derek Parfit's, where he presented an early draft of his seminal book, *Reasons and Persons*. Parfit was brilliant, and his material, intellectually intoxicating. Correspondingly, I decided to spend my extra year at Oxford, working with Parfit.

I arrived in Oxford planning to write a dissertation defending a Kantian version of morality against consequentialist rivals. But before doing that, I decided to give Parfit some feedback on one of his early drafts about overpopulation. One of Parfit's arguments contained a plausible, and seemingly innocuous, claim about inequality. But something about Parfit's claim stuck in my craw. I read and reread his argument, and as I did so I found myself, for the first time, philosophically examining my egalitarian intuitions. Ultimately, I gave Parfit a fifty page critique, which included a twenty-five page "aside" called "Reflections on Equality." Parfit's response was immediate and categorical: forget my previous plans and write a thesis on equality. Suffice it to say, I followed his advice. Fifteen years later, I published *Inequality*, and I am still working on the topic today.

What do you consider your own most important contribution(s) to political philosophy, and why?

As indicated above, I shall focus my discussion here on my contributions to the topic of equality. However, before doing that, let me note that a significant component of my research concerns problems of aggregation: how should we aggregate across different times, places, or individuals in determining the goodness of outcomes or societies? I have developed a number of impossibility arguments, showing that many of our deepest beliefs concerning trade-offs between quality and number, or quality and duration, are incompatible with each other and certain fundamental assumptions about rationality, such as the assumption that "all things considered better than" must be a transitive relation. This work has pervasive implications for one of political philosophy's most fundamental questions: when, if ever, do the interests or rights of the many outweigh the interests or rights of the few, and vice versa? Despite its importance for political philosophy, I shall not say more about my views on this topic here, since I will be discussing them in a companion volume to this one.[2]

Regarding the topic of equality, first, and most importantly, I tried to analyze and illuminate egalitarianism, introducing a new approach to understanding inequality, and exploring the nature, scope, and implications of egalitarian concern. Second, in defending egalitarianism, I have argued against what is arguably the best-known and most powerful objection to egalitarianism, the "leveling down" objection, in ways that have wide implications for political and moral theory. Third, I helped launch the "equality, priority, or what" debate. Finally, my work has prodded others to sharpen their discussions about the nature of egalitarianism. Let me comment on each of these topics, especially the first.

---

[2] For the interested reader, please see *5 Questions on Normative Ethics*, edited by Thomas Petersen and Jesper Ryberg, Automatic Press/VIP (forthcoming, 2007).

Illuminating egalitarianism

When I started writing about equality, most philosophical discussions addressed one of two questions: Is equality desirable? And if so, what *kind* of equality should we care about, equality of income, opportunity, primary goods, or what? These are important questions; but I asked a third question, one not previously addressed by philosophers: when is one situation *worse* than another regarding inequality? My question is important for two reasons. First, it can be of little practical relevance to regard inequality as bad, unless one can generally determine when one outcome's inequality is worse than another's. Second, only by addressing my question can one fully understand the nature and complexity of inequality.

In some cases it is easy to determine when one situation is worse than another regarding inequality; for example, if one situation is perfectly equal, while another is not, or if the two situations are similar in all respects, except that there are much larger undeserved gaps in one situation than the other. But often, it is unclear whether, and why, one situation is worse than another regarding inequality. This is because we have a host of conflicting intuitions relevant to assessing a situation's inequality. For example, intuitively, we often think a situation's inequality is especially bad, if it involves lots of well-off people, and only a few badly-off people. This might be so, if the badly-off people are a small group, or minority, who have been "singled" out for mistreatment, or discrimination, by a bully or tyrant. Or alternatively, we might regard such a situation's inequality as being especially bad because it seems so pointless and unnecessary, and hence "gratuitous." Specifically, it seems that everyone *could* have been equal, and well off, *if only* a tiny bit of wellbeing could (somehow) have been transferred from the many better-off to the few badly-off. On the other hand, intuitively, we often think that some of the worst instances of historical inequality involved relatively few people being well off, with the vast majority being poorly off. This, for example, is a common view about the inequality between the nobles and peasants of Medieval Europe. Yet, on still another way of thinking, intuitively, it may seem that a situation where half the population is much worse off than the other half, would be much worse regarding inequality than one where the vast majority of the population was equally well off, and just a few were better, or worse off, than the others. After all, the former situation, seems deeply divided, and seems to involve a much greater deviation from a state of perfect equality, than the latter.

Reflecting on our egalitarian intuitions about a host of different examples, I developed a new approach to thinking about equality.

Typically, the notion of equality has been assumed to be *simple*—we all know what equality and inequality are: equality is where everybody has the same amount of x, and inequality is where some people have more x than others for whatever x we are interested in; *holistic*—concerned about (in)equality between groups or societies, e.g. blacks and whites, women and men, or Ethiopians and Swiss; and *essentially distributive*—concerned with how certain goods are distributed among an outcome's groups.

In considering how outcomes compare regarding inequality, I argued that these conventional assumptions are deeply misleading. First, on reflection, it seemed clear that equality was an enormously *complex* notion. Thus, in judging outcomes regarding inequality many considerations seem relevant, including how much deviation there is from a state of pure equality, how gratuitous the inequality seems, and the extent to which individuals have a "complaint" regarding inequality. Moreover, I argued that the size of an individual's egalitarian complaint may depend on how she fares relative to the average person, the best-off person, or all those better off than she; and, in addition, one might arrive at a judgment concerning the badness of an outcome's inequality by adding individual complaints, focusing on the worst-off's complaints, or adding everyone's complaints, but giving special weight to larger complaints. On reflection, then, I argued that many distinct aspects of equality (at least eleven) underlie egalitarian judgments. Hence, importantly, much work must be done to determine how to measure outcomes in terms of each aspect, and how much each aspect matters relative to the others, and to competing moral ideals

Second, even if one grants that there may be an important holistic component to egalitarianism, I argued that a central component of the notion of equality is *individualistic*. Thus, often groups and societies aren't the proper (or sole) objects of moral concern, individuals *in* groups and societies are. So, for example, though on average whites may be richer than blacks, if inequality of wealth mattered, then in certain fundamentally important respects it would matter just as much between rich and poor blacks, or rich blacks and poor whites, as between rich whites and poor blacks.

Third, although equality *is* a distributive principle, it is misleading to think that this is a particularly distinctive feature of egalitarianism; since many principles are distributive, including many competing, anti-egalitarian, principles. Since (in)equality is a *relation* that obtains between individuals, what is distinctive about egalitarianism, I argued, or at least about one important conception of egalitarianism, is that it is *essentially comparative*; that is, it expresses a fundamental concern for how individuals fare *relative to each other*.

In my work, I noted connections between the notions of equality, fairness, and luck. Let me say more about these connections. If I give some candy to Rebecca, but none to Andrea, Andrea will immediately assert "unfair!" This natural reaction suggests an intimate connection between equality and fairness. Arguably, concern about equality reflects a concern about *comparative* fairness that focuses on how people fare *relative to others*. On my view, concern for equality and concern for a certain aspect of fairness are part and parcel of a single concern. Certain inequalities are objectionable *because they are unfair*; but by the same token, there is a certain kind of unfairness in certain undeserved inequalities. Thus, on my view, egalitarians are *not* motivated by envy, but by a sense of fairness.

Many contemporary egalitarians have been identified as so-called *luck egalitarians*, aiming to rectify the influence of luck in people's lives. A canonical formulation of luck egalitarianism is that it is bad when one person is worse off than another through no fault or choice of her own. Acknowledging the importance of personal responsibility, luck egalitarians object when equally deserving people are unequally well off, but not when one person is worse off than another due to a choice for which she is responsible, say to pursue a life of leisure, or crime.

I believe luck egalitarianism has been misunderstood. The egalitarian's *fundamental* concern isn't with luck *per se*, or even with whether or not someone is worse off than another through no fault or choice of her own. It is with *comparative fairness*. But this fact has been obscured, since most paradigmatic cases of inequality involving comparative unfairness *also* involve luck, or some being worse off than others through no fault or choice of their own.

On close examination, the intimate connection between equality and fairness illuminates luck's role in egalitarianism, as well as the scope of the "through no fault or choice of their own" clause. Among *equally* deserving people, it *is* bad, because *unfair*, for some to be worse off than others through no fault or choice of their own. But among *unequally* deserving people it isn't bad, because it's not unfair, for someone less deserving to be worse off than someone more deserving, even if the former is worse off through no fault or choice of his own. For example, egalitarians needn't object if criminal John is worse off than law-abiding Mary, even if John craftily avoided capture, and so is only worse off because, through no fault or choice of his own, a a falling tree limb injured him.

Additionally, in *some* cases inequality is bad, because it's unfair, even though the worse off *are* responsible for their plight, as when the worse off are so because they chose to do their duty, or perhaps acted supererogatorily, in adverse circumstances not of their making. So, for example, if I'm unlucky enough to walk by a drowning child, and I injure myself saving her, the egalitarian might think it *unfair* that I end up worse off than others, even though I am so as a result of my responsible free choice to act rightly.

Correspondingly, on reflection, luck *itself* is neither good nor bad from the egalitarian standpoint. Egalitarians object to luck that leaves equally deserving people unequally well off. But they can accept luck that makes equally deserving people equally well off, or unequally deserving people unequally well off proportional to their deserts. Thus, luck will be opposed *only to the extent* that it undermines comparative fairness.

Note, for the egalitarian, desert is *relevant* to issues of comparative fairness, but the concern for comparative fairness is *not* reducible to a concern for *absolute* desert, namely, that each person should get what they deserve in absolute terms. If Mary and John were the only two people who ever existed, and both were equally bad people who deserved to fare poorly and equally so, there would be no *egalitarian* objection if both fared well and equally so, though there *would* be an objection to that situation from the standpoint of absolute desert. Accordingly, were John to be hit by a tree limb and lowered to the level he deserved to be at, in absolute terms, this would unequivocally improve the situation from the standpoint of absolute desert, but it would unequivocally worsen the situation from the egalitarian standpoint of comparative fairness.

Some luck egalitarians distinguish between *option luck*, to which we responsibly open ourselves, and *brute luck*, which simply "befalls" us, unbidden. Option luck inequalities – for example, those resulting from autonomous gambles, or investments – are unobjectionable. By contrast, brute luck inequalities — for example, those resulting from birth characteristics, or unavoidable accidents —

are objectionable.

I reject the option/brute luck distinction as it is normally invoked. First, drawing the line between them is difficult. More importantly, I believe it *is* objectionable if Mary takes a prudent risk, and John an imprudent one, yet Mary fares much worse than John, because she is the victim of bad, and he the beneficiary of good, option luck. Likewise, if Mary and John are equally deserving, and choose similar options, I believe there *is* an egalitarian objection to John's ending up much better off, because he enjoys vastly greater option luck. This is unfair for the same reason that paradigmatic cases involving brute luck are. It involves comparative unfairness.

My work on equality has also addressed many other questions, including: does inequality matter more at low or high levels; does variation in population size affect inequality; should egalitarians compare whole lives, or overlapping segments of lives (e.g. today's elderly with today's youth), or comparable stages of lives (e.g. today's youth with yesterday's); and does inequality matter equally between different societies, distances, or times (e.g. should one be concerned about inequalities between societies as well as within societies, and if so should one be concerned to the same extent; or should one be concerned about inequalities between spatially or temporally distant societies, and if so, does the size of the spatial or temporal difference matter)? For each question I have argued against standard answers, and my work has a wide range of surprising and important implications regarding inequalities between young and old, rich and poor, healthy and sick, developed and developing countries, present and past or future generations, and so on. However, I cannot pursue these here.

Welfarism and the leveling down objection

Many anti-egalitarians are so because of the *leveling down objection*, which holds that there is *no* respect in which *merely* lowering someone from a higher to lower level improves a situation. So, for example, it is argued that there is *no* respect in which putting out the eyes of the sighted would improve a situation, assuming this did not increase the blind's level of wellbeing. Since, however, worsening the situation of the sighted by blinding them might (let us assume) undeniably decrease the inequality between the sighted and the blind, anti-egalitarians conclude that there is *nothing* valuable about equality *itself*; hence egalitarianism must be rejected.

I have defended egalitarianism against the leveling down objection at length. The heart of my argument follows.

Ultimately, the leveling down objection derives much of its force from an assumption, *welfarism*, that nothing matters morally except insofar as it impacts individual wellbeing, where all and only positive impacts on individual wellbeing (benefits) are good, and all and only negative impacts on individual wellbeing (harms) are bad. Welfarism is intuitively plausible and widely accepted. Nevertheless, I believe it reflects a crimped conception of moral value.

Consider the intuition that it would be *unfair* for sinners to fare *better* than saints, even if there was *no* respect in which this was worse for the sinners *or* the saints. Or the intuition that even if Hitler and his cronies were the only ones to survive death, it would be *unjust* if their afterlives were maximally happy. These intuitions reflect the fact that the concern for fairness and justice is distinct from a concern about increasing wellbeing. We value fairness and justice *beyond* the extent to which they are good *for* people. That is, their value does not rest solely on the way in which their realization benefits individual wellbeing. Similar remarks apply to the mantra of "knowledge for knowledge's sake" or Keats's famous claim, "'Beauty is truth, truth beauty'—that is all Ye know on earth, and all Ye need to know."[3]

I claim that ideals like fairness, justice, knowledge, beauty, and truth, are best understood as *impersonal* ideals, by which I simply mean that their value does not lie *wholly* in their contributions to individual wellbeing.[4] So my objection to welfarism is simple. I believe that many important ideals are impersonal, and that welfarism rules out *all* such ideals. Hence, welfarism should be rejected.

In essence, welfarists endorse the following two claims: claim one, only sentient individuals are the proper objects of moral concern; and claim two, for purposes of evaluating outcomes, indi-

---

[3] John Keats, "Ode on a Grecian Urn."

[4] I grant that this nomenclature may be slightly misleading, since it lumps together principles that might be "purely" impersonal, with those that might combine a personal and impersonal element. But I think it serves my present purposes well enough. Still, one might prefer to distinguish between (purely) personal ideals, (purely) impersonal ideals, and hybrid views that combine elements of both. My argument would then be that many ideals are either impersonal or hybrid, and that welfarism rules out all such ideals, as it only allows personal ideals.

vidual wellbeing is *all* that matters. For the sake of argument, I am willing to accept claim one, insofar as it asserts the moral primacy of sentient individuals, as opposed to groups or societies. But, importantly, sentient individuals are not merely the *objects* of moral concern, they are also the *source* of moral concerns (where this might be so for Kantian and/or non-Kantian reasons). Thus, for example, some sentient beings—rational agents—give rise to moral concerns and values that do not obtain with other sentient or non-sentient beings.

Once one recognizes that sentient individuals are not merely the *objects* of moral concern, but also the *source* of moral concerns and values, claim two loses its appeal. In evaluating outcomes, why care *only* about the *wellbeing* of individuals? Humans have extraordinary capacities beyond their capacity for wellbeing. These capacities serve as a source of impersonal value in the world; for example, the impersonal value that can be found, perhaps, in friendship, love, altruism, knowledge, justice, rights, duty, equality, virtue and truth. Perhaps none of these values arise in a world devoid of sentient beings, and that truth may partly underlie claim one's appeal. But, importantly, such values *do* arise when rational or moral agents stand in certain relations to each other or the world. Moreover, the value of such relations does not lie *solely* in the extent to which they promote individual *wellbeing*. Additionally, there may be *some* ideals, such as perfection and beauty, whose realization contributes to goodness in a way that does not depend on the existence of sentient beings, even counterfactually. If so, there is reason to reject claim one, as well as claim two.[5] Individual wellbeing *is* valuable; but it is a grotesque distortion of the conception of value to think that it is the *only* thing that matters for the goodness of outcomes.[6]

---

[5] There may, of course, also be other reasons to reject claim one which I shall not pursue here.

[6] If one has a wide enough conception of individual wellbeing, one can make room for all of one's ideals as personal rather than impersonal, including equality and justice. One could then accept the welfarist position. John Broome advocates this kind of view in his excellent book, *Weighing Goods* (Basil Blackwell, 1991). I don't think individual wellbeing is plausibly construed so broadly; but of course, if it is, then ideals like equality and justice will count as good for people, and the leveling down objection will fail. By decreasing inequality, leveling down will turn out, on this conception, to be improving the wellbeing of the previously worse-off people, and few deny that transfers from better to worse off might be warranted if the worse off actually benefit (sufficiently) from such transfers.

Isn't it unfair for some to be worse off than others through no fault of their own? Isn't it unfair for some to be born blind, while others are not? And isn't unfairness bad? These questions, posed rhetorically, express the egalitarian's fundamental claim. Once one rejects welfarism as capturing the *whole* of morality relevant to assessing outcomes, as I believe one should, there is little reason to forsake egalitarianism because of the leveling down objection.

But, the anti-egalitarian will incredulously ask, do I *really* think there is some respect in which a world where only some are blind is worse than one where all are? Yes. Does this mean I think it would be better if we blinded everyone? No. Equality is not *all* that matters. But it matters *some*.

Advocates of the leveling down objection are mesmerized by "pure" equality's terrible implications. But equality is not the only ideal that would, if exclusively pursued, have terrible implications. The same is true of justice, utility, freedom, and probably every other substantive ideal. This doesn't show that we should reject each of these ideals, only that morality is complex.

The leveling down objection's main lesson is that we should be pluralists about morality. Egalitarians accept this.

Equality, priority, or what?

In my 1983 PhD thesis, *Inequality*, I introduced a position which I then called "extended humanitarianism." According to this position, one wants each person to fare as well as possible, but the worse off someone is, in absolute terms, the greater priority one gives to improving their condition. In my thesis, I noted that extended humanitarianism was often conflated with, but should be distinguished from, egalitarianism. I suggested that many who thought of themselves as egalitarians were actually extended humanitarians, and that considerations people offered in support of egalitarianism, may have in fact supported extended humanitarianism rather than egalitarianism. I pointed out that extended humanitarianism could avoid the leveling down objection. In addition, I contended that extended humanitarianism had great plausibility, and might be regarded by many as the closest thing to an egalitarian position that might be defensible.

Derek Parfit made many of these claims, and many others, in his renowned 1991 article "Equality or Priority,"[7] though he came up

---

[7] Widely discussed, "Equality or Priority?" was first delivered by Parfit

with a much better name for the position I had called "extended humanitarianism," calling it "the Priority View." Brimming with highly original insights, distinctions, examples, and arguments, Parfit's work was the first published article explicitly defending the Priority View, and it launched the equality or priority debate. Nevertheless, I think it is fair to say that many of the key issues in the debate were first identified and developed in my thesis, and that Parfit's classic article was partially sparked and influenced by that work.

Much recent work in political theory addresses whether egalitarianism should be replaced by prioritarianism ("prioritarianism" is a term I introduced to replace Parfit's "the Priority View" and my own "extended humanitarianism"[8]). Also debated is whether one should reject both egalitarianism and prioritarianism in favor of "sufficiency" or "compassion" views, where one has a special concern for people badly off, or below a certain level, but no distributional concerns for people sufficiently well off. I have argued that while prioritarian, sufficiency, and compassion views are plausible, it would be a mistake to jettison egalitarianism altogether; as egalitarianism reflects a fundamental concern for comparative fairness that such views cannot capture. Thus, there is an important place for egalitarian considerations in our all things considered judgments, *in addition* to such other views, if one still finds them necessary once one has given egalitarianism its due weight.

Distinguishing different egalitarian positions

In many ways, equality is the common coin of contemporary political discourse, as countless current debates are framed in terms of equality. Unsurprisingly, then, egalitarians come in many stripes, and numerous, quite distinct positions—ranging from prioritarianism, to utilitarianism, to libertarianism, to Rawls's maximin principle—have been described as—or perhaps conflated with—egalitarianism. But, of course, most of these positions have little

---

as The Lindley Lecture, University of Kansas, 1991, copyright 1995 by the Department of Philosophy, University of Kansas; it has been reprinted *in The Ideal of Equality*, edited by Matthew Clayton and Andrew Williams, London: MacMillan Press Ltd and New York: St. Martin's Press, Inc., 2000, pp. 81-125.

[8] I first introduced "prioritarianism," and its cognates, in "Equality, Priority, and the Levelling Down Objection," In *The Ideal of Equality*, edited by Matthew Clayton and Andrew Williams, Macmillan and St. Martin's Press, 2000, pp. 126-161.

in common with each other.

Some believe that I have defended a narrow, etiolated, conception of equality; one divorced from its rich political and intellectual roots. For many, the essence of a concern for equality is a concern about class, race, or gender struggles, or a concern about political rights or democratic virtues. Some people believe that these concerns have gotten lost in my theoretical analysis of the nature and complexity of the notion of equality. Naturally, I believe that I have articulated a central element of egalitarian concern, one intimately connected with comparative fairness. Inequality really does seem bad, because unfair, when it involves some being worse off than others no more deserving than they. In spite of this disagreement, I trust that many might agree that my work has illustrated the importance of clarifying exactly what one cares about insofar as one is an *egalitarian*, and motivated many to sharpen their views of the matter.

In my work, I have distinguished between many different kinds of egalitarian positions. For example, I have claimed that one might have a view of equality as universality, impartiality, and/or comparability. I have also distinguished between instrumental and non-instrumental egalitarianism and, following Parfit, between telic and deontic egalitarianism, and moderate and extreme egalitarianism. I shall not clarify each of these positions here, but clearly, many self-professed egalitarians and anti-egalitarians run the risk of simply misunderstanding and talking past each other if they are not sufficiently careful in understanding and presenting their views.

I claim that many who think of themselves as egalitarians are instrumental egalitarians, where equality is valuable only insofar as it promotes some *other* valuable ideal. This is true, for example, of many humanitarians, Rawlsians, communitarians, and democratic egalitarians, who only favor redistribution from better to worse off as a way of reducing suffering, aiding the worst off, fostering solidarity, or strengthening democratic institutions. Such reasons are morally significant, but they are compatible with the rejection of non-instrumental egalitarianism, according to which equality is sometimes valuable *beyond* the extent to which it promotes other ideals, so that any complete account of the moral realm must account for equality's non-instrumental value.

My own view of equality as comparative fairness is a substantive version of non-instrumental egalitarianism. But I am a pluralist about morality, and my pluralism extends to egalitarianism itself.

So, not only do I believe that many ideals matter, besides equality, I also believe that many different kinds of egalitarianism are defensible. Similarly, I believe that there is more than one plausible answer to the "equality of what?" question; for example, that there is reason to care about both equality of wellbeing and equality of opportunity. So I believe that many views people have put forward as rivals to my own are, in fact, *part* of the truth about morality. But I have not been convinced to forsake the view of equality I have defended. Equality as comparative fairness remains a deep and important element of my thinking.

What is the proper role of political philosophy in relation to real, political action? Can there ever be a fruitful relation between political philosophy and political practice?

I'm afraid I don't have anything especially deep to say about this topic. Still, let me offer a few observations on a set of related issues.

First, as with other subjects, like physics or math, there is a useful, if somewhat artificial, distinction between theoretical and applied political philosophy. Naturally, progress in applied fields often depends, and often in unexpected ways, on progress on theoretical issues. However, in my judgment, pursuing theoretical knowledge is valuable even in the absence of practical payoffs.

Some people are theorists, others are practitioners, and some, of course, are both. There is a crucial place for both theory and practice, and while, as noted above, the distinction between them is somewhat artificial, it is important not to conflate the two. Following Aristotle, I believe that the theorist, qua theorist, must seek the truth, and follow the arguments wherever they lead. So, roughly, theorists cannot allow practical considerations to dictate their methods or influence their conclusions. Still, theorists have a moral obligation to guard against any foreseeable misuses or abuses of their positions, and in rare contexts, perhaps, must avoid pursuing or disseminating dangerous information.

Undoubtedly, political philosophy can deeply influence political practice. Such influence may be obvious or subtle, direct or indirect, beneficial or harmful. To cite a few patent examples: John Locke profoundly affected the constitutions and political life of the United States and of many other Western-style democracies; Jeremy Bentham and John Stuart Mill influenced legislatures worldwide to shape laws with an eye to "promoting the general welfare" of their citizens; Karl Marx contributed to the amelioration of working class conditions in Britain and elsewhere, but the (mis-)use of his views also contributed to countless deaths in Stalinist Russia; and Friedrich Nietzsche had a liberating impact in post-Victorian England, but a devastatingly destructive one in Nazi Germany. More recently, John Rawls has undoubtedly influenced the reasoning of deliberative bodies around the globe.

Importantly, not only the giants of political theory can influence political practice. Ideas have a life of their own, and any idea that reaches the right person can make a difference to political practice. Moreover, the right person need not be a high profile political actor; it could, for example, simply be a researcher who influences a civil servant who helps craft some legislation. I once learned that a French government department modified some distribution policies on the recommendation of a departmental economist who had been influenced by my book, *Inequality*. Of course, I have no idea if I would approve of the changes made. The uses to which one's ideas are put are rarely in one's control. But ideas clearly matter; and political ideas, in particular, can matter greatly for political practice—often in unexpected ways, places, and times. Anyone who thinks differently reveals a woeful ignorance of the course of civilization.

Political philosophy's influence on political practice is mediated by many factors, including the nature and complexity of political philosophy's results. I was once asked to advise the World Health Organization regarding how best to promote equality in global health. If my research had yielded a straightforward answer, there might have been a direct affect of theory on practice. But, in fact, my results are not so amenable to direct application. As indicated above, I have argued that many factors are relevant to assessing inequality, and that many factors matter morally besides inequality. Correspondingly, having not yet identified, and come up with a method of accurately weighing, each of morality's relevant factors, I could only offer limited advice as to how the World Health Organization should distribute its resources.

So, regarding my own work, I think one must move cautiously before prescribing practical policies. However, I hope that, in time, we will learn how best to deal with the difficult complexities my work has revealed. If this happens, then given the deep commitment to equality in many political arenas, there would be ample opportunities for my work to impact political practice. As for other, less complex, issues, there may often be a straightforward connection between theory and practice. This will be so when the results of political theory are clear and uncontroversial, and where there are the means and political will to "get things right."

Finally, the question naturally arises as to whether political theorists should also be political activists. Surely, many political theorists have activist inclinations. So, many theorists will be motivated, if the opportunity presents itself, to work to see their views put into practice. And often political theorists might be especially effective advocates for their own positions. In such cases, there may be powerful reasons for political theorists to also be political activists. But one mustn't lose sight of the benefits of a division of labor. The best theorists aren't always the best activists. And even if they were, one can't do everything. Political theorists must weigh up the full benefits and losses of trading off between pursuing theory and influencing practice. No doubt sometimes political theorists should "get involved"; but sometimes it may be better for the political theorist to focus on theory, and let others focus on practice.

What do you consider the most neglected topics and/or contributions in post-Rawlsian or late 20th century political philosophy?

As noted above, a central question in political philosophy concerns trade-offs between the one and the many. When, if ever, do the interests or rights of the many outweigh, or take precedence over, the interests or rights of the few—and vice versa? More concretely, when, if ever, is it permissible, or obligatory, for the many to be taxed, burdened, or "sacrificed" for the sake of the few— and vice versa? Associated with these are a host of related issues concerning conflicts between individual and collective rationality, problems of aggregation, prisoner's dilemmas, and voter's paradoxes. I believe that many of the most significant and pervasive social and political problems faced today are manifestations of such issues. I also believe that much important work has been done in the past 30 years illuminating these issues. While much more work remains, significant insights have been developed that could help us make genuine progress on many of our deepest social and political problems. Unfortunately, this work has been woefully neglected by society at large—to its great detriment.

Here is one example. During President Clinton's first administration, there appeared to be a golden opportunity to institute significant reform to the United States's health care system. With tens of millions of Americans lacking health care insurance, and millions more receiving substandard health care, there was widespread recognition that major reform was socially desirable. In fact, I believe that most parties to the debate could agree that, on the whole, both they, and the country, would be better off adopting the Clinton proposal than rejecting it. Nevertheless, each constituency had a special interest in trying to improve the provisions of the proposal that directly impacted them. This was true of the doctors, the insurance companies, the lawyers, the drug companies, the aged, the uninsured, and so on. Predictably, when each group acted on its own best interests to improve the proposal, the proposal collapsed; arguably with detrimental effects for virtually all concerned. To my mind, the incident represented a classic example of the conflict between individual and collective interests and rationality, and the fiasco surrounding the collapse of the Clinton proposal might have been avoided had society properly appreciated and heeded the insights scholars have revealed about such conflicts.

What are the most important unsolved questions in political philosophy and/or related disciplines and what are the prospects for progress?

John Rawls once told me that he saw the heart of his political theory as addressing Jean-Jacques Rousseau's great question: "Man is born free, and everywhere he is in chains.... What can make it legitimate?"[9] As Rawls put it to me (roughly): under what conditions, if any, can a state pass laws, use its full power to enforce those laws, and yet, in so doing, not be *unjustly coercing* its citizens?

Historically, most political philosophers have focused on nation-states. Central questions of political philosophy included the following: When is a state legitimate? When is the use of state power legitimate? And what is the nature, basis, and extent of a state's obligations to its citizens and vice versa?

Today, as ever, political philosophers must address the concerns of Rousseau and Rawls; but they must expand their discussion's scope to take account of today's global realities. Today, more than

---

[9] Rousseau famously posed this question at the beginning of *The Social Contract*.

ever, the lives and working conditions of billions globally are profoundly affected by decisions made in offices thousands of miles away, by multi-national corporations or international organizations like the World Bank, the International Monetary Fund, the World Trade Organization, and the United Nations. Moreover, unlike individual governments, these decision-making bodies do not derive their power from, and hence need not be beholden to, the individuals whose lives they profoundly affect.

Thus, political theory needs to expand its focus to address questions like the following: under what conditions, if any, can an organization like the World Trade Organization—whose most influential delegates may include politically appointed businessmen from the world's richest countries—impose trade regulations on a developing country, whose impact, predictably, will be to displace numerous poor workers, without its being the case that either the country, or its workers, is being unjustly coerced?

Important work is already being done on this topic, for example, by Thomas Pogge.[10] But much more work must be done. Similarly, the age-old questions about trade-offs between the interests and rights of the many, and those of the few, need to be addressed anew, to take account of today's global realities regarding terrorism, illegal immigration, privacy, intellectual property rights, global warming, and so on.

In countless ways today's world is much better than yesterday's; for example, regarding global rates of infant mortality, life expectancy, and literacy. Likewise, global progress is evident in the treatment of women, minorities, and the handicapped. I am optimistic that political theory can contribute to continued global progress. But I am not a Pollyanna. Progress is not guaranteed, and there are huge hurdles to overcome, both theoretically and practically. Those committed to living in a more just and equal world have no choice but to work, in their own way, for such progress. For surely the status quo is unacceptable.

Selected publications

1. *Inequality*, Oxford University Press, 1993.

---

[10] See, for example, Pogge's *World Poverty and Human Rights: Cosmopolitan Responsibilities and Reforms*, Cambridge: Polity Press, 2002, and "Severe Poverty as a Violation of Negative Duties," in *Ethics and International Affairs* volume 19, number 1, 2005, pp. 55-84.

2. "Thinking about the Needy, Justice, and International Organizations," and "Thinking about the Needy: A Reprise," *Journal of Ethics*, 8, pp. 349–395 and 409–458, 2004.

3. "Personal versus Impersonal Principles: Reconsidering the Slogan," "Determining the Scope of Egalitarian Concern: A Partial Defense of Complete Lives Egalitarianism," "Measuring Inequality's Badness: Does Size Matter? If So, How, If Not, What Does?" and "Exploring the Roots of Egalitarian Concerns," *Theoria* 69, no.s 1–2, pp. 20-30, 45-58, 84-107, and 124-50, 2003.

4. "A 'New' Principle of Aggregation," *Philosophical Issues*, 15, *Normativity*, eds. Sosa and Villanueva, pp. 218-234, 2005.

5. "Egalitarianism Defended," *Ethics* 113, no. 4, pp. 764–782, 2003

6. "Equality, Priority, or What?" *Economics and Philosophy* 19, no. 1, pp. 61–8, 2003.

7. "Worries about Continuity, Transitivity, Expected Utility Theory, and Practical Reasoning" in *Exploring Practical Philosophy*, eds. Egonsson, Josefsson, Petersson, and Rønnow-Rasmussen, pp. 95–108, Ashgate Publishing Limited, 2001.

8. "Egalitarianism: A Complex, Individualistic, and Comparative Notion," in *Philosophical Issues*, volume 11, eds. Sosa and Villanueva, pp. 327–352, Blackwell Publishers, 2001

9. "Equality, Priority, and the Leveling Down Objection," in *The Ideal of Equality*, eds. Clayton and Williams, pp. 126-161, Macmillan and St. Martin's Press, 2000.

10. "Intransitivity and the Person-Affecting Principle: A Response," *Philosophy and Phenomenological Research*, LIX, no. 3, September, 1999, pp. 777–784.

11. "Equality and the Human Condition," in a special issue on Justice, Equality, and Difference of *Theoria* (South Africa) 92, December, 1998, pp. 15–45.

12. "Rethinking the Good, Moral Ideals and the Nature of Practical Reasoning," in *Reading Parfit*, ed. Dancy, Jonathan, pp. 290–344, Basil Blackwell, 1997.

13. "A Continuum Argument for Intransitivity," *Philosophy and Public Affairs* 25, no. 3, Summer, 1996, pp. 175–210.

14. "Justice and Equality: Some Questions about Scope," in *Social Philosophy and Policy* 12, no. 2, eds. Paul, Miller, and Paul, pp. 72–104, Cambridge University Press, 1995.

15. "Inequality," *Philosophy and Public Affairs* 15, no. 2, Spring, 1986, pp. 99–121.

14
Peter Vallentyne

Florence G. Kline Professor of Philosophy
University of Missouri-Columbia, USA

Why were you initially drawn to political philosophy?

I came late to philosophy and even later to political philosophy. When I started my undergraduate studies at the University of Toronto in 1970, I was interested in mathematics and languages. I soon discovered, however, that my mathematical talents were rather meager compared to the truly talented. I therefore decided to study actuarial science (the applied mathematics of risk assessment for insurance and pension plans) rather than abstract math. After two years, however, I dropped out of university. I had always studied on my own and had never enjoyed attending classes. I therefore decided to work for a life insurance company and study on my own for the ten professional actuarial exams. When not studying for an exam, I would often go to the public library and I was drawn to the philosophy section—although I had no idea of what philosophy was about. I there saw *Logical Positivism*, edited by A.J. Ayer. I knew that I was interested in logic and I also favored an optimistic attitude towards life (!) and so I thought that the book might be interesting. I checked it out and was absolutely enthralled with the writings of Bertrand Russell, Rudolf Carnap, Carl Hempel and others (if I'm remembering correctly). Of course, I didn't really understand much of what they were doing, but I did see that they were addressing important problems in a systematic and rigorous manner. I liked it!

I then went on to read most of Bertrand Russell's books and realized that I had a deep interest in philosophy. Eventually, I returned to university—this time at McGill University in Montreal—and completed an undergraduate degree in mathematics and philosophy. After a fantastic year traveling around Greece, I went to the University of Pittsburgh intending to study philosophy of language, philosophy of logic, or philosophy of science. David Gauthier arrived at Pitt the following year, and I was exposed to his work and that of John Harsayni and John Rawls. I was very excited by the application of the theory of rational choice (decision theory and game theory) and the theory of social choice (and normative economics generally) to the foundations of moral theory and I decided to focus on moral philosophy. During graduate school, my focus was on ethical theory and consequentialism in particular. Later, I became interested in liberty and equality in political philosophy. Here, I was much influenced by the writings of Richard Arneson, G.A. Cohen, Ronald Dworkin, James Fishkin, Robert Nozick, John Roemer, Philippe Van Parijs, and Hillel Steiner. Cohen, Van Parijs, and Steiner were very important influences in getting me interested in left-libertarianism, which is my current focus.

What do you consider your own most important contribution(s) to political philosophy, and why?

My contributions have been modest, but let me identify them nonetheless.

One of my main contributions is in the area of ethics rather than political philosophy. It concerns problems that arise when, although each person has only a finite amount of goods at a given time, one must choose between options some of which contain an *infinite* amount of goods. The problem is fairly general, but the simplest version can be formulated in terms of utilitarianism when the future is infinitely long and there is at least one person alive at every point in time. For example, one might have a choice between producing a total of 2 units of happiness at each time and producing 1 unit of happiness at each time. Given that both produce infinite totals, neither of which is greater than the other, standard versions of utilitarianism say that neither is better than the other. I have argued that this judgement is implausible and defended a revised version of utilitarianism that judges 2 at every time as better than 1 at every time in the infinite case (and agrees with the standard view in the finite case). The rough idea is this: One alternative is better than another if and only if there is some time in the future such that *for all later times* the consequences *up to that time* of the first alternative are better (e.g., greater total) than those of the second alternative. This is a somewhat technical problem, but it shows, I believe, some deep tensions between basic moral principles (e.g., impartiality and Pareto efficiency). It turns out that Frank Ramsey discovered this problem in the 1920s and that economists have developed various solutions that are similar to the one I developed (but much more sophisticated!).

With respect to political philosophy proper, my contributions have been mainly in the areas of liberty and equality. On the topic of equality, I have argued (with others) that although equality is a very important requirement of justice, it is limited in a number of ways. First, there are constraints imposed by the rights of self-ownership (or at least of bodily integrity) on the means by which equality may be promoted. Second, the demand for equality does not require that one promote equality as much as possible (relative to the above constraints); it merely requires that one promote equality sufficiently (where an independent account is needed of what sufficiency requires). Third, justice leaves room for individual accountability for choices. Thus, although some form of equality is required, equality of *outcomes* is not (since that leaves no room for holding agents accountable for their choices). Equality of life prospects (e.g., initial opportunities for wellbeing) and equality of brute luck advantage are two main possibilities. (Brute luck effects are effects that are not attributable to one's choices; e.g., being struck by unforeseeable lightening as opposed to losing money on a lottery ticket.) Both base the relevant equality in part on *initial* effective opportunities, but only the latter also includes *later* outcome brute luck (brute luck in how things later turn out). I have argued that justice does not require that the effects of (later) outcome brute luck be equalized. Instead, at the level of policy, it will be included for instrumental reasons when, and only when, it is efficient to do so (e.g., when administrative costs are low and it is effective in overcoming risk aversion to social desirable activities). Fourth, equality is relevant only for choosing among Pareto optimal (or efficient) options. (An option is Pareto optimal if and only if it is not possible to make someone better off without making someone else worse off. This is a weak notion of efficiency, which requires no interpersonal comparisons of wellbeing.) In the theory of justice, that is, equality is lexically posterior to Pareto efficiency (i.e., is relevant only when Pareto efficiency is achieved) and thus justice never requires leveling down to equality. Thus, it is always permissible to make one person better off so long as no one else is made worse off, even if this results in inequality of outcome. This is called Paretian egalitarianism. Finally, the conception of equality that is relevant for the theory of justice is highly sensitive to *sum-total efficiency* (i.e., favoring the greatest total, which is a much stronger notion of efficiency than Pareto efficiency). All measures of equality hold, as does leximin, that benefits to individuals who remain *below the mean*, no matter how small, take absolute priority (with respect to equality) over benefits to individuals *above the mean*, no matter how large. I argue that a plausible conception of equality for the theory of justice will hold, as does utilitarianism, that the distribution of benefits to *individuals who remain below the mean* should be made so as to *maximize the total benefits*. This gives sum-total efficiency a maximal role in the measure of equality (anything stronger would not be a conception of equality). It avoids any requirement to channel resources to worse off individuals when other individuals below the mean would get greater benefits. On this conception of equality, for example, giving each of two below average people a benefit of two units is more equal than giving a single worse off person a benefit of three units.

The other main area of political philosophy to which I've contributed is libertarian theory in general and left-libertarianism in particular. Libertarianism is committed to the natural rights of full self-ownership. This is roughly the thesis that individuals morally own themselves in the same way that a slave-owner legally owns a slave under the strongest legal form of slavery. This, however, leaves entirely open the moral status of the rest of the world. Right-libertarians (such as Nozick) view it as largely up for grabs by whoever gets there first. Left-libertarians, by contrast, hold that natural resources (all the non-agent resources in the world prior to modification by agents; land, water, air, minerals, etc.) belong to all of us in some egalitarian manner. One of my contributions has been to promote the discussion of left-libertarianism, which has been largely ignored by recent political philosophy.

Another of my contributions to libertarian theory has been to analyze the content of the notion of full self-ownership. Full self-ownership is simply full ownership applied to the case where the owner and the entity owned are identical. Ownership of an entity consists of control rights (liberty rights to use, claim rights that others not use), compensation rights (rights to compensation if the entity is used without one's permission), enforcements rights (rights to use force to stop others from violating one's rights), transfer rights (rights to lend, rent, give, or sell these rights to others), and immunities to loss of these rights under certain conditions. *Full* ownership of an entity consists of a logically strongest set of ownership rights over that entity that is compatible with someone else having those same rights over the rest of the world. There is, it turns out, some significant indeterminacy in the concept of full ownership, since strengthening rights to compensation and enforcement weakens immunities to loss, and vice-versa. Still, there is a significant determinate core to the concept of full self-ownership, and I have defended its plausibility.

My other main contribution to libertarian theory is to articulate and defend a version of equal opportunity for wellbeing left-libertarianism. It holds that individuals have the moral power to appropriate unowned natural resources as long as they pay the full competitive value (based on supply and demand) of the rights that they claim and disburse this payment so as to promote equality of effective opportunity for wellbeing. (Michael Otsuka has also developed and defended a similar view.) This views natural resources as resources to be used for the promotion of equality of opportunity, and further holds the duty to pay the competitive value of rights we claim over natural resources is the only non-consensual source of our duty to help others. Such a view, I have argued, adequately captures the roles of liberty, security, equality, accountability, and prosperity in the theory of justice. Furthermore, it is compatible with the justice of significant state activity (significant taxation, enforcement of rights, provision of public goods, promotion of equality) but not with the justice of the state's prohibition of activities that violate no one's rights.

What is the proper role of political philosophy in relation to real, political action? Can there ever be a fruitful relation between political philosophy and political practice?

I believe that, for any domain of concern, judgement and practice must be mutually informed and mutually supporting. Our reflective judgements must have a relatively good "fit" with (in the sense of endorsing) our practices—otherwise they are not anchored in the reality of everyday living. Our practices, however, should not be taken as given. Practices are often ill grounded. They may be based on false beliefs or confusions. Or they may have been well adapted to past circumstances but not to current circumstances. Neither judgement nor practice should be considered immune to revision in light of pressure from the other. Sometimes practice should be revised in light of reflective judgement and sometimes vice versa. This, of course, is what Ronald Dworkin says about the relation between a theory of the law and legal practice. It is also the method of reflective equilibrium, but where practice plays the role of judgements about specific cases. To modify some language from Kant (writing on a different topic): Theory without practice is empty. Practice without theory is blind.

This is not to say, of course, that all theorists must be practitioners and vice-versa. There is a division of labor. Some individuals will do highly abstract theory. Others will be mainly practical. Still others will be somewhere in the middle (e.g., the way that many biomedical ethicists are). Each must to some extent be sensitive to the judgements of theory and to current practices, but there are many ways of doing this and each has some value. The only thing that is ruled out is the theorist who is totally insensitive to practice and the practitioner who is totally insensitive to theory.

What do you consider the most neglected topics and/or contributions in post-Rawlsian or late 20th century political philosophy?

I wouldn't say that any of the following issues have been neglected, but I do think that they are each underdeveloped.

One pet peeve that I have is purely linguistic. Philosophers use the term "justice" to mean all kinds of different things. Sometimes it designates the moral *permissibility of political structures* (such as legal systems). Sometimes it designates moral *fairness* (e.g., as opposed to efficiency or other considerations that are relevant to moral permissibility). Sometimes it designates *legitimacy* in the sense of it not being morally permissible for others to interfere forcibly (even if the legitimate action is wrong). Finally, sometimes it designates *the duties that we morally owe each other* in the sense of respecting everyone's rights (as opposed to impersonal duties, which are owed to no one). Each of these is an important topic. I would very much like for us to develop some standard terminology. My preference is to use "justice" to mean "violates no duty owed to someone".

One topic worth greater attention is the connection between the justice of individual actions and the justice of institutions (a topic on which Liam Murphy has done insightful work). The two topics cannot be totally disconnected, if "justice" is being used in the same sense, but what exactly is the connection? There are three main types of position: (1) The justice of actions is primary and the justice of institutions derivative (e.g., as in standard libertarian theories). (2) The justice of institutions is primary and the justice of actions is derivative (e.g., a kind of rule consequentialism according which an individual has a duty of justice to X if and only if just institutions require her to X). (3) The justice of actions and the justice of institutions are each primary and each is sensitive to the other (for example, John Rawls in *A Theory of Justice* holds that there is a natural (individual) duty of justice to comply with just institutions when they exist and to promote the existence of just institutions). These are each important views, but much further investigation is needed. (Related to this is the question of how one's duties of justice are affected by the extent to which others are fulfilling their duties of justice—another underdeveloped important topic.)

An additional underdeveloped topic is the moral limits on the use of force. A lot has been written on this, but, given its importance, more attention is needed, I think. My own tentative view is that the use of force is limited to stopping someone from violating someone's rights. Punishment for its own sake is not permissible—although forcing violators to fully compensate their victims is. (Those who murder cannot even partially compensate their victims and a more complex account is needed for that case.) Moreover, national boundaries have no intrinsic moral significance, and invasions to protect the victims of gross human rights violations are no more problematic in principle than comparable uses of force internal to a country—although, of course, there are typically significantly different practical implications. The extent to which one is permitted to use force against innocent non-aggressors is also a very important topic that deserves even more attention (although it has received lots).

The final topic for more attention that I will mention is the nature of rights. Rights protect individuals and correspond to duties owed to individuals (as compared to impersonal duties, which are owed to no one). Two broad families of theories of rights have been developed. The choice-protecting family holds that rights protect choices and thus that only autonomous agents have rights. The interest-protecting family holds that rights protect interests and thus that even animals can have rights. My own view is that (1) at the conceptual level, we should recognize both kinds of rights as possible, and (2) at the normative level, some kind of hybrid theory is the most plausible. We have, I would argue, rights that protect both our choices and our interests, with the protection of choices as lexically prior to the protection of interests. For sentient individuals with no autonomy this is equivalent to an interest-protecting account. For autonomous agents, however, it allows that, where neither consent nor dissent is given, their interests will determine whether a right is violated (e.g., when there is no time to obtain consent, or when the agent is temporarily unconscious). Obviously, all this is highly controversial. I merely mention it as an example of where further work is needed.

What are the most important unsolved questions in political philosophy and/or related disciplines and what are the prospects for progress?

In some sense, of course, almost all (if not all!) the important questions are unresolved. This is not because philosophy does not make progress, but because any solved question ceases to be philosophical. I will here briefly mention just one unresolved issue.

Perhaps, the most basic unresolved question is the nature of critical normativity. By this, I mean normativity that provides the basis for criticizing existing social norms and that is not merely an empirical description of existing social norms. This issue is not particular to political philosophy, of course. It includes, for example, moral normativity generally, prudential normativity, and epistemic normativity. It raises issues both about the metaphysics of normativity and of the methodology/epistemology thereof. The issue has been explored at great length with respect to moral normativity (moral realism, non-naturalism, non-cognitivism, etc.), and I'm inclined to think that whatever is correct with respect to morality is also correct generally. Although we've made lots of progress in understanding what the core issues are and what the main positions might be, there is nothing close to agreement. I'm not very optimistic about our being able to solve this one, but we must proceed, I believe, on the presupposition that it can be solved.

Selected publications

Luc Lauwers and Peter Vallentyne "Infinite Utilitarianism: More Is Always Better", *Economics and Philosophy* 20 (2004): 307–330.

Bertil Tungodden and Peter Vallentyne "On the Possibility of Paretian Egalitarianism", *Journal of Philosophy* 102 (2005): 126–54.

Bertil Tungodden and Peter Vallentyne, "Paretian Egalitarianism with Variable Population Size", in *Intergenerational Equity and Sustainability*, edited by John Roemer and Kotaro Suzumura, (Palgrave Publishers Ltd., 2006), ch. 11.

Peter Vallentyne, "Utilitarianism and Infinite Utility," *Australasian Journal of Philosophy* 71 (1993): 212–7.

Peter Vallentyne, "Equality, Efficiency, and Priority for the Worse Off", *Economics and Philosophy* 16 (2000): 1–19. Reprinted in *The Economics of Poverty and Inequality*, vol. 1 (International Library of Critical Writings in Economics series), edited by Frank A. Cowell (Cheltenham: Edward Elgar Publishing Ltd., 2003), pp. 112–130.

Peter Vallentyne, "Brute Luck, Option Luck, and Equality of Initial Opportunities," *Ethics* 112 (2002): 529–557.

Peter Vallentyne, "Libertarianism and the State", *Social Philosophy and Policy*, 24 (forthcoming 2007).

Peter Vallentyne and Morry Lipson, "Equal Opportunity and the Family," *Public Affairs Quarterly* 3 (1989): 29–47. Reprinted in *Children's Rights Revisioned: Philosophical Readings*, edited by Rosalind Ladd (Wadsworth Press, 1996), pp. 82–97.

Peter Vallentyne and Shelly Kagan, "Infinite Utility and Finitely Additive Value Theory", *Journal of Philosophy* 94 (1997): 5–26.

Peter Vallentyne and Hillel Steiner, eds., *The Origins of Left Libertarianism: An Anthology of Historical Writings*, New York: Palgrave Publishers Ltd., 2000.

Peter Vallentyne and Hillel Steiner, eds., *Left Libertarianism and Its Critics: The Contemporary Debate*, New York: Palgrave Publishers Ltd., 2000.

Peter Vallentyne, Hillel Steiner, and Michael Otsuka, "Why Left-Libertarianism Isn't Incoherent, Indeterminate, or Irrelevant: A Reply to Fried", Philosophy and Public Affairs 33 (2005): 201–15.

15
Michael Walzer

Professor of Social Science
Institute of Advanced Studies, Princeton, USA

Why were you initially drawn to political philosophy?

I was initially drawn to politics; I am not sure that I have ever been drawn to political philosophy, except as a reflection on what is actually happening in the political world. I grew up in a politically engaged family; I learned to read by struggling through the opinion pieces in the left-wing daily PM (published in New York in the 1940s) written by people like Max Lerner and I.F. Stone. I attended Brandeis University from 1952–56—a new school that attracted many left-leaning Jewish kids (and many "red diaper babies"), where the Sixties started in the Fifties. The magazine *Dissent* was founded in 1954 by Irving Howe and Lewis Coser, both of whom were teaching at Brandeis. I was immediately attracted to their version of anti-communist leftism and was encouraged by them to write for the magazine. They also guided my reading in those years: Camus, Orwell, Ignazio Silone, and others of that sort - literary and political intellectuals. Camus' *The Rebel* was my first, and for a long time my only, philosophical text (do academic philosophers recognize it as such?). And then I read the people you might think of as Camus' opponents – Merleau Ponty (*Humanism and Terror*), Sartre, Franz Fanon. But what I read of Sartre were the essays, stories, and plays – not then or since the big philosophical books, which I quickly decided I would never understand and didn't need to try to understand.

In graduate school at Harvard in the late 1950s, I studied political theory, but always in the same way as I had read Sartre. So I was very much engaged by Locke's *Second Treatise* and his *Letter on Toleration*, but never got through *An Essay Concerning Human Understanding*. And I much preferred Kant's *Eternal Peace*, or *Idea for a Universal History*, or *Theory and Practice* to any of the Critiques, which I suppose I labored through, though I have little memory of doing so. Among literary forms, I like the political essay best. I have never been persuaded that it was necessary to have a full-blown theory in order to have interesting opinions about the political world. Indeed, full-blown theorists often have routine and predictable opinions.

Insofar as I have been drawn to theorizing, it's been to defend the coherence or at least the non-contradiction of my own opinions. So the arguments I had already made about different wars (particularly Vietnam) led to a book about just war theory, and the arguments I had already made about the distribution of different social goods led to a book about distributive justice. Still, having written those books, I remain more interested in the particular arguments than in the overall theory. I am sometimes forced into theoretical debates, but I am never very happy there. I have always been more comfortable writing for *Dissent* than for the academic journals, though I was able to manage the journals when I thought it was necessary (for the sake of my professional career) to do so. Since I have been living in the academy for a long time, I have read quite a bit of academic political theory – by my colleagues and students, mostly – and found it most appealing when it addressed real political questions that were agitating people outside the academy. The conduct of war, civil liberties, the public schools, the culture wars, gender discrimination, religion and the secular state—these are the sorts of issues that I am drawn to, whether they are expressed philosophically or in some other way: in legal argument, for example, or in political polemic, or in literary criticism.

What do you consider your own most important contribution(s) to political philosophy, and why?

I would like to think that I have contributed something to contemporary political debates—some sense of complexity, the necessity of nuance, the value of worrying. Also, perhaps, a usable (because not esoteric) vocabulary for talking about war and justice. Also, perhaps, a version of leftism or left-liberalism that is resistant to the appeal of populist demagogues, maximal leaders, and totalizing ideologies.

The work that I have done over the last 20 years on the Jewish political tradition can't be called a contribution to political philosophy, strictly speaking, since philosophical speculation was not the common mode of the tradition. But it does present to the wider world an entire political culture, which is not well known, and in which arguments were carried on that are often similar to the arguments of political philosophers. And I have managed to entice a number of philosophers into the project, to write commentaries on critically important texts.

In the larger world of political philosophy, I doubt that my books have made much of an impact. My version of just war theory is now regarded as some kind of orthodoxy, but only for the purpose of providing an object of criticism for philosophers determined to be unorthodox. There have been some highly intelligent papers written in opposition to my views about non-combattant immunity, the equal rights of soldiers, and the relative independence of *jus ad bellum* and *jus in bello*. I suppose that I have contributed a set of refutable arguments, but I can't take much credit for that since the refutations are mostly, so it seems to me, examples of the sort of academic philosophy that I never meant to inspire. They have virtually nothing to do with the experience of war (I will say more about this in response to the 4th question).

My book about the spheres of justice is probably the most important thing I have written (though my own favorites among my books are *Exodus and Revolution* and *The Company of Critics*, which are not philosophical at all). It doesn't seem to me that the argument of *Spheres* is of great interest to younger philosophers today. I argue for a pluralist account of the principles of distributive justice, aiming to recover the ways in which people actually talk about the distribution of this good or that one. I got some very nice (both sympathetic and critical) responses, but mostly I was treated to a lecture from Philosophy 101 on the idiocies of relativism, and then ignored. If I have contributed anything to the justice debates, it is probably with regard to particular cases: people writing about money, schooling, health care, information, political power, and other social goods are much more likely to refer to my book than are philosophers looking for an abstract or general account of what justice requires. Which is entirely as it should be—the argument about pluralism illustrated in practice. Perhaps I should add that a number of sociologists and social theorists have found the argument useful.

But I don't want to accept too quickly this idea of "contributions," as if political philosophy were a kind of Community Chest to which we are all obligated to send a gift. And the gifts accumulate, and the Community Chest is more and more capable of helping the community. And the contributions accumulate, and political philosophy is more and more capable of—what? Providing guidance for political decisions? Creating a better political society? Enabling a more sophisticated political discourse? Individual articles and books can have effects like that (the work of Jürgen Habermas is a good example, though I think that it is his journalistic, not his philosophical, writing that has been most effective—no doubt the two are connected.) But I don't think that there is any actual accumulation of contributions over time. Theorists and theories come and go. Controversies flare up and subside, and many years later flare up again, and not much that could be called useful knowledge is gained in the process. The only contribution we can make is to the politics of our own time, and since politics is a partisan activity, that is likely to be a partisan contribution; it won't be universally recognized or admired. The small number of philosophers whose work survives to be cited and quoted in later generations are not really "contributing" to the politics of those times, since the cites and quotes will rarely serve their originally intended purpose. Perhaps if we defend an absolutist position, our words will legitimately be used by future absolutists. But the subtleties we more often aim at are likely to be time-bound; they are harder to reproduce in new times and places.

What is the proper role of political philosophy in relation to real, political action? Can there ever be a fruitful relation between political philosophy and political practice?

The old Marxist dream was of a unity of theory and practice. We were supposed to have a big, all-encompassing theory, such as Marxism was, which would give us a clear reading of any event in politics or political economy. Is there a strike in Detroit? We can tell you exactly how it developed, beginning with the division of labor in ancient Babylonia and moving rapidly forward, and exactly what significance it holds for contemporary politics. And from this knowledge, we can shape the "correct ideological position" vis-à-vis the strike and figure out exactly what ought to be done. And then, if things don't work out the way they are supposed to, we can go back and revise the theory, so that it will do better next time. Of course, for most Marxists, it was easier to insist that things had worked out the way they were supposed to, even when they obviously hadn't, than to make the necessary revisions. Anyway, the theory in question was not supposed to be an academic theory (which is what it eventually became, when it was cut off from political practice and protected from the consequences of failure); its home, so to speak, was the "theoretical" magazine of the mass movement. The theorists were themselves activists, who wrote for other activists, who discussed the theory in study groups before engaging in the practices it specified. So the unity of theory and practice was a matter of everyday experience.

All that is gone now. We don't have a theory of that kind, and the home of the theories we do have is the department of philosophy and the academic journal. That doesn't preclude a link to political action, but the link is likely to be fortuitous. Perhaps the theory/practice connection survives in certain professional settings—as between law professors and judges, law review articles and judicial decisions. That connection is what makes Ronald Dworkin such an exemplary public intellectual. But for the rest of us, there are no groups of activists studying our books, so it is a lucky philosopher whose ideas find their way into the world of political practice. Maybe one of his former students works on a congressional staff or writes speeches for a union leader. Or an odd and unlikely politician reads her philosophical critique, of capital punishment, say, and decides that it is exactly right and urgently important. And then, if there is some degree of integrity in the appropriation of the argument, the theorist may claim to have had an impact on a political debate or a piece of legislation or a policy decision. I think that we should welcome any such impact, but the truth is that academic work in philosophy, as in most other humanities and social science disciplines, is done in isolation from the "real world" and is subject largely to internal pressure and direction. It reflects professional imperatives, and over time it tends toward increasing subtlety and decreasing accessibility—until the arguments collapse of their own weight and some brave soul or inspired genius starts all over again.

There is one big exception to my argument so far: Leo Strauss is a philosopher who has clearly had more than a fortuitous influence on this debate or that decision. He has produced a significant group of political philosophers loyal to his teachings and a significant group of intellectuals and government officials who believe themselves to be applying those teachings in everyday political practice. For those of us who are not Straussians, this might be taken as a warning about the dangers of the "fruitful relation."

But whatever the relation of philosophy to practice, there certainly can be, and should be, a close relation between knowledge and practice. Activists in the environmentalist movement need to be in close touch with scientists. Labor activists need to know something about economics—if only to challenge the versions of economic theory that guide governmental decision-making. Defenders of our civil liberties need some knowledge of constitutional law. Critics of US foreign policy should learn as much as they can about the history of international politics and diplomacy. And if knowledge is useful, I suppose there is something – though something less – to be said for the usefulness of the sociology and philosophy of knowledge.

What do you consider the most neglected topics and/or contributions in post-Rawlsian or late 20th century political philosophy?

I doubt that I read enough philosophy to know what its neglected topics are. My sense from the journals I look at is that most of the issues that agitate the political world eventually find their way into philosophical reflection, one way or another. It's not the issues that are neglected (think of the way in which capital punishment, abortion, and noncombattant immunity have become standard topics on which graduate students test their skills), but rather politics itself—I mean politics as a human activity of a certain sort, in which the issues actually arise, are defined, debated, and (always temporarily) dealt with. My sense is that political philosophers are only rarely engaged, let alone entranced, by politics. The play of interests, the endless bargaining, the feelings of solidarity and hostility, the intense competitiveness, the love of power, the exhilaration of victory, the anxiety of defeat, the danger of dirty hands—how can philosophers talk sensibly about reason, deliberation, justice, authority, and many other topics without some sensitivity to these features of political experience? I would ask the same question about war. Just war theory is an adaptation of justice to the circumstances of warfare, and so it requires some engagement with those circumstances. That doesn't mean that theorists need to know war at first hand, but they do need to make an effort to imagine it, to think hard about the frightening, brutal, coercive character of armies in combat. They need to read anthropological accounts of warfare, memoirs of soldiers, military history, novels and poems dealing with the experience of combat—all this is more important than any philosophical texts (including my own). Some philosophical critics of just war theory are opposed to the adaptation of morality to the circumstances of war, and so they produce moral arguments that would be exactly right if war were a peace-time activity. I sometimes feel that theorists of reason and deliberation would be exactly right if politics was conducted only in academic seminars (or in artificial settings designed to feel like seminars).

What I would like to see, by contrast, is not so much a different political philosophy as a philosophy of politics—something like J. Glenn Gray's wonderful book, *The Warriors: Reflections on Men in Battle*. "Reflections on Men and Women in Political Battle" would be an appropriate subtitle for the book I am looking for. It would have many chapter titles that were close to Gray's: "The enduring appeal of battle, "Love: war's ally and foe," "Images of the enemy," and "The ache of guilt." Those are all, I would say, neglected topics in contemporary academic writing about political life. Looking at the next question, I would suggest that if they were extensively written about, that would be a kind of progress, even if it didn't happen, as it wouldn't, that the writing got better and better.

What are the most important unsolved questions in political philosophy and/or related disciplines and what are the prospects for progress?

There are no important (or unimportant, for that matter) questions that have been solved. Politics is a realm of essentially contested ideas, and philosophical argument is one version, a rather elevated version, of the contest. I doubt that there is anything like progress in political philosophy, though there probably is something like progress in politics—the abolition of slavery might serve as an example or the (partial) liberation of women. But these advances are not proof against regression. Is the widespread acceptance of the language of human rights an example of philosophical progress? Maybe so, but we don't agree on what rights are, or on how many there are, or on what realms of human life they govern, or on whether or when they can be overridden, or on how they should be enforced, or on what their standing is vis-à-vis cultural difference. And I don't see any way of definitively ending those disagreements—they certainly won't be ended by the unforced force of a good argument. We still need to make the best arguments we can, and hope that they have some local impact.

Like anyone else, philosophers can do good; they can advance the cause of justice in their own time and place, for example, as John Rawls certainly did, by helping their fellow citizens think differently about the prevailing injustices. Down the road, though, the philosophers of the next generation will have to do the same thing again, and they will probably find a different and, as they will believe, improved way of doing it (which may well turn out to be a very old way, re-invented).

16
Andrew Williams

Department of Philosophy
University of Warwick, UK

Why were you initially drawn to political philosophy?

My exposure to academic *philosophy* was a happy accident that arose after some of my teachers suggested I apply for a university place at Oxford. I'd studied too few languages to pursue my preferred course (History). I chose Philosophy, Politics, and Economics (PPE) instead, having already studied economics, and been interested in politics for most of my teens, which I spent in a Labour-dominated area (South Wales) during a period of renewed militancy (the late 1970's). I had no idea what Philosophy involved when I choose PPE but figured I could, if necessary, drop the subject. Having luckily gained a place, I spent the summer at home in Swansea hanging out with my friends, but also reading Hume, Mill, and some elementary logic. I found that reading fascinating and was intrigued by the foundational questions it addressed, and by the possibility of trying to answer them with arguments, which could be imaginative and surprising as well as reasoned.

As for *political* philosophy, the following summer I read *A Theory of Justice* and admired how Rawls showed that philosophical arguments could address the questions about economic justice and the choice between capitalism and socialism that interested me well before studying philosophy. Moreover, political philosophers could do so in a way that drew on other disciplines of interest to me, like economics. Most importantly, I was struck by the thought that with a little ingenuity it was possible to defend progressive conclusions by appeal to relatively weak assumptions, for example, about the pervasive role luck plays in explaining individuals' relative position in society and the value of sharing in each other's fortunes. The fact that only three members of my cohort went to university though the school contained about seventeen hundred pupils, and nearly all my school friends were still unemployed at the end of my first year away, encouraged me to identify with Rawls's assumptions, and so doubtless played some role in explaining why I was drawn to political philosophy.

What do you consider your own most important contribution(s) to political philosophy, and why?

If any of my papers is thought to be important, it's probably "Incentives, Inequality, and Publicity", a response to Jerry Cohen's claim that Rawls's difference principle is best construed as condemning a wider range of inequality-generating incentive payments than Rawls supposes. To defend his claim, Cohen argues that the difference principle requires workers to conform to a self-denying egalitarian ethos in their labor market behavior and not merely in their voting behavior. So, if everyone really conformed to the difference principle then many incentive payments would be redundant. In response, I appeal to Rawls's ideal of well-ordered social cooperation to argue that there are weighty reasons to restrict the scope of the difference principle to a society's basic structure, understood as the set of profoundly influential institutions that are public in various respects, though not necessarily legally enforced. I then argue that thus restricted the difference principle does not require conformity to Cohen's egalitarian ethos since the latter's informational demands are so great; for example, even in one's own case it seems impossible to know how close one's career choices come to maximizing the expectations of the least advantaged.

Whether there are principled reasons to restrict the scope of the distributive norms like the difference principle is an important issue for various reasons. Most obviously, since the incentive argument for inequality is so often invoked the issue should make some difference to our stance in real political debates, and our attitude to at least some existing inequalities. Showing that the difference principle does not require Cohen's ethos may also help prevent right-wing critics from claiming that there is a deep conflict between equality and liberty, a desirable result when many doubt whether justice favors sacrificing their vocational ambitions to make the least advantaged wealthier. The appeal to publicity is also of interest because it prompts more general questions about the nature of injustice, which Cohen has addressed in his more recent work criticizing constructivism.

For constructivists like Rawls, injustice arises when agents fail to conform to certain stringent principles whose primary function is to guide action rather than evaluate states of affairs. Moreover, the plausibility of those principles is assumed by Rawlsians to depend on the truth of various factual assumptions (including ones about limited information) as well as the principles' capacity to satisfy certain non-distributive desiderata (such as facilitating well-ordered cooperation). For others, principles of justice serve primarily not to guide action but to evaluate distributions of benefits and burdens along one dimension, and in a manner that is fact-insensitive and pure insofar as it eschews appeal to non-distributive desiderata. My current suspicion is that these two views address quite different questions, and can be combined within a complete account of our convictions about justice.

I'd also like to mention a second paper on "Equality of Resources and Procreative Justice", which was co-authored by Paula Casal. The paper asks how responsibility for individuals' reproductive choices should be distributed between the decision-maker and her society, and argues that under certain conditions resource egalitarianism requires internalizing the costs of an individual's reproductive choices but allows others to free-ride on the benefits. These issues have been relatively neglected, but I think they're important for philosophers to address. Most obviously, their importance arises because the costs and benefits our institutions attach to reproductive decisions will have profound effects on our quality of life. It's likely that our childhoods, and probably our entire lives, will differ depending on the costs that institutions attach to our parents' decisions regarding the size of their families. In societies with a gender-based division of labor within the family those costs are also likely to fall unequally on men and women. No less importantly, how a society satisfies any requirements to limit its environmental impact for the sake of future generations will depend on its members' decisions regarding the length of their lives and the size of their families as well their consumption decisions. If our institutions are to discharge our intergenerational obligations without producing unfairness within the present generation we need to decide if demographically significant decisions should be treated similarly to other decisions with comparable environmental impact. I hope the second paper will encourage others to consider these issues.

Let me add that I constantly draw on my co-author's expertise, and so asked her about my biggest contribution to political philosophy. Sadly for me she cited all the mistakes I saved other people from making by commenting on their drafts. She may well be right, but it would have been nicer had she at least mentioned the volumes I've co-edited on equality, basic income, and social justice.

What is the proper role of political philosophy in relation to real, political action? Can there ever be a fruitful relation between political philosophy and political practice?

When people advance particular proposals about legislation, public policy, or institutional design they make more or less explicit assumptions not only about the likely effects of their proposals but about which ends are worthwhile, and which means to pursue them are permissible. They also make assumptions about which political decisions possess authority over us, and so should guide us because of their source rather than content.

One important role for political philosophy is to help clarify those assumptions, their grounds and their implications, and where necessary suggest how they should be revised. This doesn't require political philosophers always to address very specific proposals rather than write at a higher level of generality. But it does favor us always asking how our work might be applied, or misapplied, in such specific disputes, and using such disputes for illustrative purposes. We should also ask how our work might be received by academics in other disciplines, especially since any practical impact it has will usually be indirect, and proceed through law, economics, or social policy.

It's easy to be pessimistic about the likelihood of a mutually beneficial relationship between political philosophy and practice, especially when we see how the outcome of many political disputes depends upon the distribution of money and the resilience of religious faith in the face of reason. It seems too hasty, however, to conclude that such a relationship can never exist. Doing so would require us to overlook obvious historical counter-examples, like J.S. Mill's *On Liberty*, a work of lasting philosophical value, which was prompted in part by the author's reflections on contemporary problems and which has exerted a positive if not uncontroversial impact on our political culture. There are also some current examples of work that explicitly relate abstract conceptions of political morality and distributive justice to concrete policy proposals in ways that display the ingenuity that drew me to philosophy, and that may well exert a positive impact on practice. Here I have in mind Thomas Pogge's work on global poverty, Philippe Van Parijs's defense of unconditional basic income, and much of Ronald Dworkin's output.

What do you consider the most neglected topics and/or contributions in post-Rawlsian or late 20th century political philosophy?

A decade ago I would have mentioned two things, namely (i) neglect for the distributive injustices that women suffer on the basis of their gender and insufficient interest in combating them with a variety of non-legally enforceable norms, and (ii) neglect for the relationship between domestic and global principles of distributive justice. Although there was some good work on each set of topics, supply fell far short of what should have been demanded given the urgency of the problems.

Now the gap's narrowing somewhat, I'll mention the more general problem that many of our best developed conceptions of distributive ethics are *ideal* theories that specify how we should act on the assumption of nearly full compliance with their demands. Some philosophers, like Cohen, Dworkin, and Liam Murphy, have done something to correct this limitation. But the implications of ideal theories under conditions of non-compliance, including the ones we actually face, are rarely examined in much depth.

Here I'm also especially struck by the fact that when philosophers do address questions of ideal theory they tend to proceed from the perspective of the beneficiaries of non-compliance, and ask how much they can reasonably be asked to transfer to its victims. Perhaps such a focus is natural given our fortunate position, and commendable insofar as it indicates some awareness that we're not doing enough. Even so, I think we should spend more time asking what losses the victims of injustice are permitted, or required, to impose on us when those losses would be an effective means to improve their condition. In short, assuming poverty and environmental degradation will cause the avoidable deaths of millions of people, we need an account of what can be done to defend to those individuals against others who, perhaps unintentionally, help maintain global institutions that impose those losses upon them.

I should add that such an account might be illuminating even if those defensive rights are unlikely to be exercised because the current beneficiaries of global injustice remain overwhelmingly powerful. Realizing that it would be permissible to impose losses on us if doing so would change our behavior in ways beneficial to the least advantaged may make it even more vivid that we are participants in a deeply unjust set of global institutions.

What are the most important unsolved questions in political philosophy and/or related disciplines and what are the prospects for progress?

Within moral and political philosophy there are longstanding debates about the conditions under which agents should be held responsible for their attitudes and decisions. We often disagree about the difference that accepting some version of determinism should make to our convictions about responsibility. Some of us are also unsure about the difference that specific scientific accounts of human psychology should make to our convictions. How should we respond, for example, if some explanation from evolutionary psychology of gender-based variations in aggression, competitiveness, or concern for offspring turns out to be true? And even if we have settled convictions about these issues, we might still be unsure about why we should hold collective agents responsible for their decisions, or what difference such decisions make to how we should treat the individuals who comprise them.

As well as raising theoretical problems, these issues could have practical implications for disputes about the legitimacy of punishment and the justice of inequality across genders and political boundaries, and so seem very important to me. We're unlikely to ever reach consensus about them, but I'm optimistic that we'll make progress in understanding our questions more clearly, and the range of reasonable positions. Here specific contributions to the debate about responsibility, such T.M. Scanlon's discussion in his magnificent *What We Owe To Each Other* and later work, give me some hope. I'm also influenced by a more general admiration for the progress in understanding that moral and political philosophy has made over the last thirty or forty years. (The material on the reading lists my students use is on average much better than the material I read as a student!) Derek Parfit is probably right that the history of ethics may just be beginning, and if so the same is true of political philosophy.

Selected publications

"The Revisionist Difference Principle", *Canadian Journal of Philosophy* (1995), pp. 257–81.

"Resource Egalitarianism and Limits to Basic Income", *Economics and Philosophy* (1999), pp. 85–107.

Matthew Clayton and Andrew Williams (eds.), *The Ideal of Equality* (London: Macmillan, 2000).

"Dworkin on Capability", *Ethics* (2002), pp. 23–39.

Andrew Reeve and Andrew Williams (eds.), *Real Libertarianism Assessed: Essays on Van Parijs* (London: Palgrave, 2003).

Matthew Clayton and Andrew Williams (eds.), *Blackwell Readings in Philosophy: Social Justice* (Oxford: Blackwell, 2004).

Paula Casal and Andrew Williams, "Equality of Resources and Procreative Justice" in Justine Burley (ed.), *Dworkin and His Critics* (Oxford: Blackwell, 2004), pp. 150–169.

"Equality, Ambition and Insurance", *Aristotelian Society, Supplementary Volume LXXVIII* (2004), pp. 131–150.

"Liberty, Equality, and Property", in John Dryzek, Bonnie Honig, Anne Phillips (eds.), *The Oxford Handbook of Political Theory* (Oxford: Oxford University Press, 2006), pp. 488–506.

"Liberty, Liability, and Contractualism", in Nils Holtug and Kasper Lippert-Rasmussen (eds.), *Egalitarianism: New Essays on the Nature and Value of Equality* (Oxford: Oxford University Press, 2007).

17

Jonathan Wolff

Professor of Philosophy
University College London, UK

Why were you initially drawn to political philosophy?

It is hard for me to remember a time when I wasn't interested in political philosophy, or at least in political questions. I think Walzer remarks that individuals who think they have achieved objectivity often see things differently simply because they are on the margins of their society. It would be absurd to claim this for myself, but probably like many people who ended up as philosophers I grew up feeling something of an outsider, and therefore was fairly reflective. My father was born in Germany but came to England as a child on the *Kindertransport*. My mother was born in England, but was also from a family of Jewish refugees, from Eastern Europe. I didn't have a self-image as belonging to an immigrant family, but we certainly felt different to those around us.

My father worked for a company that moved him from place to place as it pleased. Most of my early childhood was spent in a small town in Kent where we all felt out of place. We were a middle class, labour voting, Jewish family, and were not especially comfortable among our immediate neighbours in a predominately working class area, but even less so among the small but wealthy Jewish community: the normal cliché of doctors, lawyers and successful businessmen. Most people we knew seemed narrow-minded and prejudiced in some way. Although we were not, as far as I remember, victims of prejudice, casual racism was in the air. I can remember as a child not understanding why my classmates thought black people – not that they had ever seen any – both frightening and inferior. If you were frightened of them, surely you thought them superior? But I was more shocked that some of the Jewish businessmen and doctors we knew were just as prejudiced, even though many were from families who had suffered in the past.

Although as a child I did not know how badly my father's family had suffered at the hands of the Nazis this cast a shadow over my upbringing. My father would not buy any German products, and my mother often said that no Jewish person should vote for a right-wing party, and she despaired of her own mother for doing so. Questions about what how one should act, and for what reasons, were always there.

Later on, one of the questions which I can see in retrospect as getting me interested in philosophy concerned the justification of punishment. At the age of 13 or so I can remember asking myself what justification there could be for punishing someone who sincerely believed that what they had done was morally acceptable. I didn't take the issue very far – I didn't discuss it with anyone, or try to find readings about it – but I thought about it from time to time and found myself uncertain what to think. A year or two further on I started studying twentieth century Russian history, at school, and hence became acquainted with basic arguments in favour of communism and against private property. These arguments seemed very appealing, as, somewhat later on for me, did anarchist arguments against the state. Without signing up to anything, I read some communist and anarchist writings, which were inspiring in their way, and excellent as critiques, but infuriatingly vague about the details of what else could happen. One could detect some sort of longing to live like the watch-makers in the Swiss Cantons, which didn't sound very interesting to me. At one time I thought that my life's work would be to work out the details of how communist anarchism could function. But luckily I never got started on that.

My school career was pretty undistinguished, and after leaving school I didn't go straight to university, but worked in an office for a few years. I realized, though, that I was missing out, and as I was, by this time, living in London I applied to, and was lucky enough to be accepted by, University College (UCL). I began with the view that politics was something you should be interested in your own time, but a philosophy degree should be more serious and consist of the study of logic, philosophy of science, philosophy of language and maybe aesthetics to bring it a humanizing edge.

However, Jerry Cohen, who then taught at UCL, had just published *Karl Marx's Theory of History: A Defence*, and this book rightly had a huge impact. The idea of stating historical materialism in a way that could be assessed as being true or false, and was not obviously false, was a revelation, and created a new era in Marx scholarship. Even then – between 1980 and 1983 – Jerry was being invited all round the world to lecture, and was often billed as the 'World Leading Philosophical Exponent of Historical Materialism.' Jerry is also a brilliant lecturer and teacher, as well as being enormously entertaining. I thought I should not miss the opportunity to study with someone who was a world leader in their area, creating a new field of study, and doing so in a way I could understand and engage with. It was very exciting to be in Jerry's Marxism seminars where he would try out responses to published critics, and, even as an undergraduate you felt you had a chance that something you said might make him change a sentence in a paper he was writing. Consequently, although I hadn't planned this, I was drawn into the study of political philosophy and of Marxism, and away from philosophy of science and language, which never fully 'clicked' for me. Studying political philosophy and Marxism allowed me to take up the intellectual interests I'd had for some years, but in a much more systematic way.

I remained at UCL to read for the MPhil, under Jerry's supervision. My papers were Political Philosophy, Ethics and Marxism, and I wrote a dissertation on exploitation. There was something, I suppose, inevitable about this for me, although I had tried to resist it, thinking at first that I should study Hume and Philosophical Logic. But in the end I decided to follow my interests, rather than what I thought I ought to be interested in; advice I have given to many students since.

What do you consider your own most important contribution(s) to political philosophy, and why?

I am under no illusions about this. The main reason I am known as a political philosopher is because of the books I have written for students, especially *An Introduction to Political Philosophy*, first published in 1996, and now translated into a half a dozen languages, and widely used in introductory courses. I wrote it because I was dissatisfied with the introductory texts then available. There seemed to be a division between those who thought of themselves as analytic philosophers, and produced concept-driven texts, with a chapter each on 'authority', 'freedom', 'rights', and so on, and those who were more properly historians, with a chapter on each major figure, in chronological order. There is a place for both of these types of books, of course, but my feeling was that, on the whole, that they made a subject I find fascinating rather boring. They presumed that the reader was already interested in the subject, or, at least, compelled for some reason to read about it, and the books were written almost as a way of testing whether the reader is serious. My approach, instead, was to assume that an author needs to earn the reader's attention.

I thought that the best way of attempting this was to write the sort of book I would have liked to read myself as a student. Once I got started this turned out to be a problem-driven text, introducing analytical tools where this helps, while also showing that the great political philosophers were interested in questions which still concern us. At the same time, while I wanted to hold the attention of students, I didn't want to alienate their teachers. This seems to have worked, I am very pleased to say.

Unlike many people, my first research as a professional philosopher was not a continuation of my PhD thesis, largely because I did not write a PhD thesis. Although, as I said, I registered at UCL in 1983 to read for the MPhil under Jerry Cohen's supervision, Jerry left UCL in 1984 to take up his current Chair at Oxford. My thesis was completed under the supervision of Bill Hart, primarily a philosopher of mathematics and logician, but with very wide philosophical interests, including social choice theory. Bill was an enormous help and influence, but as he was not a political philosopher my graduate work at that time was largely self-directed.

In 1985 I was encouraged to apply for the vacancy at UCL that Jerry had left, and to my astonishment was eventually offered the job, even before completing by MPhil. UCL had decided that they wanted to find someone who could teach exactly what Jerry had done – lecture in Marxism and political philosophy, and give tutorials over a wider range of philosophical topics – and this meant that the candidate pool was very restricted. I had, though, also been offered a Fellowship to do more graduate work at Harvard, and so it was agreed that I should go to Harvard for one year, and come back to take up my post in 1986.

I was very excited about spending a year at Harvard. Scanlon had just moved there, and Rawls was still highly active. Nozick was there too, but his work was of less interest to me then. However, when I arrived I found that Rawls and Scanlon were both on leave for the entire year, and I think that there were no classes at all in political philosophy – certainly not at graduate level – in the Philosophy Department. Nozick was teaching one course on spiritual leaders and another on the nature of wisdom. In the Government Department Judith Sklar's seminars were open only to their own students and the only graduate level political philosophy course open to me was a seminar given by Michael Sandel, on liberalism and communitarianism. This was not something that had interested me before. I suppose I was more interested in debates about Rawls's difference principle rather than his liberty principle. Despite this, I did learn a lot, and a number of leading figures, including Rawls and Walzer, gave presentations to the seminar.

Within the Harvard Philosophy Department, I spent most of my time in seminars and classes with Burt Dreben, Hilary Putnam and Warren Goldfarb. Although the topics we studied were diverse and had little to do with political philosophy, all three of them influenced the way I now approach political philosophy, and, probably the message I received – or at least took – from each of them was the same. In essence, it has a negative and a positive side. The negative point was that the fact that many highly intelligent and effective philosophers have worked hard and published papers on a question is not enough to show that the question is one that is worth pursuing; and it was common at Harvard at the time to express contempt for many of the debates that then occupied the journals. The positive point is that philosophy starts with puzzlement about issues that arise in a specific context—whether everyday life, or in mathematics, or concerning art, or whatever. I understand this to mean that whatever one is working on, it should be possible to show how ultimately it has roots in a puzzle that you could explain to someone who is not a philosopher.

This was a revelation to me. My training up to this point was much more about seeing philosophy as proceeding by means of 'thesis, counter-example, reformulation, new counter-example', without stopping to see why anyone should be concerned to put the thesis forward in the first place. I came away from Harvard seeing that philosophy needed the rigour that I had been drilled in, but also needed a context in which this could be seen to have some purpose.

However, like many people who had been exposed to that Harvard regime, it became hard for me to work out a fruitful line of research. My general plan had been to write up my MPhil thesis, which was an analysis of the concept of exploitation. But on return to London this seemed to me exactly the wrong way of doing philosophy, and in fact it was about another ten years before I finally got round to writing this up in publishable form.

My first attempt to invent myself as a philosopher had me trying to be a Hobbes scholar, attempting to use the new debates about Rawls and the hypothetical contract as a way of approaching Hobbes's arguments. I spent a bit of time reading the primary and secondary sources, and trying to work up a paper, but I soon realized that this was not a fruitful way of spending my time, and that compared to real scholars I was totally out of my depth. First, I didn't have the background and training. Second, and more importantly, I didn't have the temperament. I can't sit in a library day after day, reading and making notes. I'd find myself reading chapters but taking in nothing, or, if I found myself interested in something I would want to stop and think about it, maybe go for a walk or do something else entirely, while musing on the idea. When I came back to the text I would realize that what I was thinking about would have little to do with what Hobbes had said, but rather what I would thought he ought to have said. Again I eventually got a published paper out of this work but I realized early on that this is not how I wanted to spend my life.

At the end of my first summer my colleague Michael Rosen told me that he had been asked to write a book on Robert Nozick, but didn't want to do it, and asked me if I would be interested in doing it instead. My first reaction was that this would be an absurd waste of time: why write a study of a philosopher with whom you profoundly disagree? But within a day or two I realized that this was exactly the right thing for me at the time. My attempt to define my own project had come to nothing, and so a finite project, with a defined endpoint, and a virtually guaranteed publication, was ideal. It took me probably two years to write the book. When published in 1991 it was mostly well-received, and when I last checked it was still in print. It also gave me the confidence to try out new ideas for myself.

In working on Nozick I had, for the first time, to grapple with some of the contemporary literature on the problem of political obligation. This connected with my interest in Hobbes, and I also felt that I had a number of ideas on how to approach the problem. I spent a few years working on this, greatly enjoying it at first, and always thinking I was on the brink of sorting out the whole thing. But after a while the harder I looked at the problem, the more complex the issues became, and I grew less confident I was that I could solve the problem within the liberal framework I had assumed. Although I felt that I had made some contribution to clarifying the issues, and criticizing other people's positions, in the end I ran out of steam. The problem that I came to take seriously is simply that the state is not a voluntary association, but it is very hard to understand how there can be non-voluntary associations within a liberal framework. On the other hand, assuming that the state can be understood on the model of other non-voluntary associations like the family seemed to require a complete rethinking of the issues, and I didn't have the energy to start again.

Really I had always known that my work would focus on justice and equality and it was just a matter of finding the right entry point. I had at various points tried to join the debate that was emerging in response to Dworkin's two seminal papers on equality, published in *Philosophy and Public Affairs*, but once more I found it hard to get started. I could make picky little points about the formulations of particular versions of theories, but I had a dissatisfaction with the debate that I found hard to articulate. Finally I began to see more clearly what I felt was wrong with the contemporary literature.

The argument I presented in what I think is my best-known paper 'Fairness, Respect and the Egalitarian Ethos', published in 1998 in *Philosophy and Public Affairs*, raised a number of problems with contemporary work on equality. The main argument is that the forms of conditional systems of benefit that appear to follow from theories such as those of Dworkin can create a division in society and undermine self-respect, neither of which sit comfortably with the idea of a society of equals. Very soon after my paper was published, Elizabeth Anderson published her very influential paper 'What is the Point of Equality?' which coined the phrase 'luck egalitarianism' to describe the views of Dworkin, Cohen, Arneson, and others, and made a number of criticisms which seemed to be closely related to those I had made. Since then Samuel Scheffler has done some very interesting work clarifying the distinction between distributive and social equality, which is also present in a less developed form in my paper too. But of course the distinction is well-known, and has been the topic of the work of Richard Norman and David Miller for many years.

However, because of the affinities between some of my arguments and those of Anderson and Scheffler I have sometimes been 'rolled up' with them as a critic of luck egalitarianism. However, my real target in that paper is not so much the theory of luck egalitarianism but with what would happen if we tried to implement a system of making people bear the costs of their choices when we haven't yet moved to a full, enlightened, system of equality. Essentially the argument is that the implementing luck egalitarianism requires society to filter out would-be free-riders, but to do this will often have costs (in self-respect) for those already at the bottom of the heap. In some cases they will have to declare that they lack employable talents others have, and this can be humiliating for them. I do not argue that it is necessarily humiliating, or that we couldn't imagine a society where no one is humiliated by having to admit to themselves and others that they lack employable talents, but that in the circumstances of real societies this is likely to be a fairly common response. In that paper I argued that policies required in the name of fairness can undermine self-respect, and therefore we have to accept that the egalitarian ethos can have conflicting elements which need to be accommodated in some way.

One major strand in my work since has been trying to develop points made in that paper and work them up into a more systematic form of egalitarian theory. The next stage was to think harder about forms of remedy for injustice. In the 1998 paper I make the point that paying money to people in order to compensate them for their humiliation could have the effect of compounding that humiliation, rather than compensate for it. This shows, I think, that cash compensation cannot be an all purpose cure to rectify injustice.

This then led me to think about how we go about addressing injustice, or disadvantage more generally, in actual social policy. I had, for a long time, been worrying away at the issue of disability. I was rather embarrassed on behalf of political philosophy in the way this incredibly important issue had been treated. Rawls, notoriously, explicitly decided not to discuss it. Dworkin does better, but still he seemed to conceptualise disability merely as something that is likely to reduce one's access to economic goods. While true, this is not the whole story. For some reason I cannot now remember I started reading some of the social studies of disability literature, and this was a real revelation. The more extreme social models of disability see the problem of disability as a form of discrimination exactly on the model of racism and sexism, and many disabled theorists claim that they do not see medical treatment as an appropriate way of dealing with the problems they face. This seemed to me at first extraordinary: if a medical cure was available to overcome a disability, who would not want it? Seeing disability as a medical issue is, of course 'the medical model of disability'. One problem is that proposed cures are often not very effective and involve huge inconvenience and a good deal of pain and discomfort. Philosophically more interesting however is the thought: why should I change to fit with society, rather than society changing to accommodate me?

I started writing on disability about ten years ago, and as I write these words my paper on the topic is still forthcoming: it should be published in 2008, I think. However my main idea is published in a paper called "Addressing Disadvantage and the Human Good", published in the *Journal of Applied Philosophy* in 2002. An edited version of this was published as a pamphlet for the think-tank Catalyst under the title "The Message of Redistribution" in 2003.

The main point is that in understanding what it is that determines an individual's opportunities in life, we can split factors into three. The first is that person's 'internal resources', or 'natural assets' in Rawls's terms. The second is their 'external resources', including wealth and income, but also such things as family support. The third is the social and material structure in which they operate: laws, customs, conventions, the configuration of the material environment, and so on. The idea is that your resources – internal and external – provide you with the 'pieces to play with' while the social structure determines the 'rules of the game'. It follows that we can alter someone's opportunities by adjusting any of these factors. This then provides a fairly rich range of possible strategies for addressing disadvantage or injustice, which is easiest to illustrate using the example of someone who suffers from a physical disability; the example which led me to formulate the framework in the first place.

One thing we can do to improve such a person's life or opportunities is to attempt to provide a medical cure. This would be to act on their internal resources; a policy of what I call 'personal enhancement'. This can include surgery, medicine, and physiotheraphy, but in other cases education and skills-training. A second 'space' in which we can act is on their external resources, by the provision of extra resources. However, this can come in two fundamentally different forms. The first is to provide money as a free asset, to be used however the person wishes. This, in other words, is to offer cash compensation, and I believe, much of the current literature is flawed by the implicit assumption that cash compensation is the only – or perhaps the best – form of remedy for disadvantage. However in social policy cash compensation of this form is rather limited in application. Of course societies do provide disabled people with cash to spend as they like, although typically it is spent on necessities, in order to compensate for the special expenses and loss of income generation that disabled people face. Beyond this, societies often provide disabled people with forms of equipment and personal care, but not as a freely disposable asset. For example a disabled person provided with a wheelchair is not normally at liberty to sell the wheelchair and use the cash for something else. Hence resources are provided for their use and not as individual private property. Where people are provided either with resources to use, or money with strings attached, I call this a 'targeted resource enhancement'.

Finally, it is possible to improve a person's opportunities without changing their internal or external resources. The clearest type of example would be a law ending legal discrimination; for example a law which abolished a racial bar to employment. In the case of disability the most obvious move in this direction is to try to refigure the material environment, including the work environment, to allow disabled people the same level of access as others. It is, of course, examples like this that inspire the social model of disability. This type of change – changing the world, not the person – I call 'status enhancement'.

After developing this model the obvious question is what we should do if, in a particular case, more than one strategy is available to address a particular disadvantage or injustice. How can we choose? In the papers mentioned above I suggested that different strategies make different pre-suppositions about the human good. More recently, however, I've argued in a somewhat different way. What we need to do is to consider what, in each case, will be most effective in meeting two goals: addressing individual disadvantage, and helping to create a society of equals which reduces disadvantage generally and boosts affiliation for all.

This theme is set in a broader context in my forthcoming book, co-written with Avner de-Shalit, which, finally to answer the question set out above, is, I hope at least, to be my most important work. The book is called *Disadvantage*, and looks at the question of what governments can do to improve the lives of the least advantaged and thereby move society in the direction of greater equality. It starts with a philosophical analysis of disadvantage. The first chapter argues that disadvantage is plural in nature. The second presents a pluralist view inspired by the capability view of Sen and Nussbaum, but modified on the basis of our own reflection as well as a number of interviews we carried out for the project. Next we argue that one central aspect of disadvantage is to face exceptional risks that others in your society do not have to face, and therefore insecure functionings can constitute disadvantage just as much as low functionings. To complete the analysis of disadvantage we look at the issue of individual responsibility, and, to return to a theme mentioned above, we argue that applying standard 'ideal theory' to real-world conditions will have undesirable effects. Therefore we develop a theory of when it is appropriate for people to bear the costs of their choices, based partly on the costs to them of adopting various different courses of action. Put together, this comes to the 'genuine opportunity for secure functioning' view of well-being.

With the theory of disadvantage in place we move to the question of what it can mean to be among the least advantaged on a pluralist view. Indexing disadvantage has always been the bugbear of pluralism, because deciding who is the least advantaged appears to require a way of comparing the extent of different disadvantages but, it is claimed, the essence of a pluralist view is that this is not possible. Our argument is that this overstates the difficulty. If it turns out that some people are disadvantaged in a number of different ways – if disadvantage clusters, as we put it – then there is no need to come up with a unique weighting function for different disadvantages in order to determine who is worst off. On the other hand, if disadvantage does not cluster, and who the least advantaged are changes as we change the weightings of different functionings, then there is a sense in which society is not in too bad shape, from the point of view of inequality. We think, however, that there is compelling evidence that disadvantage does cluster, and so the least advantaged are reasonably easily identified.

Finally we move on to consider appropriate social policy. Here we introduce the terms 'corrosive disadvantage' and 'fertile functionings' to explain our ideas. A corrosive disadvantage causes further disadvantages while a fertile functioning boosts other functionings. We argue that social science needs to do more to uncover these types of causal relations – not, of course, that it is easy to do so – and that governments need to shift resources and incentivise agencies so that they pay special attention to corrosive disadvantages and fertile functionings. This is the best way of helping the least advantaged and ultimately declustering disadvantage. At the same time, and again resuming an earlier theme, governments need to be very careful how they act. Attempts to address distributional problems in clumsy ways can increase stigma and division in society and thereby undercut social equality. Consequently we recommend that where possible and appropriate governments use what I called above 'status enhancements' by changing laws, public services, social attitudes and the material environment. This can address disadvantage without identifying, and thereby stigmatizing, individuals. Furthermore, it can boost affiliation and reduce risk for all, thereby having much wider social advantages. It is not always possible, but where it is, it will often be the best available strategy.

What is the proper role of political philosophy in relation to real, political action? Can there ever be a fruitful relation between political philosophy and political practice?

Recently it seems that, in the UK at least, the boundaries between academia and policy have become somewhat blurred, with ever more political philosophers becoming involved in public committees, think tanks, and in rare cases, government advisory committees. My own work has, in the last ten years or so, been as much orientated towards policy makers – or the fringes of policy making – as it has to a purely academic audience. I don't think this is the only way that political philosophy should be done, but it happens to suit me, although it has its frustrations too, as political agendas can move very quickly, and philosophers are not good at keeping up with the pace of change.

I would pick out three different ways in which my current work tries to engage with political action. The first has already been described. My book with Avner de-Shalit is explicitly written with the goal of linking political philosophy with political action. We think both sides benefit from the encounter. Political philosophy will develop a richer theoretical framework, which will allow it to engage with a wider range of issues. Political action can be set in theoretical context and provided with a basis to allow it point and justification, especially when it comes to priority setting in the use of scarce resources.

Secondly I have done a certain amount of work lately more directly in policy areas by becoming involved in a number of policy committees, governing the regulation of gambling, the ethics of animal experimentation, the law of homicide and the future of drug regulation. I have also been involved as a consultant to the railway industry on the ethics of risk. This has involved discussing questions of policy with government agencies, and those who advise government agencies. Here, though, it has been interesting to see that applying "out-of-the-box" philosophical theory is not a way of making progress. Every moral or political theory seems to have awkward and counter-intuitive consequences, and while a philosopher might be prepared to accept this as the cost of the best theory, in policy consistency is less important than avoidance of stupidity. Consequently pragmatic compromise between different views will generally be necessary.

This does not mean that there is no room for philosophical argument, but it has to be responsive to the issues as they are in the subject area, rather than trying to legislate from the outside. Distinctions have to be drawn between types of cases, analysis conducted of standard lines of thought, positions defended and criticized and so on, and so philosophical training and background can help a great deal. Nevertheless, detailed work on a small scale is much more likely to be helpful than grand theory.

A third area of my work where one day I hope there might be a connection between philosophical theory and political action is in the area of philosophy of economics. Right from the start of my research, on the topic of exploitation, I have been interested in the philosophical analysis of capitalist economics. Of course it is unlikely that any very radical critique will have any political effects, but in the last few years I have been interested in some smaller scale, but, I think, very important issues about the way the market works. Adam Smith famously pointed out that in the market self-interest works for mutual benefit. Over time the butcher and the baker can only profit in the free market if they sell decent products. Competition drives down prices and drives up quality. However there is a question about how far this argument generalizes. Some products are not consumed immediately, and, what is even more dangerous, the quality of the product remains under the control of the supplier even after money has changed hands. Long-term financial products are of this nature. There becomes a question of how best to set up the market to protect individual consumers from neglect and deception. I hold up some hope here that if compelling arguments can be made in this area, governments interested in consumer protection might listen. But this hope may well be vain.

17. Jonathan Wolff

What do you consider the most neglected topics and/or contributions in post-Rawlsian or late 20th century political philosophy?

I'm hoping that the most neglected topics are the ones that I have been engaging with in the work that I have described above: my agenda of topics has been driven more by a sense of perceived need rather than in continuing a debate.

Ten years ago I would have said that discussion of disability was the great neglected topic, but there is considerable work now. We could certainly do with more work on the understanding of the ethics of risk. This is territory that philosophers have allowed economists and sociologists to colonise, in quite different ways. There is a great deal of room for a philosophical contribution. Work has started, particularly with regard to catastrophic risk, but I'm actually a bit more interested in relatively mundane risks, and the circumstances in which it is permissible to impose risks on others, without their consent.

Another relatively new area, making up for previous neglect, is what is becoming known as population level bioethics, but what might also be called the distribution of health resources, or priority-setting in health. There is scattered, multi-disciplinary work on this and I can see an opportunity here for someone to try to pull it altogether, in a way which intersects with other issues in political philosophy.

What are the most important unsolved questions in political philosophy and/or related disciplines and what are the prospects for progress?

I am not really sure that any problems in political philosophy are solved, although some have been so worked over in detail that it will be hard for someone to say something new. But there are always surprises just around the corner.

There are, though, areas on which not much satisfactory progress has been made. I'll mention one which could have fallen under the previous heading of 'neglected question' too, in the philosophy of law. The philosophy of law is something of a puzzle to me, in that it seems to be dominated by a rather bad-tempered debate over 'legal positivism' where no two people seem to agree what the thesis is, who holds it, and why it matters, but nevertheless write extremely long papers on the topic. The central question in the philosophy of law, I would have thought, is how do we draw the line between behaviour that is wrong, but not to be regulated by law, and behaviour that we do regulate. Perhaps there is a very simple answer to this, and all I need to do is to open a jurisprudence textbook and I'll find the answer. But I haven't done that yet.

A second question concerns global justice. One could hardly call this a neglected question, but I haven't yet seen anything I find very plausible. The debate seems to be stuck. On the one side are those who insist that we have global duties of justice which mandate a massive redistribution. Those who cannot accept this consequence typically argue that we have duties not of justice but of charity, and these are accordingly less demanding in nature. Neither of these positions seems to me appealing and I feel that we need to understand a position which we could call 'justice but not the same justice'. I think I have an idea about how this could be made out in detail, but it is work for the future.

Global justice is one of the great questions of the age. The other, I think, is that of how the liberal state should deal with anti-liberal fundamentalism. Of course this has become an urgent issue, and it takes us to the limits of reason and philosophy; perhaps beyond them. It raises questions about what makes a group of people an association, and all the questions in political obligation which I found too difficult to answer. For myself I don't yet see a way out of this cluster of problems.

Principal works

Robert Nozick: Property Justice and the Minimal State (Polity Press and Stanford University Press, 1991).

'Hobbes and the Motivations of Social Contract Theory', *International Journal of Philosophical Studies* , 2, 1994, pp. 271–286.

'Pluralistic Models of Political Obligation', *Philosophica* (Belgium), 56, 1995, pp. 7–27. Reprinted in M. Baghramian and A. Ingram (ed) *Pluralism* Routledge 2000.

'Political Obligation, Fairness and Independence', *Ratio* (New Series) 8, 1995 pp. 87–99.

'Mill, Indecency and the Liberty Principle', *Utilitas* 10 1998 1–16.

An Introduction to Political Philosophy (OUP 1996, revised edition 2006).

'Fairness, Respect and the Egalitarian Ethos', *Philosophy and Public Affairs* 1998 27. 97–122.

'Addressing Disadvantage and the Human Good', *Journal of Applied Philosophy* 19 2002 207–218.

Why Read Marx Today? (OUP 2002).

'Risk, Fear, Blame, Shame and the Regulation of Public Safety' *Economics and Philosophy*. (forthcoming 2006).

'Making the World Safe for Utilitarianism', Royal Institute of Philosophy, Annual Volume, *Political Philosophy*, ed. A. O'Hear (forthcoming 2007).

Disadvantage (with Avner de-Shalit) (OUP 2007).

18

Bernard Yack

Lerman-Neubauer Professor of Democracy

Brandeis University, MA, USA

Initial Attraction to Political Philosophy

Becoming an academic, let alone a political philosopher, was the furthest thing from my mind when I entered the University of Toronto in 1971. Although an enthusiastic reader of history and historical literature, I came to university with the strong prejudice that those who can, do, and those who can't, teach. In addition, I brought with me the kind of cheap cultural relativism that so often proves irresistible to male adolescents who have read a little history. Moral and political philosophy, to the extent I knew anything about it, seemed like pompous hypocrisy to me, high-minded talk designed to hide from ourselves the ways in which we changed with the times.

All that changed when in my first year at university I encountered Alan Bloom and, through him, Plato. Long before he became famous as the author of *The Closing of the American Mind*, Bloom had made a career, first at Cornell and then at Toronto, of challenging smug young relativists like myself. He was very good at it, both at exposing our own dogmatism and giving us a sense of why the examined life might be worth living. It had never occurred to me that understanding a moral and political problem could be satisfying in itself—probably because it never occurred to me that one could make much progress in doing so. I was hooked, not on the rather conservative answers that Bloom implied we would find if we devoted ourselves to the great works of political philosophy, but on the form of self-examination that I found there.

At the core of Bloom's introductory course was Plato's *Republic*. The thing that I most remember from that first confrontation with Plato – though I can't remember whether or not it's something Bloom himself emphasized – was Plato's distinction between rhetoric and philosophy, between the love of victory in persuasion and the love of truth as motives for addressing questions of importance. This distinction, as familiar as might seem to better educated students, struck me very hard. It forced me to see that understanding and effectiveness in the world might get in each other's way, that in order to understand things you might have to sacrifice the ability to get things done, and vice versa. Like many young men, I overvalued effectiveness, especially political effectiveness, so Plato's reversal value struck me as especially daring. (At the time, of course, I was too naïve to recognize the extent to which I was being subjected to a kind of philosophical rhetoric against rhetoric.) Here was someone who taught not only that we need to be willing to sacrifice effectiveness in order to understand ourselves and our world, but that the compensation was well worth the sacrifice. More than anything else, it was this idea that first led me to consider political philosophy as a vocation.

But this distinction between love of truth and love of persuasion is very hard to hold onto in a field like political philosophy, where the questions that you consider in the study correspond so frequently to those you face as a citizen. Certainly, Bloom and his friends and students, almost all followers of the Jewish-German émigré thinker, Leo Strauss, certainly seemed willing to abandon it. For they used this distinction, and many others like it, as weapons against liberal intellectuals – something that can be seen clearly in Bloom's book *The Closing of the American Mind*. The failure to understand the true seriousness and independence of the philosophical love of truth became for them a political failure, a reason for disdaining liberal political practices, rather than just a failing of the intellect. Bloom had taught me, as he had taught many other young men and women, that the unexamined life was not worth living. But it seemed to me that he and most of his students were more interested in using this discovery as a political weapon and a source of self-congratulation than in making themselves vulnerable to the uncertainties of a life of self-examination.

Luckily, in Judith Shklar, my dissertation adviser at Harvard, I found someone who shared both my enthusiasm for the subject and my wariness about what political philosophers do with it. Shklar, as many know, was a passionate skeptic, a devotee of Montaigne and Montesquieu. For that reason she might not seem the best match for someone fired up by Platonic rhetoric about the love of wisdom. But Shklar's skepticism was rather unique. She was as skeptical of theories that told us why we could not discover the truth about moral and political issues as she was of theories that claimed to have discovered them. The way she saw things, there was simply no time for the fashionable prophets of epistemological despair, people who displayed dazzling erudition in the course of proving why we cannot know anything interesting about the world except our inability to know things. The world was simply too interesting for Shklar, too full of important problems to ponder and puzzles to try to unravel, to worry so much about the adequacy of our attempts to make sense of them. Like many others, I found this combination of openness to the world and methodological independence exhilarating, especially in contrast to the defensiveness and conformism of the Straussians. If Bloom introduced me to the idea that the unexamined life is not worth living, it was Shklar who helped me learn how to lead such a life.

One other point about what attracted me to political philosophy is worth mentioning. Like many other North American political theorists of my generation, my teachers were primarily German and Central European émigrés – or, like Bloom, students of émigrés. Their experience of Europe's 20th century self-inflicted disasters, World War I, the rise of Fascism, the Holocaust, and Soviet Communism, gave them a sense that something had gone deeply and fundamentally wrong with the modern world, something related to the way we thought about the world as well as the way we acted in it. This sense of pessimism distinguished them from most of their North American counterparts, giving their ideas a hint of urgency that was most often lacking among the latter. Jewish students like myself, born after the Holocaust but very familiar with its history, were an especially keen audience for people who recognized that something had gone deeply wrong with liberal expectations of peace, progress and enlightenment. My Ph. D. dissertation, and first book, *The Longing for Total Revolution*, was inspired in part by such concerns.

The émigré political philosophers, like Arendt, Adorno, Shklar, Strauss, Voegelin, and their many students, undoubtedly overreached at times, as if the right reading of Bacon or Aristotle might answer our questions about what caused the Europe's 20th century catastrophes. But they had a sense of history, in particular of history's discontinuities, that I fear that contemporary political philosophers are in danger of losing. When political philosophers build their theories on the "considered judgments" (Rawls) or "shared meanings" (Walzer) of their societies, they usually forget just how quickly and completely social expectations can be turned upside down. When political theorists take seriously the idea of a liberal democratic "end of history" (Fukuyama), they seem to be unaware or uninterested in how World War I and its attendant disasters shredded similar hopes in the first half of the twentieth century. So while I am aware that my particular path to political philosophy has probably disposed me to exaggerate the historical impact of the books that I read, I still greatly value the sense of historical development and discontinuity that I received from it.

Most Important Contributions to Political Philosophy

My most important contributions to political philosophy involve two related issues: the moral psychology of political life and the limitations of radical and utopian thinking. The latter is the primary theme of my first book, *The Longing for Total Revolution*, which deals with the philosophic sources of social discontent among modern European radicals. The former figures prominently in all of my scholarship, but takes center stage in my current work on nationalism, a book titled *Nation and Individual: Nationalism and the Moral Psychology of Community in Modern Political Life*.

These two issues are intertwined in a variety of ways in my writing. On the one hand, I have devoted a great deal of effort to identifying the moral psychology of the more intellectual forms of political radicalism. For example, in *The Longing for Total Revolution* I try to show that it is a new way of understanding the obstacles to human satisfaction, much more than new visions of the good society, that radicalizes social criticism among European thinkers from Rousseau to Marx and Nietzsche and their heirs. On the other hand, I have found that failure to appreciate the complexities of everyday moral psychology, in particular the variety of ways in which we imagine ourselves as connected to other human beings, is one of the major sources of utopian and unrealistic theories of political life. I develop this point at some length in my book on Aristotelian political thought, *The Problems of a Political Animal*. There I oppose Aristotle's understanding of community as an often troublesome fact of everyday life to contemporary visions of community as a promise of once and future harmony.

Rethinking the moral psychology of community is also at the core of my book on nationalism, *Nation and Individual*. I argue there that a major reason for our difficulties in explaining and evaluating the unexpected prominence of nations and nationalism in modern political life is the inadequacy of prevailing conceptions of community and human development. These conceptions teach us to associate community with the traditional world of kin and village relations that modern societies are steadily leaving behind. But the rise of nationalism suggests that at least one form of community has not only survived, but thrived in the modern world of contract and commerce. Evidently, there is something wrong with either our interpretation of nationalism or the conceptions of community that make it seem like some kind of anomaly in the modern world.

Most students of nationalism have assumed that it is our interpretations of the phenomenon that needs work, and have thus developed creative theories that try to bring nationalism back into line with our assumptions about community and human development. Some portray the nation as a *Gesellschaft* masquerading as a *Gemeinschaft*, others, as an outburst of the primitive passions that modern society has tried unsuccessfully to repress. I suggest, in contrast, that if the phenomena do not fit our assumptions about community and human development, then perhaps it is time to reconsider those assumptions. Drawing on some of the Aristotelian ideas reconstructed in my earlier book, I develop a broader and more flexible theory of community, one in which community represents a basic component of social order, rather than a special product of primitive family and village life. *Gemeinschaftliche* groups, from this point of view, represent a particular species of community, one that has less prominence in our lives than it once possessed. The nation, in contrast, represents a different species of community, one that has for a variety of reasons taken on greater political prominence in modern political life.

Although developed in order to help make sense of nations and nationalism in our lives, my hope is that this alternative theory of community will prove useful to people analyzing a variety of moral and political issues. Its most distinctive feature is its focus on the feelings of mutual concern and loyalty that frequently develop, at all levels of intensity, among people who share things. More familiar conceptions of community, which focus on collective identity or subordination of individuals to the group, make it hard to recognize its everyday impact on our lives because they teach us to associate community with the rare occasions when we sacrifice our own interests or our principles for the sake of others. I suggest, in contrast, that our lives are lived in a rich patchwork of more or less intense communal relationships, relationships that we regularly rely on to balance, check and reinforce our calculations of self-interest and our beliefs about the justice. Nationalism, I argue, is such a powerful and explosive force in our lives because it lines up all three of these motivations, community, self-interest, and justice, against our communal rivals, not because it suppresses self-interest and principle in a frenzied outburst of group loyalty.

Political Theory and Practice

A "fruitful relation" between political theory and practice depends, I believe, on maintaining a clear distinction between them. This view reflects years of study of overreaching thinkers who claimed to have discovered what Marx called history's "line of march." But, more fundamentally, it is drawn from my understanding of the distinction between understanding and effectiveness, the love of truth and the desire to persuade, that first drew me to political philosophy. Philosophy serves politics best when it preserves its independence from considerations of what it takes to make something happen in the political world.

Many political theorists today talk about engaging in what they call "public philosophy." To me, this concept is a contradiction in terms. Public speech is directed at action and must therefore seek to persuade people to do things. Philosophic speech is, or should be, directed at understanding the way things are, not at persuading people to do things. A philosopher can speak publicly, but not as a philosopher, just as a public figure can philosophize, but not as a public figure. When political theorists engage in "public philosophy" they usually end up invoking either philosophic or academic authority as a means of persuading people to follow their political opinions or, worse, current political needs as a reason for accepting a particular view of the way things are.

This distinction between philosophy and rhetoric is especially important to insist upon in democracies, which, as Michael Walzer suggests (in *Spheres of Justice*), are regimes in which power is distributed to the persuasive. As Plato dramatically illustrated in his variation on the ship of state metaphor, what gets you power in a democracy is the ability to persuade a majority (or plurality) of people that you know the right thing to do, not the possession of the truth, let alone the ability to discover it. Such a disjunction between philosophy and democracy is hard to swallow for many contemporary political philosophers, since, unlike Plato, they think of themselves as democrats. That is why so many of them seek means of narrowing this gap, the most influential of which today is probably the Rawlsian idea of "public reason."

According to this idea, a commitment to democratic institutions implicitly obliges one to accept certain limits on the way in which free and equal citizens address each other in the deliberation of public matters. Rawlsian public reason improves democratic deliberation by raising the general level of political speech, rather than by focusing attention on the speech of a few philosophically inclined individuals. As such, it is less offensive to my understanding of both democracy and philosophy than the celebration of public philosophy and public philosophers. Nevertheless, if implemented, it would still challenge a basic tenet of democratic sociability: that we decide matters by our ability to persuade each other to do things in one way or another. If, like defenders of Rawlsian public reason, you suggest that we should only listen to a certain kind of speech, you give people an excuse to ignore opposing arguments that are put to them. And if, like them, you suggest that we should be protecting proposals that "no one could reasonably reject" from rhetorical assault, then you give public speakers a powerful excuse to ignore and subvert negative public judgments.

So I am unsympathetic to attempts to develop distinctly political ways of engaging in the pursuit of philosophy and distinctly rational or philosophic ways of engaging in politics. In my view, political philosophers have no business participating in the democratic process *as* political philosophers or trying to redesign that process according to their own conceptions of what counts as reasonable speech. As citizens, we have much to contribute to public life, since we bring to the marketplace a perspective on things that receives little support from a society that values effectiveness, and therefore the virtues associated with persuasiveness, above all other qualities. But we need to remind ourselves constantly that this different perspective, no matter how valuable it may be, deserves no special privileges. In this respect, at least, I insist on leaving Plato's legacy behind.

Neglected Problems and Contributions

Political philosophy has become such a large and thriving field in recent years that few contributions of real merit are completely neglected anymore, even if they do not all receive the attention that they deserve. Like all other fields, political philosophy has its trends – the liberalism-communitarianism debate in the 1980s or the obsession with "deliberative democracy" today – that divert attention from more interesting issues and more original insights. But it is rare nowadays for really fine work to fall through the cracks.

There are, however, some new bodies of knowledge that political philosophers have been slow to integrate into their thinking. One example that strikes me as especially important for our work concerns the evolution of human morality and sociality. We political philosophers tend to rely on assumptions about human nature and motivations that have been rendered obsolete or, at the very least, questionable by recent studies of human and primate evolution. For example, only by ignoring what has been learned about the evolution of our moral dispositions can one treat rational choice theory as a descriptive account of human behavior, as opposed to a prescription for self-improvement. Human beings are disposed by nature to express concern for the well-being of others, as well as to seek their own good. You cannot explain human cooperation or conflict without taking both dispositions into account.

That does not mean that the answer to our normative questions lies in some account of how we came to inherit our current genetic makeup. Evolutionary accounts of human nature teach us about our dispositions – which, as I have suggested, are a very mixed bag – rather than about what is right and wrong. The naïve identification of the natural with the good in the overreaching claims of Social Darwinists and, more recently, sociobiologists has made it easy for political philosophers to dismiss these accounts and persist with their traditional assumptions about human nature and motivation. But in doing so, they are throwing the baby out with the bathwater. The best work in social and moral evolution now disdains both the naturalistic fallacy and the gleeful celebration of aggressiveness and selfishness – of nature "red in tooth and claw" – that marred Social Darwinism and sociobiology. These works, for example, Franz de Waal's *Good-Natured* or Christopher Boehm's *Hierarchy in the Forest*, invoke evolutionary knowledge to help us ask the right questions about morality and politics, rather than as a guide to the right answers to these questions.

Unresolved Issues and Prospects for Progress in Political Philosophy

Of the many unresolved issues that face political philosophers today, the most pressing, I believe, are those that concern the nature and limits of the form of democracy that we currently practice. I do not think that we adequately appreciate, let alone understand, the oddness of this political regime in which it is generally agreed that popular approval is the only legitimate source of authority, yet extraordinary concentrations of power are not only allowed, but constitutionally protected, in the economic, political and legal systems. The familiar distinction between participatory and representative democracy is not sufficient to explain these peculiarities, since there are much more egalitarian ways of selecting and empowering representatives than we currently practice. (On this point, see Bernard Manin's important but under-appreciated book, *The Principles of Representative Government*.) And the constraint of democracy by liberal conceptions of individual rights merely poses, rather than answers, the question about what kind of democracy we practice and prefer.

My own inclination, like Manin's, is to treat contemporary democracies as a kind of mixed regime. Modern representative governments combine a relatively egalitarian form of election, in which all adults share the franchise, with an aristocratic or oligarchic form of representation, in which we seek to choose the best or most noteworthy people to represent us. As in classic mixed regimes, this combination of democratic and aristocratic or oligarchic practices promotes an appreciation of both egalitarian and inegalitarian principles of justice. (That is one reason that Tocqueville's fears about tyranny of the majority proved so exaggerated: the representative system of government itself promotes an appreciation for the inequalities that raise individuals above the crowd.) If true, this understanding of modern democratic practice would have many complex and interesting implications for the relationship between elitism and egalitarianism in modern social and political life.

For example, it would also help us begin a more honest accounting of just which areas of our lives we can and should seek to democratize in the modern world. Such an accounting is often limited these days by a kind of democratic piety that makes it hard for political philosophers to acknowledge frankly the limits of their attachment to democratic ideals. Fearful of being unmasked as elitists, they work very hard to portray practices that limit democracy and egalitarianism, like the endorsement of Rawlsian standards of public reason in political deliberation, as means of perfecting democracy. But the recognition of the limits of democracy does not necessarily undermine the value of its practice within these limits. For example, if one concludes that in modern political regimes democracy can and should focus on popular accountability, as opposed to, say popular participation, that might lead one to devote one's energies to developing much more effective practices of accountability than we now possess, rather than seek vainly to find ways of equalizing participation in politics. So the kind of analysis of what C.B. MacPherson called the "real world" of democracy that I am looking for could help improve the democratic features of modern politics precisely by looking more frankly at their limits.

A second unresolved area that I hope will be pursued by more political philosophers is the relationship between sovereignty and human rights. This relationship is much more complex and uncertain that it would appear in current debates, especially in the growing literature on globalization. State sovereignty, in that literature, is generally treated as an obstacle to the extension of human rights, since it impedes intervention against a state's cruel and tyrannical treatment of its own citizens. But state sovereignty is, at the same time, the means by which human rights have generally been delivered to individual citizens. For example, I only have an effective right to free speech if there is some singular and generally recognized structure of authority within my political community that will stand in the way of all the individuals and groups who want to impede my speech. Of course, having constructed and endorsed such an authority I have to worry about how to keep it from interfering with my speech. But that is the problem of limited government as it has developed in modern politics. Extending it beyond borders does not make it go away. In the absence of establishing a world sovereign, which very few of even the most ardent globalists seem to want, one needs to recognize multiplying the number and levels of authority creates problems as well as opportunities for the advancement of human rights.

A final area where I believe that unresolved problems should inspire a lot more work concerns questions about the justification of moral and political claims. Sustained criticism of natural rights, utilitarian, and historicist arguments have left appeals to consent – actual, implied, and hypothetical – as pretty much the only method of justifying substantive normative assertions that is widely recognized by political philosophers. Whether it is as simple as an appeal to shared opinion or as complex as the Habermasian belief that our desire to communicate commits us to a very particular way of determining moral principles, it is our explicit or implicit acceptance of some proposition that we tend to rely on now for our first principles. As a result, debates among us often devote more attention to identifying the nature and implications of our beliefs than their adequacy. The problem with this subjective focus, as many of these debates amply demonstrate, is that it is often no less difficult to come up definitive answers to questions about what "we" believe than it is to come up with definitive answers about the direction of history, the content of utility or the naturally just. More often than not, a definitive answer is found by writing a philosophically derived notion, like Rawls's Kantian view of moral personality, back into our "considered judgments" and the democratic public culture that they supposedly inform.

I believe that we have exhausted the value of these subjective approaches to justification and the pendulum is about to – or, at least, should – swing back to more substantive or objective forms of argument. The challenge is how to engage productively in such arguments without reproducing the exaggerated claims of foundationalist appeals to nature, history, and utility. I do not believe that this is an insurmountable problem, but it will take considerable rethinking of the way in which we justify arguments. The belief that we possess arguments that should compel our opponents' approval, were they only willing to be honest with themselves about their own commitments, is tremendously empowering. I don't think that political philosophers will give them up lightly. But I think that we must if we want to reconnect our inquiries with the full variety of our interests in the political world.

Whether or not we will see much progress in resolving these or other issues is hard for me to say. When I first began to study political philosophy, in the early 1970s, it was just beginning to recover from the premature announcements of its death as a worthwhile field of inquiry. Its place in philosophy and political science departments was still marginal and insecure at that time. That is much less the case today. The field has grown tremendously in both the numbers and acceptance of its practitioners. As a result, I am confident that there will be a fairly large number of well trained people setting out to resolve these problems for the foreseeable future.

How well they will succeed in doing so is another matter. There are many fewer intellectual charlatans in the field these days. But there has also been a considerable narrowing of intellectual imagination and ambition as research increasingly comes to be focused on engagement with the last round of round of scholarly books and journal articles. Perhaps this "normalization" of the field is inevitable, given its increasingly secure place in the academic world. Unfortunately, there is not much room for "normal science" within the field of political philosophy, apart from the editing of classic texts. The subject is inherently interdisciplinary, a child of the marriage – or dalliance – between history and philosophy. We need therefore to make sure that we do not let conventional acceptance lead to the conventionalization of the field. Otherwise, I fear that we may end up trading intellectual insight and excitement for professional security.

Selected publications

Books

The Longing for Total Revolution: Philosophic Sources of Social Discontent from Rousseau to Marx and Nietzsche, Princeton University Press, 1986. (Paperback edition, with new preface, University of California Press, 1992.)

The Problems of A Political Animal: Community, Conflict, and Justice in Aristotelian Political Thought, Berkeley: University of California Press, May 1993.

Liberalism without Illusions: Essays on Liberal Theory and the Political Vision of Judith N. Shklar (edited volume with preface and two articles). Chicago: University of Chicago Press, 1997.

The Fetishism of Modernities: Epochal Self-Consciousness in Contemporary Social and Political Thought. Notre Dame: University of Notre Dame Press, 1998.

Articles

"The Problem with Kantian Liberalism." In R. Beiner and W. J. Booth (eds.). *Kant and Political Philosophy: The Contemporary Legacy*. New Haven: Yale University Press, 1993, 244–64.

"The Myth of the Civic Nation." *Critical Review*, 1996. Reprinted in R. Beiner (ed.), *Theorizing Nationalism*, Albany, SUNY Press, 1998.

"Active and Passive Justice in the Liberal State." In *Liberalism Without Illusions*, Chapter 13.

"Putting Injustice First." *Social Research* 66 (1999): 1103–20.

"Popular Sovereignty and Nationalism," *Political Theory*, August 2001. (Revised version in J. Hall and T. V. Paul (eds.), *The State in Question*, (Princeton: Princeton University Press, 2003), Chapter 1.

"Rhetoric and Public Reasoning: An Aristotelian Understanding of Political Deliberation," *Political Theory* 34 (2006): 417–38.

About Political Questions

Political Questions is a collection of original contributions from a distinguished score of the world's most prominent and influential political philosophers. They deal with questions such as what drew them towards the area; how they view their own contribution to the field; and what the future of political philosophy looks like.

> I have long thought that there is too much emphasis in political philosophy on theories. What matters is what real people – theorists – think. And also why they think what they think. This fascinating collection of interviews with a wide range of some of today's most influential political thinkers is a huge help in understanding their views and where they came from. It's the kind of book that once started is difficult to put down.
>
> —**Roger Crisp**
> St Anne's College, Oxford University

> For those of us who have found their vocation in political philosophy or theory, the interviews in this volume make for fascinating reading. How could it be otherwise when eighteen distinguished Anglophone political philosophers explain what drew them to this vocation and what they see as their most significant contributions to it? There are surprises along the way, too, including the fact that as many of these luminaries seem to have begun their intellectual journey in mathematics or the sciences as in history or literature. Less surprising is the fact that all eighteen are academics, and one occasionally notes a tension between what the "profession" demands and what the philosopher's sense of vocation requires. Even so, there is little in these interviews to support the claim that contemporary political philosophy is "academic" in the pejorative sense – that is, an arid, abstract enterprise that

has little connection with real politics. On the contrary, one finds in almost all of these interviews a firm commitment to bringing philosophical analysis to bear on the problems of what the editor calls "real, political action." In this and other respects, Political Questions is not only fascinating but inspiring. Anyone contemplating a career in political philosophy should read this book as soon as he or she can.

—**Richard Dagger**
Political Science and Philosophy, Arizona State University

This collection of interviews with political philosophers makes fascinating reading. Free of professional jargon, and firmly focused on the big picture, their responses combine to yield an unusually accessible guide to the state of the art, and stimulating insight into the sheer variety of ways that political philosophers think about what it is that they do. The range of views on the proper relation between political philosophy and political practice is particularly interesting. The result is an absorbing conversation about what the discipline has to offer, where it has contributed most, where it should be going, and how it should get there—and powerful evidence of its strength and vitality.

—**Adam Swift**
Fellow in Politics and Sociology, Balliol College. Author of *Political Philosophy: A Beginners' Guide for Students and Politicians*

About the Editor

Morten Ebbe Juul Nielsen, Phd, MA (phil), BA (psych). Currently Post Doc at Roskilde University. Awarded Copenhagen University's Gold Medal for Master's Dissertation on Communitarianism, 1999. PhD from Copenhagen and Oxford Universities 2004, *Liberalism, Neutrality, and Perfectionism*. Several publications, mainly in political philosophy. Reviewer for *Synthese*. Editor of *Political Questions* and *Legal Matters: 5 Questions on Legal Philosophy* both appearing with Automatic Press / VIP. Commentator for Danish main intellectual Broadsheet *Weekendavisen*.

Index

9/11, 58

abortion, 7, 137, 184
abstraction, 23, 68
academia, 123, 206
accountability, 173
accountancy, 68
action, 36, 68, 79, 163
Adorno, T., 213
Affirmative Action, 135
Africa Diaspora, 2
African-American Studies, 3
AFT, 123
aggregation, 150, 163
Al-Quds University, 94
Althusser, L., 99
anarchism, 196
animal experimentation, 206
anti-communist leftism, 179
Apartheid, 29, 65
Appiah, J., 2
Appiah, K.A., 1
Appleton, 148
Aquinas, T., 87
Arendt, H., 213
Aristotle, 4, 8, 42, 44, 47, 84, 87, 93, 161, 213, 214
Arneson, R., 129, 170
ascription, 4
assertibility, 1
atomism, 106
Austin, J.L., 94
Australia, 65, 69, 106
Australian Aboriginal, 64
Australian Capital Territory, 114

Australian Institute of Aboriginal Studies, 64
Australian National University, 63
Ayer, A.J., 169

Bacon, F., 213
Bagwhati, J., 123
Baran, P., 123
Barry, B., 3
BBC, 115
Beccaria, B., 16
Beirut, 94
Belgium, 100
belief, 29, 36
   belief, 32
Bellamy, R., 13
belonging together, 76
Bentham, J., 92, 107, 161
Berlin, I., 17, 45
Betts, J., 130
bigotry, 148
bioethics, 30, 32
biology, 101
biotechnology, 32
Black Panthers, 122
Bloom, A., 42, 211
Boehm, C., 218
Bosnia, 38
Bossuet, J.-B., 16
Braithwaite, J., 107
Brandeis University, 179
Braverman, H., 123, 126
Brazil, 91
Brennan, G., 116
Bristol University, 75

Broack, D.W., 32
Buchanan, A., 29
"bumiputra", 65

Cambridge University, 3, 14
Camus, A., 179
Canada, 31, 90
Canberra, 41
"capabilities approach", 85
capitalism, 124, 126
Carnap, R., 169
Casal, P., 189
Cicero, 92
citizenship, 87
Civil Rights Movement, 83, 148
climatology, 101
Clinton administration, 44
Clinton, B., 41, 46, 163
Cohen, G.A., 78, 127, 170
Cohen, J., 127, 188, 191, 196, 198
Cole, G.D.H., 44
Columbia University, 29
communication, 59
communism, 196, 213
communitarianism, 4, 6, 19, 76, 199
Community Chest, 181
compromise, 58
conditional, 1
consequentialism, 110, 130, 170, 175
Constitution, 91
constitutionalism, 18
constructivism, 188
Cornell University, 41, 211
Cornwall, R., 124
corruption, 58
Coser, L., 179
Cripps, I., 2
critical normativity, 176
Croce, B., 16, 20

cruelty, 58

Danto, A.C., 30
Darwinism, 218
de Waal, F., 218
de-Shalit, A., 204
Debreu, G., 124
decision theory, 1, 170
decision-making, 18, 34, 59, 117, 138
deliberation, 47, 56
democracy, 18, 42, 56, 117, 132, 219
  constitutional, 60
  deliberative, 56
  global, 22
  liberal, 18, 42
democratic
  policy, 57
democratic education, 55
Democrats, 121
demography, 101
desert, 136
Devlin, L., 17
Dewey, J., 93
difference principle, 188
disadvantage, 204
discrimination, 135, 148
Dissent, 179
distribution, 10, 67
  of assets, 127
  of benefits, 172
  of goods, 130, 143
  of means of production, 127
  of money, 190
  of opportunities, 143
  of outcome, 131
  of property, 126
doctrinal paradox, 112
Dodgers, 121
domination, 109
Dowding, K., 17

Dreben, B., 199
drug regulation, 206
Du Bois, W.E.B., 2
Dubai, 94
Dummett, M., 2
Durkheim, E., 25
Dworkin, R., 17, 25, 100, 113, 127, 131, 170, 191, 201

economics, 14, 24, 88, 91, 101, 122, 187, 190
   capitalist, 207
   Marxist, 123
   mathematical, 124
   normative, 170
education, 55, 87, 137
egalitarian ethos, 188, 202
egalitarianism, 76, 128, 132, 149, 150, 189, 219
   luck, 153, 201
   non-instrumental, 160
   Paretian, 171
Eisenhower, D., 41
Elkin, S., 49
Elster, J., 8
Emerson Hall, 121
emotion, 84, 87, 92
English Revolution, 63
Enlightenment, 15, 49
environmental degradation, 191
epistemology
   social, 32
   social moral, 32, 36
equality, 88, 147, 150, 171, 173, 188, 192, 202
   democratic, 69
   sex, 86
ethics, 5, 32, 149, 170
Ethiopia, 31
EU, 18, 22, 141
eudaimonia, 4, 5
euthanasia, 67

exploitation, 124, 197
   capitalistic, 125
   feudal, 125
   social, 125
'extended humanitarianism', 158

fairness, 147, 153, 156, 202
   comparative, 153
Fald, W.D., 30
Fanon, F., 179
fascism, 213
feasibility, 78
Feldman, D., 148
feminism, 86, 95
feudalism, 124
Fielding, H., 15
Figgis, J.N., 44
Finnis, J., 17
Fishkin, J., 170
Forbes, D., 14
Free Speech Movement, 121
Freeden, M., 17
freedom, 58, 60, 107, 109
full self-ownership, 172

Galston, W., 41
gambling, 206
game theory, 170
Gauthier, D., 170
gay rights, 67
Gemeinschaft, 215
genomic science, 32
geogrpahy, 101
Germany, 53, 90, 162, 195
Gesellschaft, 215
Ghana, 2
'global village', 140
Glover, J., 33
Godwin, W., 15
Golden Rule, 36
Goldfarb, W., 199
Goldman, A., 32

good life, 84, 137
goods, 170
governance, 140
　trans-national, 143
government, 53, 58, 59, 141, 207
government advisory committee, 206
Gramsci, A., 19
Gray, J., 17, 64
Gray, J.G., 185
Green, L., 17
group, 111
Gutmann, A., 53

Habermas, J., 22, 110, 182
Harman, G., 149
Harsanyi, J., 131, 170
Hart, B., 198
Hart, H.L.A., 17, 25
Hart-Devlin debate, 17
Harvard University, 121, 179, 198, 212
hatred, 148
Hayek, F.A., 64, 71
Hegel, G.W.F., 15, 30, 70
Heidegger, M., 42, 140
Held, D., 22
Hempel, C.G., 169
history, 14, 18, 79
Hitler, A., 135
Hobbes, T., 30, 49, 63, 64, 70, 94, 108, 111, 117, 200
Holland, 90, 91
Hollins, M., 18
Holocaust, 148, 213
homosexuality, 115
Howe, I., 179
Human Development and Capability Association, 86
human morality, 218

human rights, 58, 175, 220
human sociality, 218
Humboldt, A.v., 4
Hume, D., 13, 25, 64, 94, 187, 197

ideal, 110
idealization, 23
identification, 4
　norms of, 5
identity, 59, 76
　ethical, 4
　group, 57
　social, 4
ideology, 1, 3, 138
ignorance, 131
India, 53, 90, 91, 93
individualism, 106
individuality, 6
inequality, 149, 152
infinite series, 121
injustice, 202
institutions, 32, 48, 79, 88, 111, 136, 139, 174, 217
interest, 59
International Monetary Fund, 165
Iraq, 38
Islam, 94
Italy, 90, 91

James, C.L.R., 2
Japan, 91, 123
Jerusalem, 94
judgement, 173
Just War Theory, 34
justice, 23, 25, 42, 57, 66, 71, 79, 85, 92, 132, 136, 147, 156, 171, 174, 180, 189, 202
　compensatory, 135, 137
　democratic, 57

distributive, 100, 191
egalitarian, 77
gender, 86, 92
global, 209
of inequality, 192
social, 85, 88
justification, 221
of moral claim, 220
of political claim, 220

Kafka, F., 99
Kant, I., 41, 44, 47, 49, 56, 90, 93, 94, 174, 179
Kent, 195
Kindertransport, 195
Kitcher, P., 32
knowledge, 43, 72, 78, 156, 161, 184
sociology of, 43
Kojeve, A., 42
Kosovo, 38
Kripke, S., 106
Kukathas, C., 17, 63
Kymlicka, W., 4, 69

Lacey, N., 17
Ladrière, J., 99
language, 2
Laski, H., 44
law, 25, 32, 101, 113, 174, 190
international, 32, 38
law of homicide, 206
Lerner, M., 179
liberalism, 4, 6, 19, 35, 67, 76, 137, 199
'political', 85
libertarianism, 6, 67, 159, 172
liberty, 171, 173, 188
linguistic diversity, 100
List, C., 113
Locke, J., 43, 50, 93, 94, 161, 179
logic, 2, 13, 187

London, 196
Longino, H., 32
luck, 153
brute, 154
Lukes, S., 17
Lyttleton, H., 117

MacCormick, N., 17
Macdonald, G., 106
Machiavelli, N., 25, 116
MacPherson, C.B., 220
Madison, J., 44, 91
Magdoff, H., 123
Malaysia, 63, 65
Malcolm, N., 41
Manchester, 2
Manin, B., 219
Marx, K., 30, 63, 125, 214
Marxism, 63, 182
Mason, A., 18, 75
math puzzle, 60
mathematics, 49, 53, 121, 122, 169
maximin principle, 159
McCarthy, G., 83
McGill University, 169
Mendelssohn, M., 94
Merleau Ponty, M., 179
metaphysics, 13
Middle East, 26
Mill, J.S., 4, 56, 64, 66, 70, 87, 89, 92, 116, 161, 187, 190
Miller, D., 17, 64, 201
Mona Lisa, 70
Montaigne, M. de, 212
Montesquieu, C.-L. de, 115, 212
Montreal, 169
moral compromise, 137
moral judgment, 33
moral justification, 35
moral motivation, 33

moral reasoning, 33
moral theorizing, 33
morality, 5
Morishima, M., 124
Morton, C., 63
Mosca, G. de, 17
Mounier, E., 99
"multi-cultural citizenship", 69
multi-culturalism, 4, 69
Murphy, L., 174, 191

Nagel, T., 149
nation, 215
nationalism, 3, 76, 214, 215
    liberal, 76
    Negro, 2
NATO, 38
nature of rights, 175
Nazis, 196
neurophysiology, 132
New York City, 29
Nietzsche, F., 13, 99, 162, 214
Nkrumah, K., 2
non-atomism, 106
non-domination, 109
non-welfarism, 130
Norman, R., 201
Nozick, R., 4, 9, 55, 64, 68, 100, 130, 170, 172, 198
nuclear deterrence, 137
Nuffield College, 17
Nussbaum, M., 47, 83, 204
Nusseibeh, S., 94

Oakeshott, M., 69
Oakland, 122
Okin, S., 86
opportunity, 129
oppression, 58
option, 154
Organization of African Unity, 2

Oriental Studies Institute, 29
orthononomy, 108
Orwell, G., 179
Otsuka, M., 173
overpopulation, 149

Paine, T., 91
Pakistan, 91
Paley, W., 107
Pan-African Congress, 2
Pan-Africanism, 1
Pareto efficiency, 171
Pareto, V., 17
Parfit, D., 17, 149, 158, 192
Pelton Junior High School, 123
person, 111
    orthonomous, 108
Peterhouse, 15
Pettit, P., 21, 105
Philip, M., 17
philosophical logic, 197
philosophy, 66, 69, 75, 90, 91, 99, 101, 121, 141, 183
    feminist, 86
    Greek, 83
    Islamic, 94
    methodology, 199
    moral, 29, 33, 67, 147, 170
    of language, 1, 29, 30, 169
    of law, 32, 37, 208
    of logic, 170
    of mathematics, 2
    of science, 41, 64, 170
    political, 3, 7, 25, 46, 60, 66, 68, 81, 88, 102, 138, 142, 187
    ideal, 33
    influence, 88
    non-ideal, 33
    'public', 216
    Roman, 83

Plato, 43, 45, 54, 63, 71, 87, 93, 211
PM, 179
Pogge, T., 165, 191
Poland, 148
policy, 69, 206
policy making, 206
political action, *see* action
political culture, 190
political life, 138, 161, 214
political moralism, 48
political obligation, 200
political practice, 22
political radicalism, 214
political realism, 48
political science, 24, 91, 101
political theory, 18, 22, 65, 179
  history of, 54
politics, 13, 23, 25, 26, 80, 83, 88, 109, 139, 184, 187
Popper, K., 64
popular culture, 90
Porter, R., 14
Portofino, 99
poverty, 142, 191
PPE, 187
practice, 173, 182, 190, 216
Priestley, J., 15
Princeton University, 14, 149
prioritarianism, 159
Prisoner's dilemma, 163
private property, 196
probability, 1
  subjective, 1
Prynne, J., 14
psychology, 8, 14
  evolutionary, 192
  moral, 214
  'political', 85
public committee, 206
punishment, 115, 137, 175, 192, 196
Putnam, H., 199

quality, 153
quasi-egalitarianism, 77

race, 1
racism, 1, 29, 122, 202
  administrative, 122
  causal, 195
Rapallo, 99
rape, 86
rationality, 150, 163
Rawls, J., 3, 9, 17, 30, 45, 55, 68, 84, 86, 93, 100, 103, 113, 121, 130, 149, 159, 164, 170, 175, 187, 198, 203, 213
Raz, J., 17
Reichstag fire, 30
relativism, 138, 181
  cultural, 85, 211
religion, 94
religious liberty, 80
republicanism, 18, 107, 114
Republicans, 121
responsibility, 139, 192
rights, 7
Roemer, J.E., 100, 170
role morality, 137
Rosen, M., 200
Rousseau, J.-J., 30, 87, 93, 164, 214
Royal Military College, 64
rule-following, 106
Russell, B., 169
Russia, 148
Rwanda, 38
Ryan, A., 17

San Francisco, 122
Sandel, M., 199

Sartre, J.P., 13, 105, 179
Scanlon, T., 149, 192, 198
Scheffler, S., 139, 201
Schmitt, C., 42
Scholem, G., 42
science, 49, 75
Searle, J., 122
secession, 31
security, 173
self-respect, 202
semantics, 1
Sen, A., 17, 84, 91, 100, 204
Seneca, 87
sexism, 202
sexual
   harassment, 86
   orientation, 86, 148
Sher, G., 135
Shklar, J., 55, 199, 212, 213
shtetls, 148
Sigman, F., 148
Silone, I., 179
Sils-Maria, 99
Singer, P., 66
singularism, 112
skepticism, 67
Skinner, Q., 14, 16, 21, 107
slavery, 124
Smith, A., 87, 207
Smith, M., 108
social choice theory, 170
social contract, 86
social discontent, 214
social policy, 190, 205
social practice, 139
social science, 24, 26, 54
social unity, 66
socialism, 63
society, 25, 60, 79, 102, 106, 115, 126
   liberal, 67
   topology of, 131

sociobiology, 218
sociology, 8, 14, 101
South Africa, 65
sovereignty, 220
Soviet Union, 31
Spinoza, B. de, 87, 94
Starr, R., 124
statistical analysis, 68
statistical journalism, 123
Steiner, H., 170
Stoicism, 93
Stone, I.F., 179
Strauss, L., 42, 183, 212, 213
structuralism, 105
Sugden, R., 18
Swansea, 187
Sweezy, P., 123
Swift, A., 17

Tagore, R., 93
Tanner Lectures on Human Values, 6
Tanzania, 2
targeted resource enhancement, 204
Taylor, C., 4
technology, 139
Temkin, B., 147
Temkin, L., 147
Temkin, L.S., 147
Thatcher, M., 106
think tank, 206
Thompson, D., 56
Tocqueville, A. de, 219
toleration, 67
totalitarianism, 71
truth, 1, 138, 156
Tuck, R., 14, 17
tyranny, 58

Ulysses, 110
UN, 84, 141, 165

236   Index

Development Programme, 85
Security Council, 35
University College London, 127, 196
University College, Dublin, 105
University of Bielefeld, 100
University of Bradford, 106
University of California at Davis, 124
University of California, Berkeley, 100, 121
University of East Anglia, 18
University of Edinburgh, 17
University of Louvain, 99
University of Minnesota, 75
University of Oxford, 64, 75, 100, 149, 187
University of Pittsburgh, 169
University of Reading, 18
University of San Diego, 6
University of Toronto, 169, 211
University of York, 13
USA, 3, 87, 142, 148, 161
    health care system, 164
use of force, 175
utilitarianism, 15, 86, 115, 130, 159, 170

Vallentyne, P., 169
value theory, 149
Van Parijs, P., 99, 170, 191
Vico, G., 13
Vietnam, 30, 122
Vietnam War, 53, 121, 148, 180
virtue
    epistemic, 32
    liberal, 45
Voegelin, E., 213
voter's paradox, 163

Waldron, J., 17, 80

Walzer, M., 54, 58, 179, 195, 213, 216
war, 58, 180
    just, 181
Ward, B., 123
warfare, 58
Weber, M., 20, 25, 49
Welcome Institute, 15
welfare, 129
welfarism, 130, 155
wellbeing, 157, 171, 173
Whitlam government, 65
WHO, 162
Williams, A., 17, 18, 187
Williams, B., 48, 84
Williams, R., 94
Wisconsin, 148
Wittgenstein, L., 13, 41, 106
Wolff, J., 195
women, 67, 107, 165, 185, 191
Women's Liberation, 148
World Bank, 89, 165
World Institute for Development Economics Research, 84
World War I, 213
Wormald, B., 15
Wright, R., 2
WTO, 165

Yack, B., 211
Yale University, 1
Yankees, 121
Yugoslavia, 31

Zapatero, J.L.R., 114
Zeno's paradox, 121

www.ingramcontent.com/pod-product-compliance
Ingram Content Group UK Ltd.
Pitfield, Milton Keynes, MK11 3LW, UK
UKHW042318200426
11947UKWH00048B/170